Finding
Freedom
in the
LOST
KITCHEN

ALSO BY ERIN FRENCH

The Lost Kitchen: Recipes and a Good Life
Found in Freedom, Maine: A Cookbook

Finding Freedom

in the

LOST KITCHEN

Erin French

Aurum

First published in 2021 by Aurum
an imprint of The Quarto Group.
The Old Brewery, 6 Blundell Street
London, N7 9BH,
United Kingdom
T (0)20 7700 6700
www.QuartoKnows.com

A catalogue record for this book is
available from the British Library.

ISBN 978 0 7112-6533-2
Ebook ISBN 978 0 7112-6535-6
Audiobook ISBN 978 0 7112-6608-7

10 9 8 7 6 5 4 3 2 1

Cover design by Anna Morrison

Typeset by SX Composing DTP Ltd, Rayleigh, Essex, SS6 7EF
Printed and bound by CPI Group (UK) Ltd, Croydon, CR0 4YY

CONTENTS

PART FOUR: LIBERTY

PART FIVE: FREEDOM

PART ONE

HOPE

1

BACON AND ICE CREAM

It was ten past three in the afternoon, the time of day I looked forward to the most. This was the hour each afternoon that offered a bit of much-needed semi-peacefulness in the kitchen at my father's diner. It was the time of day when, for a split second, I could finally take a break. Over the past four hours I had flipped at least two dozen burgers, fried an equal number of clam baskets, plated a dozen meatloaf specials and made a few BLTs and egg salad sandwiches in between.

After the frenetic lunch rush ended, the grill was finally empty, the Fryolators idled hot and peaceful and the ticket bar sat quiet and vacant of orders. Here it was, my chance to sit down, grab a quick bite, or take my first pee in five hours. But it was also the only moment quiet enough in the kitchen to get ahead with prep for home fries and bacon for tomorrow morning's crushing breakfast service. The ten-pound bag of pork on the counter was glaring at me impatiently. I pulled a fistful of the fatty strips from the huge bag and laid them one by one into four long rows on the giant griddle that sat centre stage on the old diner line. I fried each length until it was just barely brown and stacked it between layers of brown paper towels to absorb the warm fat, then laid out four more rows again, then again and again and again. Every day it felt like an endless task, the sputtering grease pelting my wrists with tiny burns. I couldn't help cringing, even though I was well used to it by now. And then there was the smell of rendered pork fat that came with it. It seemed to permeate every strand of hair, every thread of clothing, every pore: I flat-out reeked of bacon. God, I couldn't wait for a long hot shower, but that was easily seven hours away. I had more pork to fry and home fries to dice and then a full fucking dinner service ahead of me.

After the last batch was tucked between paper towels, I twisted each of the four knobs on the griddle to the right and killed the ignition to the pilot lights below. I grabbed the grill scraper and, using it like a squeegee, began to move the puddles of hot grease down the perimeter of the grill, guiding the smoking liquid to the stainless-steel trap in the lower left corner below. Finally a clean grill, a still-empty ticket board and a moment to sit. *Yes!* I walked over to the soft-serve ice cream machine that was tucked in the front of the kitchen and pulled on the lever, letting the soft and creamy vanilla squiggles twist their way into the sugared wafer cone in my hand. It took a lot of practice to twist a good-looking cone, but I was a pro by now, after all these years. And then you needed to know the difference between a small, a medium and a large. It was important; it mattered. Believe me, I got bitched at more than once by my dad for making cones 'too big'.

'Why don't you just give the fucking place away?!' he'd yell. 'How many times do I have to tell you?! Three twists around for a small, four for a medium and five for a large. What do you want me to do?! Work for nothing?! One, two, three! That's three twists for a small! Four for a medium and five for a large! *Get it?!*' His anger seemed so wild, so unnecessary, but not out of character. His lack of patience with me had become old news.

Meanwhile, my younger sister, Nina, had been dishing out parfaits and banana boats to her stoned friends through the dairy-bar window every day after school and ruining cases of whipped-cream canisters by doing whippets, yielding him net nothing. She was younger, so maybe he went easier. Or maybe he was worn out by his disappointment in me.

Finally I took a perch at the back of the restaurant for my afternoon pause. Sitting on an overturned milk crate, I propped my feet on an empty plastic bread rack and lapped up the cold, delicious and perfect small one-two-three vanilla cone. I was far enough away from the kitchen to catch a breath, but close enough, still in earshot, to hear the ding of the call bell on the cook's counter should an order come in from the dining room.

I remember the first day I ever set foot into the diner. I was just five. En route to kindergarten one morning, my mom veered our old Volvo off our normal path to school. We bounced over a few potholes in the wide dirt parking lot before coming to a stop in front of the little diner we had passed many times before, perched on top of Knox Ridge. RIDGETOP RESTAURANT read the prominent sign on the front gable. BEST MEALS FOR MILES in dull brown and yellow paint.

'What are we doing *here*?' I asked my mother from the backseat, puzzled by the unexpected stop.

'We're going to visit Dad before school. This is where he works now. This is our restaurant. We bought it!' It was genuine excitement. My sister and I were speechless for a split second. Our eyes widened and we squealed with delight. 'What? We own a restaurant?!' It was as though we both simultaneously pictured all the free burgers, fries, milkshakes and soft-serve ice cream our bellies could hold. We jumped out of the car and raced for the front door, trying to fling it open in our joy, but the big plate-glass door was heavier than expected and it opened far more slowly than the speed of our pounding heartbeats. A string of bells tied to the handle clanged gently as we pulled it open with all our might, announcing to everyone that we had arrived. Inside we paused in amazement, taking in *our* new surroundings: before us was a long row of faux-wooden booths. The tabletops were adorned with paper place mats and simple tableware, red plastic ketchup bottles, pink packets of sugar and stacks of assorted tiny jam cups. The smells of fried onions and bacon filled our nostrils. To our right was a tall breakfast counter, lined with wooden stools and topped by glass containers stuffed full of baked goods. A few patrons sat at the counter, quietly sipping their coffee from shiny brown mugs and sucking on cigarettes. They noticed us for only a split second before going back to their plates of hash and eggs. I remember marvelling at the thin plumes of smoke wafting from their lips and ashtrays, up toward the asbestos drop ceiling yellowed with nicotine stains, the pattern mimicking the shape of the breakfast counter below, representing years of loyal regular patrons.

We were greeted by a kind waitress wearing stonewashed jeans, a soft purple T-shirt, white leather high-top sneakers and a frilly black apron. She had thick curly brown hair that stood tall and firm (Aqua Net, to be sure), her eyelashes were caked with blue mascara and she had a Bic pen tucked behind her ear, her hairspray-drenched locks helping to keep it firmly in place.

'Hi there. I'm Viola. You must be Jeff's girls,' she said in a bubbly voice as she bounded toward us. But before we could even respond with a nod, our attention was diverted by the familiar voice of our grandmother from behind the breakfast counter. There she was, her soft and sweet face coming into view through the haze of smoke.

'Girls!' she exclaimed with a chuckle as she motioned for us to join her behind the counter. We ran to her, eyes still wide, our backpacks swinging behind us. We each received big hugs and a warm kiss on the head.

'Let's get you two a doughnut and a glass of milk,' she said as she whisked us away into the back. We pushed through the swinging wood door into the kitchen and there he was – our dad. He was standing in front of a giant stainless griddle, a white apron around his waist, a large spatula in his hand, effortlessly flipping oversize golden pancakes high in the air, all the while whistling happy tunes through his teeth. Each cake he flipped made a *hiss!* and *splat!* as its uncooked side hit the hot grill. I liked it. He glanced over at my sister and me and we were staring at him in honest amazement, our jaws slightly agape. We were mesmerized by the sight of this man, our father – there was something about him we didn't quite recognize. His smile was so big that his blue eyes were squinted small enough so you almost couldn't tell what colour they were. His dark blond sideburns stretched with his face and his moustache twitched as he bared his big white smile, still whistling through his teeth. In this very moment his immense joy was overwhelming and obvious. It was rare and strange, to see him like this – happy, whole. Look at me! Loving life! he said, without actually saying a word. It warmed me inside. 'I didn't know Dad knew how to cook,' Nina said without blinking, without moving or taking her eyes off him, her eyes large like a little fawn's.

Further down the vast line I could see my grandfather, fiddling away with something in a large Fryolator. His black-rimmed reading glasses were smudged with grease and had slid down to the very tip of his nose, where they miraculously managed to stop and stay. He was whistling loudly too, with joy. His tune would mingle with my father's from the grill to the fryer and back and forth again. From the hot oil we watched him pull one, two, three – six – piping-hot doughnuts and place them on a parchment-lined plate that my grandmother was patiently holding beside him. He turned in our direction, his white apron splattered with egg and batter, adjusted his glasses and blew Nina and me a kiss, before dropping more raw dough into the hot fryer and resuming his joyful tune.

Gram stood before us now with the plate of freshly fried doughnuts. We each grabbed one and bit in. Steam rose from our mouths. The warmth, the crunch on the outside that yielded to the softness inside, the delicate hints of nutmeg and vanilla and the subtle sugary sweetness. It was the best thing I had ever tasted in my entire life. We cooled our mouths with swigs of fresh cold milk in between. We were all so happy in this moment. It was poetic and romantic. What *is* this magical place?! I thought as I took my second bite.

'*This* is *our* restaurant,' my dad said out loud, glowing. And I was in love.

I was twelve years old when my dad first pulled me onto the line. I remember the Sunday morning clearly. I woke early, filled with butterflies and excitement that I was going to work at the diner for the very first time. I jumped into the passenger seat of my mom's car and honked the horn impatiently.

'Come on, Mom!' I yelled from the side window.

'All right, all right!' she yelled back as she made her way through the front door. She got into the driver's seat and turned on the ignition. 'I can't wait for you to get a driver's licence,' she said, tired and slightly annoyed.

'Mom, I'm twelve. I'm saving for a bike.' I rolled my eyes.

I had stepped in all those years ago to help my dad out at the diner, mostly because I needed the cash to buy that bike, then eventually to fill the tank of my Volkswagen Rabbit, or to buy Janet Jackson cassettes. I worked my way up the rungs of the line and learned every basic kitchen skill a cook would need to know: how to cook a burger a nice pink medium-rare. How to cook eggs – hard, sunny, over easy, scrambled, poached and boiled. How to roast a chicken and extract every bit of meat from the carcass (we always saved and dried the wishbones – for wishes, of course, which Nina and I would duel over). How to perfectly bread and fry clams, scallops, shrimp and fish. How to balance the ratios of mayo, vinegar, salt and butter. I learned about timing and multitasking – minding the grill with a half-dozen burgers (in an array of different cooked temperatures) or composing chicken and egg salad sandwiches while warming stews in the microwave and monitoring the fry basket, just to name a few of the varied and simultaneous tasks I was charged with. Left alone in the kitchen without my dad to answer my many questions, I was learning how to use my intuition, to rely on it. To taste and test and figure out what seemed just right. All those years of experimenting – out of necessity – had started shaping me as a cook.

Now, nine years later, I was holding my own on the line, though not without its own sacrifices, evidenced by my quick ice cream break before returning to another twelve-plus-hour-long shift. The cone was melting fast in the summer heat. I couldn't keep up with the vanilla custard dripping down my hand and onto my very pregnant belly. I was twenty-one years old; single, nine months pregnant and fighting through a sixteen-hour workday. I was tired, uncomfortable and particularly angry with my father, who had left me in charge of *his* diner while he was off manning a blooming-onion booth at a nearby county fair for Labor Day weekend. There was too much money he'd miss out on by not going – every year he'd sell through hundreds of pounds of fried onions and come home with garbage bags filled with cash – but to me it still made no sense. 'What if I go into labour.' I asked him. 'I don't care,' he had told me with the most sincere lack of concern over the phone earlier that day. 'Lock the fucking door if it comes down to it.' My pregnancy was not only a major inconvenience to him, since I would need time off from work at the diner to have my baby, but a genuine embarrassment. 'Do you see the problem I've got on my hands here?' he snapped at the Sysco salesman one afternoon, pointing squarely at me and my belly as I worked in the corner salad station. The disdain was no different from what he once showed toward the female kittens on our farm. They were useless creatures – it was just a matter of time before they got knocked up, forsaking their mousing duties and creating more mouths to feed.

I wanted to lock the door, go home, take a bath and a nap. But I didn't. I finished my cone, washed up and went back to the kitchen. There was more work to be done for the following day and with the baby due any moment, it was best to get ahead on prep. There were home fries to be made. And bacon.

2

TAPIOCA AND KITTENS

Freedom, Maine, population 719, was the town you passed through when you were going somewhere bigger. A little town of nothing, a rural mix of farmland and thick woods. It didn't offer a lot – a church, a small general store with a couple of gas pumps, a sleepy post office that was open for only a few hours a day. At the centre of town was an old shingled mill, sitting vacant and crumbling, overlooking the Sandy Stream. This mill was long ago the backbone for the town, harvesting power from the stream to grind grains like flour and corn. Eventually it would transform into a saw- and wood-turning mill, putting out timber and shingles and handles for shovels and screwdrivers. The work of the mill came to a quiet halt in the sixties. It sat for the years that followed, the water rushing past it and flowing over the falls, forgetting it. It slowly faded and became the heap of crumbling wood and granite that I knew it to be in my childhood.

My sister and I would parade past the old mill every Fourth of July in our retired dance recital costumes from the year before and attend Sunday school just up the hill at the Congregational church each week. We ice-fished each winter and skated along the clear ice of Freedom Pond, which fed into the Sandy Stream, running past the mill and washing bits of it away. The sad and neglected structure listed dangerously to one side, its rusted metal roof warped from the many years it had been forgotten. It appeared as if it could collapse with a single gust of wind. The only souls foolish enough to explore its rotting interior were a few of the local teenage boys who would mark the walls with their graffiti and piss, or throw rocks through the few panes of glass that remained in the dark holes that used to house windows. To me the building represented everything I thought Freedom was: if you stay here, you will rot. Freedom didn't lend a lot of promise. We were raised with unspoken reminders: if you wanted to be something or do something with your life, then you had to go somewhere else; you couldn't live out dreams in Freedom. You couldn't be successful in Waldo County; there was no good life to be found in Freedom. The mill whispered a ghostly reminder of what would happen if you stayed – you'll just end up like me, a crumbling junkyard that nobody cares about. If you were born in Freedom, you would most likely die in Freedom and whatever you did in between wouldn't matter all that much.

The old shingled farmhouse we lived in sat at the end of a pothole-ridden dirt road, just three miles away from the mill at the centre of our town. With twenty-six acres of farmland and woods to play in, Nina and I spent countless summer days from breakfast until dinner running wild through the seemingly endless pastures and wilderness. We both lived barefoot in the white cotton tank tops that came in packages of three – with ribbon straps and bows on the sternum – and faded jean shorts that my mom bought for us at JCPenney in nearby Waterville. On bright July afternoons we'd heist fresh cucumbers from our dad's garden and eat them then and there, cool, prickly and crunchy off the vine, while we tended to our daily chore of picking potato bugs off the plants one by one and drowning them in a preserving jar of petrol. We made mud dams in the streams surrounding our house with the farm boys from next door and built elaborate stick forts in the sumac bushes. We climbed trees and collected abandoned bird's nests, caught frogs and tadpoles in the pond, which we stored in clear jars so we could watch them grow before releasing them carefully back into our farm pond to become the strong and wild full-grown frogs they were supposed to be. We sang songs from *The Little Mermaid* at the top of our lungs in the middle of the field as if we were the only humans on the entire planet and we sold fresh eggs and herbs by the roadside to the maybe six cars that passed the house each day. On rainy days we'd climb around the hayloft, building hay-bale forts, tormenting our cats with dress-up, or cleaning out our rabbit hutch, if Mom made us. It was simple, it was honest, it was dirty and it was real. It was glorious.

Over the years we had everything from ponies and horses to geese and chickens, llamas, bunnies and dogs – and barn cats, so many barn cats. It started with one cat whose outside duty was to keep the mice at bay. 'Cats *not* rats' was the household motto. The single cat fast became pregnant and there you have it: the cats started multiplying like, well, rabbits. On many occasions we found a clutch or two of surprise newborn kittens nestled in the warm hay at the back of the hayloft. We followed the sounds of tiny mews, sometimes for hours, until we joyfully uncovered the fluffy cluster of baby cats, their eyes like little slits, still tightly closed. It was like the most exciting Easter egg hunt you could imagine – black ones, buff ones, grey calico ones. Cute, sweet, fluffy balls of cunning fur. Our mom was kind and fair and would let us keep them long enough until their eyes popped open and they were on kitten chow, which meant Nina and I were already deeply emotionally attached to them all and past the point of giving them up easily. We made a FREE KITTENS sign out of cardboard and Magic Marker, which we hung reluctantly on our mailbox each time we had a litter. We'd give them names like Pumpkin, Panda and Ritz and hope that our parents would let us keep our favourites out of each litter. We would beg and plead and show them off, shrieking and bragging.

'Mom! Look at this one. She is just the cutest! Have you ever seen a more beautiful kitten?'

'But, Dad! This one is smart. Look! He comes on command and knows his name. He's a keeper for sure.'

The odds of keeping them were slim, but we knew the best chance was to fight to keep the boys. Farm cats didn't get fixed. It was expensive and we were told they weren't real pets. They were working animals with a job – to kill rodents. The boys were coveted because they didn't get pregnant; the girls were a liability, a major inconvenience. My dad made his opinion on this fact of farm life painfully clear on so many occasions, not a far cry from the way he felt about his own children.

I had spoiled his plans, born a girl, a liability, a major inconvenience. Caught off-guard, he hadn't wrapped his mind around having a girl or a name to go with her. I was hastily named after a couple of Walton girls: 'Goodnight, Erin Elizabeth.' My father was the only son, flanked by two sisters and his duty to make boys to carry on the family name held a heavy weight in his heart. His own father had put a great pressure on him to keep the family name alive. Instead he produced two soft blonde girls who played with kittens. My mother told me about the look on my father's and grandfather's faces when it was announced that my mother had delivered a healthy baby girl. It was one of letdown and disappointment and the inebriation that quickly followed for both of them was more out of sorrow than celebration, while she hemorrhaged alone in her hospital bed. It seemed to me the disappointment was a weight that my father would carry for years in his heart, most evident when Nina or I acted up. He would tell us that we were lucky to be girls because 'If you were born boys, I would beat you with my bare hands right now.' His words seemed to hurt just the same.

Yes, we were soft blonde girls who played with kittens. And the kittens, in all their sweet and soft glory, taught my sister and me a lot. They taught us about fragility and how to care for something small and helpless. They taught us how to love and laugh. They taught us how to cry and mourn loss, each time we had to give them up, or even worse, if they died.

When I was ten, I watched my father place my favourite cat, Ritz, who had been hit by a car on our quiet dirt road, in a pillowcase and walk toward the barn to drown him in a five-gallon pickle bucket full of water. The cat was doomed and there was no saving him, but it was still inconceivable for me to understand finishing the poor thing off as mercy. Dad had learned about this way of living, or dying, from the dairy farmer next door. Mr Connor couldn't keep up with all the barn cats and would frequently 'keep things even on the farm'. He would fill a hessian grain sack with a fresh litter of female kittens and dip the entire clutch in a trough full of water, drowning them while the mother cat circled, mewing with wild anxiety, knowing her babies were inside the sack. My father, taking a cue from Mr Connor, was using the same technique on *my* cat. I couldn't watch, couldn't stand by and couldn't understand the reasoning. I couldn't stop it either. I begged and pleaded and realizing it would do no good, I ran.

I ran, sobbing, into the back field and hid among the tall strands of goldenrod, hoping that if I ran away, the trouble would too. I threw my body into the tall grass and flailed as if I were making a snow angel. I just wanted to move my body and release these wild emotions that I was feeling for the first time. The energy in the air had shifted. It felt grey and depressing even though it was summer and the sun was shining. I stared up into the sky, the smell of hay all around me in the field, like the day I had found Ritz in the hayloft, huddled in the nest of fur with his siblings. I understood why Dad had to do what he was doing – the poor cat was a mangled mess and in severe pain – but I didn't understand how it was fair.

Why did Ritz have to get hit by a car in the first place? If there *was* a God, why was he taking his shit out on my little helpless cat? What kind of a God would do such a thing? This was bullshit. God was a kitten killer. What an asshole!

This was gnawing at me hard the next day during Sunday school at the Freedom Congregational. I sat through all of the hymns, singing alternate lyrics under my breath and sneaking in a few words for God, if he was even listening. As I looked around at everyone else sitting in the pews, singing along to all the lies that seemed so obvious to me – 'to give him the glory, great things He hath done'? I *couldn't* 'Rise and shine and give God [my] glory'! I couldn't hold in my anger anymore. I lost it. I started preaching loudly that 'God is *not* good!' He was a heartless man who took cute, soft, kind, sweet things from this world! My grand finale was lifting up my Sunday dress in protest, flashing my pale pink tights and underwear to the congregation. Granted, I was ten and therefore hadn't thought out the protest clearly, so I exited quickly to avoid waiting around for the reaction.

After the service my mother arrived to retrieve my sister and me. The story of my tantrum was recounted by my Sunday school teacher while I hid in the grass at the edge of the parking lot, plucking forget-me-nots. Nina was in trouble, too, for standing over the big forced-hot-air vent and letting her dress fly up and wild, flashing her undies for all of the congregation to see. We both had nicks on our behaviour sheet from last week for breaking into arguments more than once. We couldn't seem to resist fighting each other, even under God's eye. I handed a fistful of little blue blossoms to my mother in some attempt to soften the blow that was about to come my way. Her cheeks were flushed with colour; she pursed her already thin lips and glared at me for a moment in deep disapproval, which was sobering because it was so rare that she expressed anger. She didn't have to say a word. I knew she was angry and most likely embarrassed. She motioned for me with her eyes to 'get in the damn car'. Nina and I got kicked out of Sunday school that day, for protesting against God, for bickering with each other and for flashing our underwear for all to see. We were asked not to return until we had pulled it together. The three-mile ride home was quiet and it was clear Mom was not pleased with us. But she also never made us go back to Sunday school again. Maybe it was because she was just too embarrassed that we had been such jerks. Or maybe it was because she also believed the whole God thing was a sham. She never prayed or sat through a sermon or spoke of the guy up above, but for some reason she wanted my sister and me to give it a whirl and see what stuck. Frankly, I think she was just using Jesus as an excuse to celebrate holidays and used the special occasions to make a nice meal and memory to go along with it.

I never stopped cursing God for the death of animals on our little farm, though it also brought unexpected solace. It gave me rare glimpses into my father's heart and showed me that he actually had one. The first tears I ever saw him shed had streamed from his eyes the day he had to put Ritz in that pickle tub. Tears streamed the day he dug the shallow grave in the back woods for our old Doberman after he collapsed playing fetch with my sister and me at our nearby swimming hole. He lay on the couch in grief for two days following the death of that dog. I remember thinking it could be possible he loved that dog more than he ever loved either of his own girls. He wept hard one late September afternoon when the local vet came to put our old pony down before winter. I could hear his sobs echoing in the distance as he walked off into the back pasture to try to conceal his sadness from us. I hid at the back end of the barn, peering from around the corner of the weathered shingled wall, watching his figure in the distance, witnessing his pain as he yelped, his anger as he shook his fists up toward the sky, at God, I imagined. His grief made my heart break for him and it scared me at the same time because he seemed so fragile, emotional and vulnerable. These were not the characteristics I had ever associated with this bear of a man. This was one of the rare, emotional moments that he hid, because he was raised to believe that men don't show emotions and that emotion was a sign of weakness.

My understanding of my dad was gathered in the brief moments I saw of him between his comings and goings from the restaurant. The little diner he had bought and had been running for the past few years had been consuming him. Six days a week he'd rise at 5:00 A.M., well before us and head up the hill to the restaurant to get the grill fired up and the coffee made in time for the first customers at 6:00. He'd arrive back home just before 10:00 P.M. after cleanup from the dinner shift, well after our bedtime, with just enough time to get some rest before doing it all over again. This little restaurant that once appeared to be this bit of excitement and great joy was no longer that place. It was consuming him alive with stress, burning up his heart and soul. His smiles and whistles while working had turned into curses and cans of beer. How could this place that I had witnessed giving him so much joy for life be the same place that was now killing all the joy inside him?

It was becoming clearer that he was never going to be the soft kind of dad that I secretly wished for on more than one occasion. He would never be the dad who would lift you up high into the air, kiss you on the cheek, give you a big squeeze and tell you that he loved you with all his heart. Instead he was unpredictable and explosive. You just never knew when he was going to blow. When he'd get angry, his eyes would get big and his face red, his blond hair wild and wispy, veins popping at his neck, F-bombs frothing from his mouth. Sometimes he seemed happier after putting down a six-pack of Budweiser, or maybe three or four Absoluts with tonic and limes, but sometimes they just seemed to make him angrier. He didn't offer hugs, kind words or tokens of affection. The closest he came was twice a year, in the simple form of a plain white envelope with a crisp fifty-dollar bill, one for my birthday and one on Christmas.

The evening of my Sunday school stunt, our family sat around our kitchen table eating my dad's meatloaf in silence. Sorrowful silence for me and my sister, still processing the fresh death of a beloved kitten; passive silence for my mother, whom I believed was still stewing over our behaviour that afternoon, or perhaps it was over the six-pack of beer she watched my father put down while making dinner. I knew killing the cat hadn't been easy for my dad and I imagined the beer was to drown his own sorrow. The air softened a bit with each bite, the familiar taste of the tender glazed meat mixed with a forkful of airy, perfectly salted mashed potatoes. By the meal's end, the warmth of a home-cooked dinner had turned the cold silence into mild content. For dessert my mother had made tapioca and the soft and creamy vanilla pearls were a salve we all happily gobbled up, curing whatever was momentarily ailing us all. Nobody could fix the fact that my cat was dead or that God was an insensitive meanie, but these were the grievances of a ten-year-old. I didn't know then about what greater injustices lay ahead, or that the faith I'd placed in my family would begin to erode too. But for now all it took was meatloaf and tapioca to soothe me.

3

WE WERE SPEEDING;
WE WERE SPOILED

My grandparents were born-and-bred Mainers and a couple of the hardest-working people I have ever met. Growing up in my dad's diner, I thought of them idol-like, my grandfather running the busy breakfast line alongside my dad, my grandmother scrubbing dishes until someone had to physically drag her out of the dish pit at the end of a shift. She was fierce and relentless, the way she had been raised and the way she had instilled a work ethic into her own children and then her grandchildren. My grandparents saw hard work as respectable – honourable, even. If you wanted something, you worked for it. Even though they were Yankee and frugal, they still splurged on occasional luxuries with the money they worked wicked hard for. They always drove a smooth-riding Lincoln with a big backseat where my sister and I would ride with so much space between us that we couldn't touch each other if we tried, which kept our fighting to a minimum. We'd slide around the slippery leather seats listening to country music while my grandfather would accelerate, changing the speedometer from miles to kilometers, watching us in the rearview mirror as we squealed with excitement, thinking we were really going a hundred miles an hour. 'Now don't you girls go telling your parents about this,' he'd tease, making race-car noises with his mouth, making us feel special and a bit like little rebels. His love for us was deep and true, he bore no resentment that neither of his granddaughters would carry on his family name. He spared us any such feelings, leaving them all for my father.

My grandparents spoiled us with treats that were forbidden by our mother and we were sworn to secrecy, even though my mother knew full well what was going on. Sometimes it was a bowl of Lucky Charms, or a brown sugar–frosted Pop-Tart. There was always a box of Jell-O Pudding Pops in the freezer, each pop coated in a thin layer of ice that I liked to meticulously remove with my teeth before devouring the cold and creamy treat in order to make the joy of it last just a little longer. I'd eat the chocolate ones first, then the marbled and leave the vanilla ones that I didn't like for Nina. Sometimes my grandmother would drive us to town to the Shop 'n Save and set us loose in the frozen food aisle, letting us pick out whichever boxes of TV dinners we wanted – forbidden by my mother, who favoured home-cooked meals and only shopped in the freezer section if she needed petit pois to throw into a beef stew. Running down the glass-lined aisle with fluorescent lights would always leave me feeling a bit guilty, though mostly with a sense of awe. I went with the fried chicken, mashed potatoes in one corner, a bit of corn in the other and a gooey undercooked chocolate brownie in the centre (or sometimes a cherry crisp). There were Happy Meals with nuggets and sweet-and-sour sauce, and hot fried apple pies and creamy cones with a crispy cherry-dip top from the Dairy Cup that was next to the hospital. And Chinese food, a favourite that we ate over and over and over again. Egg-drop soup for my grandfather, beef with pea pods for my grandmother and a pupu for two for Nina and me just so we could have the excitement of fire on the table and the equity of the same meal so we wouldn't argue over who got what. My grandfather would playfully take a big spoonful of hot

Chinese mustard, put the entire thing in his mouth and pretend it was so hot it was setting his mouth on fire, his eyes popping out real wide, his mouth leaking imaginary smoke. It never got old, making us laugh every time. He'd finish the meal by reading our fortunes and throwing us a couple of pennies to toss into the bubbling fountain with our wishes before filling our pockets with a handful of chalky mints from a bowl on the hostess stand on our way out. Creating these moments for us brought them genuine joy and it made me and my sister feel so very loved.

My grandfather was plump and kind. He would whistle almost all the time, tweeting little tunes that he knew from his childhood or some that he just made up on the spot but sounded practiced and perfect. He'd sing songs with silly rhymes that always felt a year or two too mature for our age, sending my sister and me into fits of giggles and my grandmother into fits of scolding. 'Jack!' she'd chide, giving him eyes of disapproval from behind her glasses, with a smidge of a smile in the corner of her mouth, because he was undeniably funny and she knew it. He was also a fantastic cook. He would rub big slabs of meat with garlic powder and pepper and roast them to perfection, nice and rare. Prime ribs, roast beef and slow-cooked pork roasts too. He'd use his big fingers to drop giant globs of dough into boiling pots of chicken stew for the most perfectly soft and pillowy dumplings. His hot dogs were unrivalled, cooked in a cast-iron pan with a knob of butter and a handful of sweet onions alongside. He'd grill the rolls until they were toasty but still soft and moist inside and serve the dogs topped with the caramelized onions and a sweet pickle relish made by my great-aunt the year before. But it was his corned-beef dinner that I craved the most. There was nothing better than that slow-cooked piece of succulent cured brisket, laden with delicious layers of fat, served with carrots, cabbage and potatoes that had boiled alongside the tasty hunk of meat. We'd smash the potatoes and carrots together, adding butter from the block that always sat at the centre of the table, along with a good sprinkle of salt and pepper. My grandfather could also cook eggs like a pro, any way you liked 'em – boiled, poached, scrambled, fried. He would take a few medium-boiled eggs and mash them with a fork, the bright orange yolks breaking into bits with the whites, then throw on a nice big tablespoon of butter and sprinkle it with salt and pepper. We quickly learned that everything tasted better with butter, salt and pepper and we stuffed ourselves silly with the jammy-egg treat on Saturday mornings.

My grandmother was the clear boss. She kept our grandfather in line, gently scolding him when he did or said things she thought were outrageous, which was often. He had his occasional vices, like sneaking a cigar, or a nip of whisky from the bottle of Crown Royal he kept hidden in the grain bin at my parents' farm. (Later in life it made sense why he loved to feed the horses so much.) Even with all her seriousness, my grandmother was witty and quick. She could send my sister and me into stitches in seconds. She also had incredible strength, lifting and moving things that would otherwise take men twice her size. Together my grandparents loved family and visited their nearby relatives often, bringing us along to help can piccalilli at Aunt Bessie's or make a batch of her famous sour pickles. We'd go for drives just because, cruising the roads to see the sights, discovering new places or revisiting old, frequently stopping by old cemeteries to trim the grass with a set of hand clippers from around the corners of the gravestones of relatives and add a fresh geranium for the season. We'd visit the grave of my grandmother's father, who died the month before she was born and the plot where my grandparents buried their first child, a daughter who died of spina bifida at eight months old. Here at the grave sites of these relatives, whom my sister and I had never met, we learned little snippets from our family's past. It was a rare tear that once fell from my grandmother's eye that made me realize that this woman, whom I idolized and believed to be invincible, was in fact human and woundable. I was too young to fathom the depth of her feelings, but I knew that losing a child must have hurt a thousand times more than losing a kitten. And maybe my grandfather's disappointment on the day of my birth was only a reaction to his own memory of his firstborn, a daughter, who was buried in the ground below me. The visits to these old gravesites provoked lots of questions from our young minds.

'What does a dead person look like, Gram?' I nervously asked her. 'Like they're having a nice long sleep – peaceful,' she responded in a soft voice, with a warm smile on her face. So soft and warm that I felt comforted, enough so to lob in a grim question or two when they came to mind. After all our queries about life and death had been answered by my grandmother and the plots tidied, there was usually a cone or a fried snack to follow our cemetery visits. Most likely to keep our mouths busy with the treats instead of available for more questions.

Along our drives we also frequented spots from their childhood foraging – a way of life for most Mainers who grew up not having much and they never let it go, passing it down through the generations as a family ritual. There were fiddleheads (young fern fronds eaten as a vegetable) that popped up from the mossy earth in the woods in the spring and teaberry leaves in the summer that tasted like the freshest wild wintergreen when you broke them down between your teeth. And there was always a bit of jewelweed that my grandmother would stuff into a glass jar and cover with witch hazel and keep under the kitchen cupboard to cure a case of poison ivy should we encounter it. I thought my grandmother had gone mad the day she pulled me out into the yard and started hacking down long thick stems from a patch that looked like burdock, which I knew well. I'd never forget it after I had been thrown from our old pony (which I shouldn't have been riding, bareback in a swimming costume, in the back pasture at my parents' when I was seven) straight into a patch of burdock. The small, round thistle-like balls covered my costume like Velcro and made a matted nest of my thin blonde hair. Only these shoots my grandmother gathered weren't burdock, but something far more magical. My grandmother took one of the stalks, cut it in half, gave me one of the pieces and told me to try it. I took a bite of the fibrous green and red stalk and started to chew before an intense sourness made me pucker and spit it out. My grandmother was doubled over with laughter – she had done it on purpose, knowing it would elicit such a reaction. Then she handed me the other stalk and a small bowl of sugar and showed me how to dip it into the granular sweet stuff and suck on the stalks. It had transformed! The sweet with the sour was like nothing I had ever tasted before. We made a pie with that rhubarb that night, with an old-fashioned crust made from shortening. From then on, I was determined to walk the pastures of my parents' property in search of the stuff, hoping that I had mistaken it for burdock all along. Sure enough, I discovered a small patch at the edge of the pasture – which I later discovered was surrounded by poison ivy. But we had a cure for that under the kitchen sink.

The love that my grandparents gave us was strong. It was a different kind of love from what a parent gives you and they were receiving a different kind of love from us than from their children. It was a special bond and one that I felt at times my father was resentful of. He didn't have the kind of relationship that I did with his father. My grandfather didn't make jokes with my father, or sing him songs, or spoil him with food. He pushed him hard and had high expectations and sometimes wasn't there for him in moments of need. The father my father knew and resented was not the grandfather I knew and loved so very much. I wondered sometimes if we were even talking about the same person.

My grandparents ran an egg farm (the reason we ate so many eggs over the years) and, for a time, a small convenience store and sandwich shop on one of the main drags of Belfast, Maine. Their retirement eventually turned into helping out on the breakfast line of Dad's diner, flipping pancakes and eggs and helping out with us kids when needed. But all that came after my father did his time working for his own parents at their shop. The convenience store shaped my father into a sandwich-making pro and the cook he eventually became, thanks to pumping out hundreds of sandwiches a day to the factory workers from the chicken-processing plant down by the water. They'd line up each afternoon in their chicken-blood-splattered white jackets to pick up an Italian sandwich, a pack of smokes, a soda and a bag of crisps. Running the little grocery store was hard, hands-on work. It was the only kind of work my grandparents knew and they were proud to do it. So it was with every intention that they taught their kids the same. They bought the store in the late sixties and raised their kids there, my father flipping fresh pizza dough in the back kitchen and my aunt Rhoda taking the orders, running the cash register and helping out with the bookkeeping. Sure, Rhoda would heist a pack of Marlboro 'hards' on occasion, but it was my father's sticky hands for the beer cooler that ended up driving them to call it quits. He had questionable friends who were coming around and my grandmother didn't like it. She could sniff out that something shady was going on. And she was right. Later she found that a small drug ring had formed in the little town of Belfast and my grandparents were glad to have taken him out of town. They sold the store in the early eighties, hoping that would put an end to the trouble my grandmother could smell brewing. My father needed a redirect; an old farmhouse in the middle of nowhere that would keep his hands busy with its constant upkeep and maybe a business of his own, might just do the trick to keep him distracted and out of trouble. My grandfather whistled all the way to Freedom, thinking about how his son's freewheeling days were about to become filled with loads of responsibility. But beneath the whistles, I think it's likely he secretly held a bit of resentment in his heart toward his son for the sacrifices their family had to make to keep him out of trouble.

4

DAYS, NIGHTS,
YEARS IN A DINER

Growing up in a diner wasn't the worst of things. There were loads of delicious moments like those fresh-from-the-fryer nutmeg-laced doughnuts and a mug of Swiss Miss hot chocolate – complete with a squirt of whipped cream from a canister – while waiting for the school bus. Or a make-your-own hot fudge sundae as an after-school snack. On weekend mornings when your grandfather asked you what you wanted for breakfast, he really meant it – 'What do you want? A nice egg sandwich? A couple of scrambled eggs and Texas toast? Over easy with corned-beef hash? White, wheat or rye?' There was a menu a mile long and it was all yours, unless we were running low on something while waiting for the Sysco truck to arrive with a fresh order. There were few rules when it came to what my sister and I could have, except maybe: 'Keep the Coke intake from the soda fountain to a minimum, please.'

But the bottomless treats weren't exactly free. The trade-off was that the restaurant seemed to be holding my father hostage. Long, grueling days spent overseeing things at the diner meant we didn't get to spend a lot of quality time with him. The restaurant made it hard to get close to my dad and perhaps easier for him not to bond with us. Work consumed him and kept him from us and when it didn't, he was irritated and tired after his long shifts. There was little energy left at the end of the week to put into being a fun-loving dad and we tiptoed around him, avoiding his short fuse at all costs. His drinking was predictable, every day washing down beer after beer or vodka tonics galore. It was who he became after a few drinks that wasn't predictable. Maybe he'd loosen up, reveal his fun-loving side – or maybe the booze would send him into fits of anger, filling the room with a flurry of profanity-laced rants. We tiptoed around him when he was sober; we tiptoed around him when he was drunk. We never knew when he might blow and the last place we wanted to be was in the crosshairs.

My father had always been resigned to the fact that he'd be stuck to this patch of earth in Maine for all of his days. He struggled as a student and ended up dropping out of college. He fell back into the only thing he knew how to do: work. He spent his days turning out pepperoni pizzas and Italian subs by the hundreds in the kitchen at his parents' convenience store. He picked up lots of basic cooking skills, eventually becoming quite good in the kitchen himself – especially when it came to pizza dough. He could toss and spin the dough so high into the air, stretching it over his fists each time it landed, forming the perfect fresh crust. He also learned about running a small business from watching his parents, from tending the cash register to ordering products and taking inventory. They had trained him well and after years of hard work he was ready to fly on his own. The idea of having his very own place was a slice of pride. He could finally be his own man and not have to live under the scornful eye of his father. It would maybe even be a chance to make his father proud of him for once. God knows he had tried over and over again, yet somehow nothing he did seemed to work. He was a star football and basketball player in his high school teams, but his father rarely went to games because he was stuck running the convenience store. He had always wanted to do right by his father, but the bar seemed to be set unattainably high for some reason. Much higher than that set for his sisters. It was a man's responsibility to perform, excel and succeed and, no matter what, never to show weakness. Trudging through sixteen-hour workdays at the diner was the norm for him now. My parents found balance in the best way they could with the near-impossible task of running a restaurant and raising two kids. On school mornings my mother would drop my sister and me at the diner to wait for the bus. She'd continue on to work a full day of teaching special ed at the public school a few towns over. Dropping us at the restaurant made it easy on her, like having before-and-after care (food included!), just at a greasy spoon diner instead of some kind of school-related enrichment. It also served as our interaction with Dad for the day, even though he seemed indifferent toward having us around. We knew enough to stay out of the way if things were really hopping and to avoid a tongue-lashing. He would feed us breakfast and we would sit at the counter with the locals, munching on English muffins and bacon while waiting for him to fix us sandwiches to take to school for lunch. As long as we stayed out of the way and let him get on with his work, we were no bother to him. My sister and I knew to clear our own plates and leave little trace that we had even been there. He was sober during the breakfast shift, which didn't mean that his fuse was any longer or his patience any deeper. He was overworked morning, noon and night and stressed through breakfast, lunch and dinner. We'd get on the bus smelling of fried food and cigarettes, but we had long become immune.

I was never one of the popular kids, but I was the envy of the lunch table whenever I pulled a nice long professionally made Italian sub sandwich from my bag. A soft white sub roll with slices of deli ham, American cheese, tomatoes, onions, green peppers, pickles and black olives, a sprinkle of salt and pepper and a dash of oil, wrapped up tight in shiny clingfilm. My dad put great care into making these sandwiches and I could taste it. They were always perfectly balanced, not too many olives, just the right amount of salt and pepper, tomatoes sliced with precision, just enough drops of oil to make the sandwich moist but never soggy. Even if he was just making diner food day in and day out, he had a great palate and I learned from it, too. He knew how good, simple food should taste. It was in him, innate and natural, a quiet knack that maybe should have received more appreciation over the years than it ever did. His food made me feel warm inside in a way that I was too young to fully understand. It was like an emotion. It was like love. And sometimes a sub sandwich felt like a fair-enough replacement for the hugs my father never dished out.

After school the bus would drop off Nina and me once again in the parking lot of the old diner. Come 3:00 P.M., there was a lull between the lunch and dinner rushes. When the mid-afternoon ticket line was finally empty, the bacon fried and the home fries boiled for breakfast service the following day, my dad would spend those few quiet hours back in the office making orders or counting cash while soap operas flickered over a small television he had jerry-rigged with tinfoil to get decent reception. We were hungry, growing girls and when the griddle sat hot and clean, my sister and I would play on the quiet line by ourselves, making after-school snacks. A simple grilled cheese sandwich made for a nice treat, or maybe we'd drop a handful of fries into the idling fryer. Sometimes it was a soft-serve cone dipped in rainbow sprinkles, or maybe a bright-red cherry Dip-Top, if we liked. The ice cream machine was ours for the taking and the drawers full of fixings too. Then, while nobody was looking, we'd grab a handful of quarters from the cash register. We discovered early on that if you hit the button on the keypad that said NS (no sale), the drawer would spit open and there was a buffet of change to be had, so we spent hours upon hours in the empty afternoon dining room, pumping quarters into the tabletop Pac-Man machine, working on our joystick skills and trying to get to the highest level we could. When we ran out of quarters, we'd retire to a quiet booth in the back dining room to do homework and wait for our mom to pick us up after work. If it had been a really long day – and it often was – and she didn't feel like cooking, we'd stay at the restaurant through the dinner hour and order as we pleased from the menu. A hot chicken sandwich, perhaps, with freshly roasted meat between thick slices of soft white bread, slathered with rich chicken gravy, a side of mashed potatoes, a round scoop of tinned cranberry sauce and a side of peas was a favourite. Or, if it was meatloaf night, we couldn't resist having a slab – it was Dad's specialty, with a sweet brown-sugar-and-ketchup glaze, plus a big hot baked potato on the side with a cube of butter, a dollop of sour cream and a few spears of broccoli to round it out. We weren't all sitting at the same table, but still we were sharing dinner together in our own unique way.

Most of the time we'd enjoy our meal outside on the deck, at a picnic table meant for afternoon breaks. We could sit there and look out at the cornfields and mountains in the far distance. It was relaxing, shielded from the chaos of the dinner-rush dining room, with only distant echoes of the bubbling Fryolator and ding of the counter bell. But mainly we'd sit back there because it was too stressful for my mother to sit in the restaurant, watching the young waitresses not clear the tables quickly enough, or not bring drinks in a timely manner, or forget to bring out dinner rolls with individual pats of butter before the meal. The imperfections drove her crazy and it was hard for her to sit by without feeling the need to hop up and help out – which more often than not is what happened. She always knew as she approached Route 137 and the parking lot came into view how her evening would pan out. If it was jam-packed, her long day of work wasn't over. She couldn't leave my father to be crushed on the line with the dinner tickets waving from the breeze of the exhaust fan. She'd throw on a fresh white apron and join him in her best school outfits to man the fry station or grill by his side, trying her best not to get grease stains on her good tights and khaki skirts. The fury of the line was stressful and you could see it on both of my parents' faces, flushed and red, sweat beading on their brows as they scrambled back and forth from the walk-in to the counter, whipping out plates of hot food, hitting the loud handbell each time an order was up.

My sister and I found ways to distract ourselves, keeping clear of the chaos and avoiding the restless boredom that could easily consume us after countless hours hanging out at the diner each day. We'd run through the neighbouring back fields, playing hide-and-seek among the rows of tall cornstalks, sometimes stealing a few ears to munch raw when they were young, sweet and tender. We'd dig through the Dumpster for boxes to make box forts or cat houses for our kittens. We'd climb the old cherry tree out back, jamming plastic milk crates between the upper branches to give us sturdy perches to sit and nibble on the ripe fruit when it was ready. And sometimes we'd crawl under the deck and collect beer cans for five cents apiece from the mysterious pile of cans that never seemed to disappear. Occasionally we would get to go home with one of the Ingraham girls, whose parents ran the tractor shop across the street. We'd have a playdate until my parents were done on the line, my father sending us along with a hot pizza in exchange for letting us come by. Other nights we'd get restless and it would get late, the magic of the diner and its surroundings dimming as we longed for our own beds.

But there was one day a week that was unlike any other. Tuesdays were the one and only day the restaurant was closed. The one and only day my father could take a break from the stress of the line. He would only set foot in the restaurant on those days to raid the walk-in for food, grabbing supplies to make us a big and beautiful family dinner. Sometimes it was thick rib-eye steaks that he'd grill outside and serve with slices of potatoes and carrots that he'd roast over the hot coals in aluminium-foil packets stuffed with onions and butter, sprinkled with fresh chives to finish. Some nights it was lobsters, fresh from the ocean, that he would get from a friend for a steal, boiled in a big pot of salty water, served with ears of freshly picked corn and a platter of sliced ripe tomatoes from our garden dotted with dollops of mayonnaise and a few twists of fresh black pepper. Tuesdays were special, filled with good food and Dad, who could be found on occasion in rare good spirits.

But the best was the winter, when the wind and snow blew too hard and cold on the ridge for the diner to stay open. The kitchen and dining room were unbearably cold and the hood over the grill would suck out all the hot air that blew out of the heat registers, making it hard to make costs with the wild heating bill. In the depths of winter, my father became resident home chef. Bound to the house by the snow and frigid Maine temperatures, he would spend his days concocting family meals on the small commercial stove he had installed in our kitchen, complete with four big cast-iron burners and a small built-in griddle. We'd return home from school to delicious aromas and happy whistles of joy wafting from a warm kitchen. It was refreshing to see him like this, becoming human and himself again. He cooked because he loved it. Sometimes it would be simple roast chicken with crispy skin that we'd fight over, with wedges of roasted squash sprinkled with nutmeg and a dab of butter, mashed potatoes and peas. Or baked stuffed haddock, with a seafood bread stuffing with lemon and dill, or homemade chop suey with bell peppers and hamburger, served with wedges of buttery garlic bread. He'd make big pots of New England boiled dinner, cooking tender corned-beef briskets all day long with potatoes, carrots, wedges of cabbage and turnips, serving it simply with mustard and a bottle of vinegar on the side, a staple meal from his own childhood dinner table. In shrimp season we'd come home to a heap of thin shells covering the kitchen counter and the smell of a fish shack taking over the room. He'd spend hours shucking the sweet pink meat from the iridescent shells, then fry it for mere seconds for crispy treats that we'd dip in homemade cocktail sauce, then bag up the rest into quart-size Ziploc bags to freeze for eventual winter stews.

There were special occasion dinners, too. On holidays our kitchen would be full of activity all morning long, pots on all four burners bubbling away while a hunk of good meat roasted slowly in the oven. There were traditional turkeys for Thanksgiving, beef Wellingtons slathered with store-bought pâté and wrapped in puff pastry for Christmas and bone-in hams pierced with whole cloves for Easter, served with my grandfather's old-fashioned raisin sauce on the side. There was always a split-pea soup made with the ham bone that would last us for days to follow. And if my father was in a particularly good mood, he'd make something really special, even if it wasn't a holiday. His home kitchen gave him a space where he could play and experiment, maybe make a few fancy dishes that he would never be able to sell to the clientele at the greasy diner. There were prime-rib nights, when big slabs of rib-eye roasts had been rubbed with garlic powder and secret spices, just as his father had taught him, then slow-roasted all day in the oven and served with the pan drippings and fresh hot popovers to sop them all up. Or nights when he would splurge on a rack of lamb if he found it on sale, giving us a little tablespoon of mint jelly on the side for dipping the rare meat. There were even times when he would go so far as to make elaborate menus, planning out courses. On these nights we wouldn't eat at the kitchen table, we'd eat in the side dining room, a room we usually only used for holidays or special occasions, or on a winter Sunday for a roast pork supper.

I remember a particularly special meal my father made one night – he had been inspired by something he had seen on TV that had sparked his need to be extra creative in the kitchen. He took notes on a piece of ruled paper as he watched Emeril Lagasse move back and forth on the set of his own kitchen. He made a list of ingredients, went shopping and laid everything out so carefully, which was unlike him. (He was a great cook, but an even better mess maker.) He started with serving a few small appetizers, my sister and me picking up the unrecognizable bits with questioning eyes: what is it? A different-tasting soup, an out-of-character salad that we both picked at and moved bits we didn't care for aside. Then came the main course. A big flaky piece of pink fish, topped with a slice of lemon and a few sprigs of fresh dill. He sipped at the red wine he had poured for himself and my mother, waiting for our reactions. Red wine on the dinner table meant it was a special dinner, like holiday special. I could feel the pressure that our reactions better be 'special' too.

'What is it?' both my sister and I asked with a smidge of nervousness. My father had poached salmon steaks in a flavourful brine with white wine, fresh herbs, leeks, a bay leaf and peppercorns. He served the fish perfectly cooked medium, with a side of a homemade tartar-like-sauce that he had made with fresh citrus and capers. I was first taken aback by the oiliness of the fish. It wasn't like the mild, light white fish I had eaten all my life. There was a different taste to this fish that I found off-putting and unenjoyable. As I looked across the table to see my sister's face, I knew I wasn't the only one who thought so. But it was the crunch of the tiny bones in my mouth that made me involuntarily gag and spit the fish out onto my plate. My sister followed, spitting out the half-chewed pink meat, as my mother politely pulled the bones from her mouth.

My father, witnessing our reactions, began to turn red in the face. He was mad and he let us know it. How dare we spit out the dinner he had shopped for, prepared and cooked for us! He had put so much time, energy and love into this meal and as he saw the regurgitated bits of pink fish make their way to our plates, he took it as a symbol that we didn't appreciate what he had done for us. He had given us his heart and we were spitting it out on our dinner plates. It was painful to see his feelings hurt, his anger too, but I just couldn't choke down the fish no matter how hard I tried. A cloud of shame formed over the table from my father's visible anger. He ordered us to finish that fish, saying we would not be excused from the table until every bite was gone. My sister and I splattered our dinner plates with tears on top of the chewed-up fish, sitting alone in the dining room after our father stormed out and threw his dish in the sink. My mother followed timidly behind to clean up the mess. We sat there with our heads in our hands, in shame, both bleary-eyed, my sister raising her fork here and there, trying to take another bite and chucking it up again. It wasn't going down.

After my father's anger had subsided by watching whatever TV show he had immersed himself in while finishing the bottle of red wine, my mother quietly shooed us up to bed. It was proclaimed from there on out that my sister and I had only punished ourselves by not eating the meal. 'It's gourmet!' my father had protested. 'You're just too young to appreciate it. What a waste.'

5

MEMORIES OF A
MEATLOAF

By the time I was twelve, the diner had become a second home to me. Spending as much time there as I did at home or school or anywhere else, I knew the place like the back of my hand. I knew where every dish belonged, where all the ingredients lived, how the equipment worked, how each paper placemat setting was supposed to look and even how to cash out the register. The drawer started with $72.50 in cash each day (two tens, two fives, twenty-five ones and a roll each of quarters, dimes, nickels and pennies). If a handful of quarters had been swiped by a couple of bored girls in the middle of the afternoon, it was easy to figure out. I didn't care so much about playing hide-and-seek in the cornfields anymore or climbing trees and making cat boxes. Pac-Man never got old, but I needed new ways to entertain myself while stranded at the diner before and after school. So I started to pay more attention to the food.

When you grow up in a restaurant, it's inevitable that bits of it will rub off on you. It's an intangible something that seeps its way into you until it sears itself in your belly, then your heart, as it did to both my sister and me, whether we wanted it or not. There is romance, there's magic, there's love. The ability to touch a complete stranger with a plate of food, to feed them and awaken their senses while filling them up with joy – it's an intimacy that you can't help craving. It's an intimacy that can only be made with food – a reason why restaurants can be so enchantingly addictive. And sitting there in that diner, day after day, that attraction was seeping into me, whether I liked it or not. There were times when I resented the place because I blamed it for taking my father and turning him into a stressed, mean and angry man all the time. But it also gave me the best of my father – inspired, creative, enthralled with the delicious. Even the greatest resentment couldn't stop my insides from pounding with love and excitement for the greasy spoon.

From the very first day I ever set foot in the place, that little diner on the ridge had burrowed its way into my heart. It made me start to see the world differently – food, service. It was a way to care for people – something that struck at the core of who I was and what drove me. As a daughter, I wanted to please and make proud; as a girl and eventually a woman, it was innate in me to nurture people. When I wasn't puttering around the diner, I was at home playing restaurant. By the time I was eleven, I would dig through the refrigerator and cupboards and rummage through the garden at the back, looking for ingredients to inspire the evening menu for my sister and mom. If it was pasta and a jar of tomato sauce that I found, it was proclaimed to be Italian night. I would fold a blank piece of paper in half so it would open like a menu. On the front I would name the imaginary place ('Luigi's') and set the table with a red-checkered tablecloth and a couple of candlesticks. I'd make garlic bread like my dad did with butter and garlic powder, dousing sub rolls with the delicious liquid and baking it in aluminium foil in the toaster oven. I was the chef and Nina was the waitress and we would wait on my mother hand and foot, tickled by her delight with the whole thing. There were diner nights with grilled hot dogs and baked beans and vegetarian nights when I would just use veggies from the garden to make a simple salad. There was always a drink menu, scribbled in pencil with an array of choices that we thought would suit our single diner – and happened to be what was on hand in our refrigerator (milk, juice, Kool-Aid, wine, or Baileys, from the back of the bottom cupboard). My sister and I would both wear tidy aprons and serve the food and beverages on napkin-lined trays. A small tip would be expected at the end of the meal, left on the table, just like at any real restaurant. If not, the diner would be expected to do the dishes.

Then one weekend at the actual restaurant, my play quickly turned real. My father had been feeding the weekend breakfast crush when I was bringing my plate from the back office to the sink. He beckoned me over to the line, which was covered with eggshells, toast scraps and leftover slices of orange that he would use for garnish. He wasn't the clean-up-as-you-go kind of guy.

'Hey, I'll give you five bucks if you clean up this mess for me,' he offered.

Sure. I thought. Five bucks! Big money for a twelve-year-old.

My dad continued on, working through the orders that were lined up on the ticket line, cracking eggs onto the griddle and popping different varieties of toast into the toaster. I threw on a clean white apron, wrapping the long strings in loops around my kid-size waist. I swept eggshells into my hand with a damp rag and dusted off the toast crumbs from the white laminate countertops. I mounded up the orange slices and reorganized the little packages of jellies that sat in a box next to the pickup counter. I wiped up the splatters of pancake batter and egg yolk and pulled sausage patties from the cooler on command, all the while mindful of my father's movements, trying to anticipate where he'd need to be in order to avoid getting in his way as he moved between the griddle and counter. It was a dance. But there was fire and heat and hot grease involved.

At the end of the shift, as promised, he pulled a five-dollar bill from his back pocket and put the crisp bill in my hand. The reward of the money felt good, but so did being helpful on the line – and to my dad. It was the first time he had rewarded me for anything. It only took once to show my father that I could be useful and from there on out, my presence became more of an interest for him. He liked having someone around whom he could pay a few bucks to clean up the messes he made and I didn't mind it one bit. He treated me like a kid, like *his* kid, not like a girl or a daughter. Even if the time with him was spent working, it was time he gave me. And if I could keep up with him, he might even give me more, plus a little respect, in the shape of five-dollar bills.

Over time I learned how to keep up, dancing around him on the tight line as he picked up his pace with the increasing number of incoming tickets. Eventually I graduated to making toast. My dad taught me how to use a pastry brush to paint each freshly griddled piece of bread with a slick of warm liquid butter substitute that we kept in a bowl on the line, then cut it into triangles and place it on the edge of each breakfast plate he filled with hot eggs and home fries, just so. As I watched him work, I picked up his little tricks, like how to make the citrus twist that was added to each dish and how to call out tickets:

> 2OE, BAC, HF, W = *two eggs over easy, bacon, home fries,*
> *white toast!*
> 2OM, SAS, HF, WH = *two eggs over medium, sausage,*
> *home fries, wheat toast!*

At the end of the breakfast shift, I'd wipe down the line and scrape down the grill, clearing away the overcooked home fries and scrappy pieces of egg into the grease trap below. At twelve years old, it felt like a grown-up accomplishment to be allowed to play with the hot grill. I felt a sense of pride in the trust my father was giving me.

* * *

On my thirteenth birthday my father announced that I had achieved the age where I was no longer eligible for spankings. It was a coming-of-age and one I threw in my sister's face, reminding her to not be a jerk to me because she had two more years of spankings ahead of her. It also meant I was ready to graduate to the lunch line at the diner. Buttering toasts and cleaning up eggshells over the last year had just been training – a cinch compared to what was required for lunch. Breakfast was confined to the griddle, toaster and occasional pot of oatmeal over a single burner. Lunch? It was a whole different beast. The griddle was hotter, the fryers were fuming, the pizza oven was cranked and the line was filled with even more components and garnishes. The menu was four times as big, featuring everything from fry baskets to burgers, stews and pizzas. Timing was everything and multitasking was a must.

The fry station would be as good a station as any to start. It was narrow in focus; I could just keep my hands in the batter, breading different seafood and dropping in ready-made chicken fingers straight from the freezer. My father instructed me carefully: he wanted a perfect product and expected me to deliver. If I fucked up, he'd tell me, red-faced and fast-paced, 'Goddammit. Now I'm gonna show you once and that's it.' Or, 'Jesus Christ! I don't have time to show you twice. Just watch me, for Christ's sake.' Or, 'What are you tryin' to do, put me out of business? I work too fucking hard to just give shit away. You're giving them way too many shrimp!' If I perfected it, he kept quiet. The reward was letting the hot dish make its way out to the dining room. There was enough pride to be had in knowing it was up to his standards. And the feeling of a stranger out there in the dining room eating something I made was damn good. With more practice, I started to rule the fry station like a queen, whipping out baskets of perfectly golden seafood and chicken, French fries and onion rings. Through service, my father's voice became my inner monologue:

Scallops, shrimp and fish get rolled in egg wash then dipped in the flour; clams skip the egg and go straight to the flour mix. Not too much; don't make it cakey; nobody likes a thick, greasy batter.

Haddock is expensive; pollock is cheap. Full-bellied clams are like gold. Treat 'em like that. Use your fingers to gently stretch the clams into rings so they spread out in the fryer – it makes them look bigger.

Be light with your hands; toss the pieces back and forth gently, letting the excess flour fall off. If you don't, it'll end up in the fryer and gum up the heating elements – you don't want to see the wrath that will take over if you blow a fryer. But at least I wouldn't get spanked.

Don't overfry. Bits of seafood take only twenty to thirty seconds. Think golden, not brown.

Give the basket a good shake when you pull it from the fryer, it will keep the seafood light and greaseless and help it not stick to the bottom of the basket.

Serve it fresh and hot, immediately from the fryer. Nobody likes soggy, cold clams. Ding the bell like hell when that hot fried food is up so the waitresses come running.

Scream over the bell if they don't run fast enough. Food is money.

The closeness and connection of feeding a complete stranger a plate of food that you had made with attention and care, created with your own two hands, to witness the reaction on their faces when they took the first bite and felt the flavours and textures on their tongue – it was a satisfaction built out of the greatest simplicity, even if it was just a plate of fried food. I could peer out from the back of the line and watch the patrons at the counter as they munched on the dishes I had fried up that my father deemed good enough to send out. They didn't need to see me; heck, words didn't even have to be exchanged, because the food did all the talking and the emotions it was capable of producing were so powerful. I could see their faces; I could feel their satisfaction. It brought me more joy than I had ever felt. And the side dish to this joy was that I was secretly gaining my father's attention.

I had watched my father long enough and practised hard enough – spending hours on the line with him so I could eventually keep up – that I must have shown him a glimmer of promise, because he started to introduce me to tasks that required more precision and skill than just dropping random things in a bath of hot oil and waiting for them to turn the right colour.

'This is rare, this is medium, this is medium-well, this is well.' He showed me by taking his finger and pressing it into the fleshy meat of burgers and steaks. 'Feel it?' he'd ask. 'It's like the palm of your hand.' He took his pointer finger and pushed on the fleshy edge of his palm, showing me the give that each temperature should feel like when it's done to liking. 'It's all in the feel,' he explained. And sure enough, when he cut into a steak, it was the exact temperature he had told me it would be. His cooking was old-school – no thermometers, no gadgets, no beeping timers or fancy equipment. He was cooking with instinct, with touch and with feel and he was teaching me how to do the same. From seasoning to doneness and proper measures, food would give you all the signs it was perfect if you paid enough attention and took great care. Care to slice the wheat bread to the perfect thickness, toasted just lightly so it was crispy on the outside but still warm and soft in the middle; care that each slice was just slightly slathered with a thin layer of mayo, just enough to keep the crispy layer of iceberg lettuce in place and the chicken salad not too dry, not too wet but just right and flavoured with a balanced sprinkling of salt and pepper. If you could make a perfect chicken salad sandwich, you could master a perfect anything in the kitchen. My dad shared his skills with me by letting me watch and learn. It was as though he were teaching me to tie my shoes but only showing me once. There was not enough time or energy in a tiring sixteen-hour day to show someone how to do something twice. But while sharing skills and techniques was one thing, sharing a recipe would be another.

My father placed a huge stainless bowl on the counter and, very cool and casual, told me he was going to show me something. Over the next ten minutes he didn't say much as he moved more slowly than usual, giving me a better chance to soak it in. 'See this?' or 'Watch' was all he needed to say at each step as I watched him intently. He pulled packets of ground meat from the walk-in and dumped them into the bowl, using his hands to combine them. He sprinkled the meat with a good bit of salt and pepper and kneaded it a little more. He took a box grater and grated a handful of raw carrot straight into the bowl, then a handful of grated pizza cheese. He took a bread bag that was filled with the unused heels and broke them into pieces. He chopped up a white onion and tossed it in, wiping a few tears from his eyes. A few raw eggs and a splash of milk, then he used his hands to churn the mixture into a big cohesive ball. He stuffed a casserole dish with the mixture and patted it nice and level. In a small bowl he added a mound of brown sugar and drowned it with ketchup and a small squirt of yellow mustard, mixing it into a smooth paste before spreading it over the meat with a spoon and popping it into the oven. And when the glossy dish of meat emerged from the oven an hour later, bubbling hot with rivulets of fat running around the edges, I could smell it immediately: it was Dad's meatloaf. He had given me the secrets to the dish that he had made for our family so many times. It was the dish that warmed my stomach, warmed my heart and made me feel okay no matter what. His moment of sharing was intentional. It went beyond just being part of the job; it was part of him doing the best job he could as a dad. He was patient with me, tender even. It was a rare feeling, just the two of us. I couldn't help thinking that maybe, just maybe, if I continued to do right by him in the diner, there'd be more to come.

6

THE SOUND OF HARLEYS

On the occasional warm summer afternoon, the sound of rumbling motorcycle engines would fill the parking lot of the diner. I could hear the growls echoing through the screens of the dairy-bar windows all the way into the kitchen where I was working over high school vacation. I had come to recognize the warning signs that I'd be working the lunch line alone. When the sun was bright and the air was warm, it meant it was a good day to take a motorcycle ride, have a few beers and maybe some fried food. My father would yearn for the days when he too could feel the warm summer wind on his face while riding his Harley, but the busy shifts at the diner kept him anchored to the line. But that didn't stop his friends from finding him. A slow but steady stream of middle-aged men sporting leather jackets and greying handlebar moustaches would file through the kitchen and past the hectic line with a case of beer or a handle of vodka under one arm, en route to the private back deck. Even as customers were filling the dining room for lunch, my father would peel off to entertain the growing crowd of rowdy men out back. He felt the lure, he was a host and his private back deck was calling him to join the crowd of rough dudes that had gathered for a good time on a warm summer's day. He was more than a host, he was an entertainer, which he enjoyed as much as he enjoyed being a part of a good party. He was all too excited to leave me to tend to the mounting orders that flowed in so he could entertain the circus of beer-drinking clowns with raunchy jokes. He couldn't resist orchestrating the afternoon's activities of drinking and eating and drunkenly hitting golf balls into the neighbouring cornfield driving range–style. As I continued to plough through the lunch tickets my father would reappear here and there, set his perspiring Budweiser down on the line, slap a hamburger patty on the griddle and disappear again into the growing swarm of laughter that billowed through the back door. But after two beers he'd stop coming back to help, like clockwork. I'd be on my own to finish up the crushing rush of service. Again.

'Hey, Erin! Fix us up a platter of fried clams and bring them out back for us,' he'd yell from the back door with another beer in his hand and a half-buzzed smile on his face, pretending he was oblivious to the never-ending line of chicken salad sandwich and fried fish basket orders. I had learned how to dance between the griddle and Fryolator while making quick stews by filling ramekins with mixed raw seafood, big pats of butter and a thick pour of half-and-half, then microwaving them on high for a minute or two before garnishing them with a sprinkle of paprika, a wedge of lemon and a packet of oyster crackers. While they cooked, I stuffed the fry baskets with fresh-cut French fries and chicken fingers, dropping them into the hot vat of oil before bouncing to the griddle to flip the assortment of hamburgers and steaks on the hot top, checking their doneness with a quick touch of my finger, a rare, two mediums and a few well-dones. There was toast to toast for BLTs, one white, two wheats and one rye. This one wanted mayo, that one wanted cheese, another one wanted no onion or pickle. Baked potato and sour cream for the meatloaf special at the bar and a side of peas, please. Mashed potatoes with extra gravy, a side of broccoli with the roast beef. I kept a bowl of fresh nasturtium blossoms that I picked each morning from my mother's backyard garden before my shift and would pause to dot special plates with the bright garnishes, even in the busiest of lunch rushes. It brought me joy in those stressful moments. And when the last order had been filled and the bell on the counter sat quiet, I would go to the walk-in to fetch the plastic tub of shucked clams that the rogue group of men out back had been waiting for. One by one I would dredge a few giant handfuls of full-bellied clams through the soft, floury fry batter and drop them gently into the bubbling oil, frying them just long enough to turn a soft gold before pulling up the wire mesh basket and shaking them vigorously. I dumped the tender and crispy fried pieces onto a platter, mounding them high, and sprinkled them with a dusting of parsley flakes and a few lemon twists before delivering them to the impromptu private party.

The men would be circled around my father, listening intently as he sputtered crude stories laced with profanity, all erupting into laughter. I would be able to smell the beer from their breath.

'Oh, beautiful. Look at this! Fried clams,' my father would say, as though it was always a surprise, something new. He'd motion for the group to clear the way for me and the platter and the men would swarm the pile of food vulture-like, as if they hadn't eaten in days. They'd lick the crumbs from their moustaches, looking me up and down.

'Jesus, you are growing right up,' they'd slur. *'You even sprouted a little pair of titties. Jeff, had I known your girls were all grown-up with tits, I woulda been coming around more often.'*

'Hey sweetheart. You got any red stuff? Bring us a side of that red stuff – I love to dip in the red stuff. You get your red stuff yet?'

'Ketchup? Yeah.'

'Easy now, easy now,' my dad would chuckle as my fifteen-year-old cheeks flushed hot with embarrassment. He had been laughing, too. I wanted him to stick up for me, I wanted him to punch the guy for saying these things. I wanted him to protect me – like the one and only time I could remember, when I had wandered into our chicken coop at five years old and had been pecked in the eye by the giant hostile rooster that ruled the coop. I emerged with blood trickling down my face, shrieking in pain and shock. My father had gone straight to the coop and let the rough and tough bird out. He let him graze on the lawn for a split second before turning to our Doberman and exclaiming, 'Have at 'im, boy!' The dog could have snapped that bird's neck in a split second, ending its life mercifully, just like that. But he didn't. He took his time circling the old rooster, gnashing his teeth and licking his lips. He lunged, attacking the bird, gnawing and stripping him down with mouthfuls of feathers in a way that seemed so intentional, like he was taking his time, savouring this moment – enjoying it, even. I looked up at my father to see a cracked smile on his face, an unspoken satisfaction that the bird was getting what he deserved. He turned to me and gave me a promise that the rooster would never hurt me again. So, while I didn't expect my dad to rip this raunchy cock friend of his to shreds, a black eye or even a few stern words would have sufficed. But there'd be no such luck.

Eventually someone would ask – usually with a raspy, cigarette-gravelled voice—whether I could bring out a few cups of ice, 'Sweetheart'. It meant they were heading for the vodka and I would be working the dinner shift alone. Between bringing out more fried clams and fresh ice for a few dollar bills here and there, I would be prepping for service, pushing buckets full of Yukon gold potatoes through the French fry press on the wall and readying the fry station for what would always be a busy night. If there was any time between service, I'd go out back to fetch the golf balls the guys had been pitching into the cornfield-turned-drunken-driving-range. I used my kitchen apron to collect the balls in the field, ducking and dodging the whizzing hard white things as they continued to shoot in my direction. Upon return I'd endure all the ball jokes they thought were so tastefully hilarious before they handed me wads of cash, a buck a ball, in exchange for the retrieved balls. Some afternoons I'd make as much as seventy-five dollars in less than thirty minutes.

As the sun fell lower in the sky and the afternoon turned into evening, I'd watch the moustached men stagger out of the diner, straddle their bikes and light up the parking lot with one last thunderous roar of their Harley engines. Inevitably there was always one who would get so falling-down-stupid drunk that he'd have to wait it out and sober up in the back office with my dad or get drunker and wait for me to drive him home after finishing the dinner shift. I knew it to be the latter when a certain order would come in from the back room: two rib eyes, cooked rare. Baked potato with sour cream. Greek salad with oil and vinegar. My father's meal of choice to sop up a drunken afternoon, often topped off with a few shots of peppermint schnapps to freshen up. They would ramble drunkenly to one another as they waited for me to scrub down the grill and put the Fryolators to bed. After the floor had been mopped and the cash-up completed, I would hand my dad the cash from the register for the day's shifts and in return he would hand me the keys to his car.

'We're going to have to swing by Billy's house and drop him off on our way home,' was the usual refrain. 'He's in no shape to drive.'

Billy's house wasn't on the way to our house – it was thirty-four miles out of the way round-trip. But I wouldn't be surprised because being designated driver had become typical ever since I had gotten my learner's permit. It had become one of the hot new perks that was valued (besides my budding tits). As long as there was an adult in the car over the age of eighteen, drunk or sober, my father had discovered I could legally drive all over the place. He and his friends paid me good cash to drive them home and I figured it was the least they could do for what I had to put up with from them. Somehow, though, even the biggest bill never felt like enough.

I would climb into my father's Lincoln Town Car and pull the electric seat forward so I could reach the pedals. The two men would slide into the big backseat and pour a few more shots for the road. We would make our way in the dark around the curved bends of Route 137 as I practised my nighttime driving skills, switching between high and low beams as we met another car here and there. I'd pull over to the shoulder of the road on request when passengers were in need of a roadside piss. There were occasions when a passenger would lose his balance while urinating on the edge of the road. When the drunken tumble into the ditch occurred, I would dig through the bramble on the roadside, following the drunken babbles and laughter to find the intoxicated man buried in the brush. I'd pull him up, then help him crawl out of the ditch and back into the car and hope he had finished what he had started before the fall. Sometimes they wouldn't make it to the road and there'd be a wet splotch on the front of their Levi's as I helped them out of the car, barely able to stand on their own because my father – ever the host – had yet to stop feeding them shots. I'd get them to their kitchen table – my job was to get them home safely, not tuck them in – and they'd give me a handful of bills.

When I'd come back to the car, my dad would be in the front seat, signalling that he was done entertaining; I wasn't his servant anymore.

'We can go home now, Erin.'

I would buckle my seat belt, check the position of my mirrors and put the car into drive, but first making a full and complete stop before flicking the blinker to the right and pulling onto the road to head home. In time for the breakfast shift to start tomorrow at 6:00 A.M.

7

THE FULL BOAT

The idea of college was an exciting escape plan. It was a one-way ticket to get the hell out of Waldo County. It was a chance to take the first step toward living my own life. I could choose what to study, where to live and *how* to live. My mother was her usual supportive self, gently urging me to finally go for the things she knew I wanted. 'You've lived a country life; now you need to try the city life. Once you've lived them both, your heart will be able to decide who you are and the life you want to live.' Unlike many parents, she was able to separate her own dreams from mine.

Born into in a large family an hour south of Boston, my mom grew up craving something different. She wanted the wilds of Maine, the smell of clean, fresh air and a patch of dirt to call her own. She wanted to settle down on a quiet road where the only sounds would be peepers in the spring when the ground started to thaw, crickets in the summer and the slow engine of the occasional car or two that would pass each day. She wanted a simple life in a quiet corner of the world. When she met my dad in the late seventies, her dream started to take shape. They met at a party in the sleepy seasonal seaside town of Bayside, Maine. My father was living in a gutted and converted school bus on my grandparents' property and she was blinded by the silly details, overcome with the romance of living wild and free. It was a bold move for a woman as shy and timid as she, but she was seduced by the land and the visions of her future here. She would build a life, make a home, have children and raise them right here, giving them a different childhood from her own. My parents had given me a rural life, with chicken shit between my toes and the starry sky above my head. But I always wanted to know what it would feel like to walk on pavement and be surrounded by the bright lights of the city. I wanted to hop a train downtown in the middle of the night, maybe try Indian food for the first time. I wanted to feel the electricity pulsing through my veins; I wanted crowds and noise. Northeastern University, in the heart of Boston, seemed like my ticket to that life.

My father was less forthcoming with his support. He had been clear that he had no intention of contributing to my tuition. After all, he never had the chance to get away from here, so why should I? 'I'm not slaving away working my ass off through sixteen-hour days just to pay for you to go to school, so you'd best be getting good grades and getting yourself a heap of scholarships.' I wasn't surprised. He had always been telling me: 'Figure it out on your own,' but that didn't make it hurt any less. He was brutally honest that the cost of tuition for a year at Northeastern was as much as a brand-new Harley-Davidson and there was no way in hell he was going to put a penny into the ridiculous cost of a college education before buying himself a shiny new bike. But that didn't stop me from applying.

I was a pretty well-rounded student. I played soccer, ran track, took viola lessons, studied hard and did well in school, all while working at the restaurant after music and sports practices, on weekends and all summer long. I started to dream about medical school, so I had to take school seriously. I took French and German, eager to learn new languages, sure I would put them to good use and be the first person in my family ever to travel outside the United States. We didn't travel much as a family. The restaurant managed to keep us tethered and close to home. My father was also consistently not interested in going anywhere that would put him outside his comfort zone. If you were uncomfortable, it meant you weren't in control and he was the kind of guy who liked to stay in control. My mother held dreams inside of distant travel (the lavender fields in Provence or the sheep-filled fields of the Cotswolds, perhaps) but kept the secret to herself, knowing full well her husband would never go for such a thing. She didn't want to start any trouble, so instead she'd stick to being satisfied with our predictable family travels, which consisted of a once-a-year trip to Florida over our winter school break and a few car rides a year to Massachusetts to visit my mother's family south of Boston.

Boston had become a romance of mine from a young age. Each year my mother would load my sister and me up to make the trek from Freedom for our annual family Christmas party. Driving through the city always sparked a wild excitement inside me. I made sure to never doze off in the backseat as we drew closer to the city, fearful of missing the view as we rounded the bend on the highway. I could see all the shimmering lights of the city skyline as the Tobin Bridge and its tollbooth stood before us like a gateway. I never ceased to be mesmerized by all the lights, the three lanes of fast-moving traffic, the Citgo sign flashing by Fenway Park in the far distance, the sight of the trains moving in and out of North Station and the blinking white-and-red spires atop each skyscraper! It felt so bustling and alive. I had a big crush on the place.

Boston seemed like the perfect fit for me. It was close enough to the Maine border to keep me comforted on the rare chance that I became homesick, I had family who lived just an hour south of the city and some friends who were also attending Boston-based schools. But the city was also starkly different enough from where I was coming from to make me feel like it was on the other side of the world. So I submitted my application to Northeastern University, crossed my fingers and hoped for the best. And when the acceptance letter arrived in our mailbox one early winter afternoon, it was my golden ticket out of there. The tuition was steep, but I had done as my father asked and worked hard for the grades that allotted me some scholarship money. I'd still have to apply for student loans to pay for the rest that remained, knowing it would put me into debt that would take me decades to pay off, but that didn't seem to matter at the moment.

Not more than a week later, another envelope arrived in our mailbox. This one was from the University of Maine (my fallback school) offering me a full ride – tuition, books, housing, you name it. The only thing I'd have to purchase myself was the meal plan. I knew the smart thing to do would be to buck up and take the handout. But something felt dirty about giving up on Boston. I didn't want to live a life where dollar amounts dictated dreams. Sure, there was a load of debt that would come along with choosing Northeastern, but I could find a way to dig out from under it. Though it also wasn't completely up to me; I would need the blessings of my parents.

My mother was never one to ruffle feathers or cause a scene. She didn't stand up to people, even when she thought they were wrong. She was submissive after living for years under the great tension my father was so good at producing. She had learned that the best way to avoid stepping on his wide radius of broken glass was just to keep quiet and to herself. But in the case of advocating for me and my college decision, she didn't want my life to be shaped by my father's jaded and unreasonable opinions.

My mother held both of my acceptance letters in her hand, asking me for one last confirmation – did the thought of the city really make my heart pound? *Yes.* There was only one thing to do: we would tear up the acceptance letter from the University of Maine; we would never tell my father about the free ride. So he got his new Harley and I got a ticket to Boston.

My grandparents had a special send-off in mind for me. They picked me up on a Friday night, my grandfather in his best sport coat, which meant it was a special occasion because I had only ever seen him wear it if he was going either to a funeral or to the horse races in Bangor for the night. We rode over the winding woods roads from Freedom to the coastal town of Camden, nearly forty-five minutes away. They took me to the finest restaurant at the time down on the docks, the Waterfront. There were real candles on the tables and cloth napkins and a fireplace with a big roaring fire. The menu was studded with pricey starters and main courses costing over twenty dollars! A lavish contrast to the diner food I was accustomed to. I had never been to such a fine place before. Order anything you like, they told me. I ordered a fancy salad, with mesclun, dried cranberries and goat's cheese. It reminded me of the time I snuck a bag of the fancy mix into our Sysco order at the diner, eager to replace the basic iceberg salad we served with a bright and colourful mix of baby lettuces. I couldn't forget the sight of all the melamine bowls coming back to the dish station with handfuls of the red lettuces tossed aside, uneaten. It had been too groovy a move for some of the local farm boys, who only knew iceberg to be the one lettuce of the world. I ate every last drop of this salad that night, savouring the balsamic vinaigrette and the fancy company of my grandparents.

I ordered a thick filet mignon, with a twice-baked potato and a side of garlicky green beans. But it was dessert that really got me – a shallow dish of vanilla custard, topped with a crispy layer of burnt sugar – crème brûlée. My God, what was this magical creation I was eating for the first time in my life? Its creamy thick pudding soothed me with warm thoughts of my grandmother's instant stovetop pudding, but it took me to new levels with its crunchy, sugary shell. It was a sweet, celebratory and eye-popping moment for me. It was a decadent moment that would fondly come back whenever I tasted that rich vanilla custard with the crisp burnt crust.

And on that following Sunday, I would make one final stop at my dad's diner, our car in the lot stuffed full of all my possessions that would fill my dorm room, my mother and I en route to Boston. One more breakfast at the diner, whatever I liked, one last squeeze from my grandparents and one rare and awkward hug from my father before my grandmother tucked a warm doughnut in a sack into my hand for the ride south. I left them in the breakfast rush that morning, with their grease-stained aprons, flipping pancakes and eggs on the griddle as I hit the pavement, trading the bright starry sky for one filled with city lights. Nina was nowhere to be found. It wasn't surprising; it wasn't unusual. Our years as a couple of teenage girls under the same roof only cemented the fact that we were different, very different and far from being the best of friends. There would be no hugs good-bye, no well wishes, no warmth on that day between two sisters, but her cold silence and lack of presence that day couldn't bring me down. I was filled with too much excitement over the prospect of this new free life to be dragged down by our complex relationship. I had freed myself from Freedom.

PART TWO

UNITY

8

IT BETTER BE BLUE

The stars had seemingly aligned. I had made it out of Freedom; I was living a city life of dreams. But the fragility of it all was so unexpected. I didn't know it would only take one false turn, one fateful night, to send all the hard work, hopes and dreams crashing to the ground. They thought I was the good girl, the one it would never happen to, so cautious, smart, responsible and filled with prospects and big dreams. Yet here I was, two years into college, twenty-one years old, pregnant and under great pressure to abort the baby that was growing inside of me. Pressure from my family; pressure from myself. Because my father said so, because I was too young, because my life had promise before all of this mess and because if I didn't, I'd just be throwing all my hopes away. If I kept it, I'd be sure to end up back in Waldo County, back in Freedom, on that quiet dirt road that would, without a doubt, become my dead-end future. It was my choice and for that I was thankful, but that never meant it would be easy. The truth was, it felt like failure no matter what I chose. Both decisions carried a crippling hand-ful of life-altering changes and neither left me feeling good about the life that would be left. Getting pregnant was like dropping an anchor. All the dreams of what I thought my life would be sailed past me as I came to a screeching halt. I'd never finish college, I'd never go to medical school and I'd never become the doctor I dreamed I'd one day become. There would be no escaping Freedom and no living out big-city California dreams because I had squandered my one chance. I could feel the ball and chain in my belly, the result of one night with an ex-boyfriend and a bottle of cheap Chardonnay while home during Christmas vacation, pulling me back to the rural town I had worked so hard to escape from. I knew that if I chose this baby, I'd not only be sacrificing dreams but I'd also be raising it alone.

'You just couldn't keep your fucking legs together,' my father barked while frothing at the mouth. 'Now look at the big fucking mess you've made.' I was already beating myself up inside, feeling worthless and loose. His angry words only confirmed what I already believed: I was a disgrace. I had only ever wanted to make my parents proud. It had felt like my profound duty as the firstborn, the dutiful daughter. They expected trouble from Nina, but never in their wildest dreams expected this from me. I had pushed through high school so I could get into a good college that would take me somewhere far away from here. I worked hard to get good grades, played soccer and ran track, avoided hanging out with the kids who did drugs, I didn't drink and I worked weekends and summers at the diner to save money and show my dad I was a hard and loyal worker. Even though this eventually meant that I was admitted to Northeastern University to study medicine with the hopes of becoming an obstetrician (the irony didn't escape me), it never felt like enough. I had always been a letdown to my father. I was a girl and now a pregnant one at that. I'd only armed him with more ammo to constantly remind me of my failed existence. If I had been a cat, he would have drowned me in a hessian sack. He never shied away from reminding me that the child I was carrying was a bastard, that I had ruined my life and maybe his too by spiking his blood pressure daily. He was burning mad that he couldn't control my decision to keep or abort this baby. He was burning mad that the high school boyfriend who had gotten me pregnant wouldn't be involved. It was my choice to keep the baby; it wasn't my choice to do this alone. No one could force me to have an abortion and I couldn't force anyone who had no interest in doing so to be a part of raising a child. I knew the chances were good that I would raise this child on my own.

The father had waffled at first, thinking maybe he could wrap his head around the responsibility. *How hard could it be? A pack of nappies here, an occasional sleepless night there . . . ?* But in reality the responsibilities were far greater than either of us could have fathomed and this wasn't supposed to be part of the plan. The challenge of choice didn't make the situation easy; the conflict and separation between us made it that much harder. I didn't stop hopelessly dreaming he'd rise up, grab my hand and say, 'I got you, girl, whatever you decide,' because deep in my heart I still had love left for him. The reaction to my pregnancy was as if I had been infected with a wild virus – *steer clear of that girl*. My feelings of heartache were intertwined with feelings of guilt. I felt that I was the one who got knocked up. I was the one ruining our lives. And no matter what I did, what I decided, I couldn't repair the fact that our lives were forever changed because of what was happening inside my body.

My father demanded that he '*Be a man*; step up,' and when that (not surprisingly) didn't happen, he grew increasingly aggravated that he had no control over the situation. He would throw himself into angry fits and release his frustrations with verbal explosions or, occasionally, threaten to pop a few nails into a tire or two of the car of the guy who had knocked me up. I still wonder how many sets of tires he went through over the course of those nine months. Because despite the swarm of pleas around me to end the pregnancy, I chose to keep the baby. And with just a few years of college under my belt, recognizing full well that girls like me who come from the middle of nowhere don't get second chances, I dropped out.

Inevitable harsh judgment and a slew of opinions followed. Some predictable, some not so much. I was anticipating my sister's glee, her bright moment to shine and look down upon me in my moment of weakness and imperfection, the moment she had been craving all these years, licking her lips and waiting for me to tumble down beneath her: *Look at Little Miss Perfect all knocked up! And they all thought it would have been me! How does it feel to be a fuckup, dear sister?!* I could hear her cackle with enjoyment. But she didn't – she didn't laugh, she didn't gloat, she didn't trample me with excitement over my downfall. She didn't speak of it to me; instead she sent a message through our mother: *'Tell Erin she needs to have this baby. I know her. I know her.'* She recounted a story to my mother about a baby robin I had rescued after it had fallen from its nest. I kept it warm with a heating pad and the warmth of my hands, fed it chopped-up bits of worms that I gathered in the garden and gave it water using a tiny eyedropper. I raised it up into a strong and healthy bird until it was good and ready to go off into the world on its own. *'She'll be a good mother,'* she confirmed to our mom. She recounted the farm animals that died over the years and the tears I cried for them and she couldn't imagine me aborting my own baby, growing inside me, and not living to regret it one day. Her reaction was uncharacteristic, surprisingly affirming and a rare and tender moment of near-sisterhood between us. It was a feeling that I'd hold on to and cherish, knowing it would likely be but a momentary glimmer and it would get me through all her prolonged absences over the months to come.

My mother wasn't outspoken like my father. She was his antithesis, soft and calm. She made up for all the ideas of inadequacy that my father continually fed me. She showered me with love and support and quickly grew excited about the arrival of her first grandchild. She looked to the future and, instead of hardship, saw a baby coming and she insisted there would be joy. She insisted that, despite my father, we would eventually find our own way to a better, happier place. There was a different feeling between us than ever before. I felt closer to her. Maybe it was because Nina had moved out years ago and here I was, back home, just me, like an only child. She was ever present, ever loving, no attention to divide between two same-same but very different sisters. I soaked up the attention like a salve, using it to treat my emotional wounds.

Eventually my mother became more than just Mom. She was becoming my birthing partner, my confidante, my biggest cheerleader in what would be one of the most challenging times of my life. She was becoming my best friend when most of mine had drifted away. When I became pregnant, some had quietly distanced themselves out of embarrassment (or apparent fear that it might be contagious). Some were swayed by the disapproving glares of their mothers. There was a handful of fair-weather friends who conveniently fell out of touch. Those who stuck by me were separated by distance, as I was now living back in rural Maine and the great divide of our contrasting lifestyles was growing wider. The good girls were on track, studying and pursuing their college hopes and dreams. While they were studying for bio exams and figuring out what party to go to over the weekend, I was taking Lamaze classes and figuring out which breast pump had the best ratings and how to deal with gestational diabetes.

There was no one who could tell me what to expect, what contractions felt like, or that breast-feeding was hard work and made your nipples sore as hell. Well, except one. One friend who was by my side every day lifting me up and rooting me on more than any other – sisterlike, even; my mother. Sure, times had changed and we were years apart in our birthing experiences (my mother had given birth to me in 1980 and brought me home from the hospital on her lap in the front seat of the car), but at the root of it all, our ability to understand each other and this journey would be forever timeless.

We were forming a most sacred partnership, bringing this kid into the world together. She knitted drawers full of tiny sweaters and hats from skeins of soft organic yarn. We found my old crib in the barn and stripped it down, repainting it a soft sage green. Then we found an old dresser and unfinished rocking chair and did the same to match. We made bunting together from some inexpensive white eyelet cloth, as well as batting to wrap around the edge of the crib. We set up a nursery in my childhood bedroom, the same one that I had come home to. She filled the sometimes heartrending vacancy of the standard male role at my Lamaze classes, hugging me tight and drying my tears as needed. Each week I was reminded of my rejection, failure and heartache as I looked around the full room of the stereotypical couples sitting cross-legged on the floor. The men placing their hands on the growing bellies of the women, who basked in the comfort and intimacy of their partners.

For every brave face I tried to put on, acting as if I were just fine doing this without him by my side, I secretly wept inside – or out loud when I was alone. My broken heart felt more like a broken bone and I was learning there was no quick fix to heal the pain. Months had passed since the initial shock and break, but it became clear that it would take ages to heal. I still woke at 2:00 A.M. some nights, tossing and turning restlessly, dousing my pillowcase in quiet tears, beating myself up, wondering what I could have done differently. I knew we would never be together again, but I'd always be reminded of him every time I looked into the face of his child. He had been my first love. We had parted and gone in different directions, but no matter the distance we were connected for life now, whether we liked it or not. It hurt like hell at first, then slowly a little less, then eventually a little less. But even as my heart healed, I sensed there would always be a lingering hairline scar. Pangs of pain would come to me in the most random of moments, much like when my left shoulder ached ever so slightly on damp days, a reminder of the time I broke my arm in fourth grade.

'It better be blue,' my father sputtered as I hung up my apron, peeling off from the lunch line at the diner early to head to an ultrasound appointment. 'You might want to think about not coming back if it isn't,' he said as he reached into a ten-pound pack of raw beef on the counter, pulling a fistful of meat out and throwing it back and forth between his hands angrily before forming it into a patty and slapping it onto the grill. He was angry I was leaving him alone in the kitchen to man the busy lunch at the diner to go to this appointment and he'd be even more irritated if I returned to tell him I was having a girl.

With my mother by my side, the ride to Bangor was especially long and quiet. Any excitement about learning the sex of my baby was clouded by the fear that if I were having a girl, my relationship with my father would plummet to new lows that I was terrified to discover. I hadn't cared one way or another about the sex of my unborn child until now. As much as I resented my father for his unfair prejudice against me and as much as I knew, deep down, that there might have been nothing I could have done to please the man, I wanted to. As children so naively do, I wanted to please my father, make him proud, give him the boy he always wanted. And even if it wasn't enough to heal our relationship, at least my child wouldn't grow up feeling as worthless and weak as my father had made me feel for as long as I could remember.

As the cool ultrasound gel hit my bare stomach, panic set in even deeper. I could feel the angst building inside me as the nurse moved the plastic wand around my belly with circular motions, like a fortune-teller with a giant fleshy ball, looking to see what gender the future would bring.

'Do you want to know the sex?' the nurse asked. I looked at my mom. Of course I wanted to know, because keeping it a surprise seemed pointless. The surprise of finding out I was pregnant in the first place seemed like enough to last me for years. And any insight I had on the gender of this baby might give me time to brace for my father's backlash. I nodded my head up and down because the word 'yes' couldn't come out of my mouth. I just wanted a healthy baby, girl or boy, to whom I would give all my strength, to raise to feel valued, respected and loved. I didn't care about the gender because I would give my love equally.

'I see a baby boy in there,' the nurse exclaimed. 'It's a boy!'

I sighed with strained relief and looked to my mother, who was sighing too, knowing that my father's pleasure would make all of our lives a little easier. The fear of my father's disapproval was slowly exiting me with each exhale. My mother and I were both relieved, I could return home without greater judgment and we followed our relief with tears of joy. The excitement that had been clouded by fear exploded, triumphant. I was carrying a boy and maybe, just maybe, this child – like a young King Arthur – could pull a sword of reason and kindness from my father's stony heart, softening him and perhaps exposing a capacity to love. But at the very least, he would be born with a shield that I never had against the emotional trauma my father inflicted. I was carrying a baby boy and in an instant, the perceived would-be wrong had become the only right that my father would ever recognize. For a brief time I felt his love and respect.

9

MAKING A MOTHER

They say that when babies are born, they look like their fathers. It's nature's effort to help male creators recognize their offspring, facilitating the bonding that didn't happen during the nine months they spent in utero. But mainly so they feel more compelled to stick around.

He was born on a Tuesday afternoon, seven pounds, six ounces, twenty-one inches long, with a full head of dark brown locks – just like his father. From the very first moment I held my new baby boy close to my bare chest, my mother and sister at my bedside, I silently processed the strikingly obvious resemblance to his dad. (My father stood to one side, keeping his distance, showing little emotion.) I sobbed with joy that he was here and I wept with sadness that I'd see his father forever in him, every time I'd see those curly locks, those dark brown eyes. Would I be reminded every day when I looked at my child that his father stopped loving me, seemingly cold and easy? Would I feel the heart-crushing pain of his walking out on me every day for the rest of my life? No. I couldn't live like that. I had too much hope in my heart for this fresh, newborn boy. I would name him Jaim, a twist on *j'aime,* French for 'I love'.

In what seemed like a flash, Jaim had left my arms. A quick cuddle with his new grandmother and aunt before being whisked away to be washed, weighed and checked from head to toe. What had just happened? In what felt like the blink of an eye I had become a mother. I felt a shift in the air, like when autumn seems to come in one quick afternoon near the end of August. The world was forever changed now. I was no longer one; we were two.

'You must be feeling so hungry by now,' one of the nurses said. 'What can I get for you? What would make you feel really good and comfortable?'

I wiped the tears from the corner of my eye with my hospital gown and paused for a moment.

'A doughnut? And a glass of milk.'

It was the first thing that came to mind and it was not lost on me that it was the very same breakfast my grandparents would serve me some mornings at the diner.

After my family had departed to get some rest, the nurse returned to my room, rolling a plastic crib with my newborn baby toward me.

'Now it's his turn,' she said as she handed the fragile little bundle to me to feed. 'I'll let you two get acquainted.' She smiled and left the room, closing the door behind her. There we were, just the two of us, alone for the very first time. We were together and yet I had never felt so alone. I sat in the hospital bed with my legs outstretched in front of me, cradling him in my forearms, just staring at this unbelievably tiny being. It was the most beautiful and yet most terrifying moment I had ever felt. I had never felt so much love and I had never felt so much fear – all at the exact same time. He was so beautiful, so small and so sweet smelling, with tender pink skin. He was perfect. His tiny fingers slowly caressed his own face as he stretched a bit, his dark locks hiding beneath his tiny knit cap. He was here and I – just me – had the incredible responsibility to never let him down, to lift him up and to love him forever. I promised him right then and there that I would give him my all.

* * *

The nine months that I had carried Jaim in my womb felt like an eternity, waiting, anticipating, knowing his birth was imminent. I was excited to meet the tiny being that had been growing inside me over all these months, but anxious about what having him here in the outside world would look like. Was I prepared to care for him, raise him strong? Would I know what to do once he was here? Was motherhood instinctual; would it just come naturally? Would I know how to hold him just right or soothe him when he cried? What if I didn't? Even with my mother's support, I couldn't escape the reality that I was bringing this baby into the world partnerless. Could one person give a child enough love to make up for the love of two?

Days dragged on for what felt like weeks and the weeks felt like months. Even his birth moved slowly, with five days of contractions, stuck at four centimeters. But when he arrived, time made up for its lagging. The first few days were terrifying and emotionally rocky as my hormones bounced around, trying to find their way back to normal. I was sleeping deeply in short spurts after days of not sleeping at all before his birth and would wake, fearful and confused, to his foreign-sounding cries in the crib beside my bed. I'd sit up, heart pounding, sweating, discombobulated. *Was I dreaming?* I'd come to eventually and realize – *Oh my God, I'm a mother to a living, breathing, crying baby. Now wake up and pick him up! You have to swaddle him! You have to feed him! You have to burp him! You have to comfort him!* It was the strangest feeling, being in my childhood bedroom, the same soft rose wallpaper, with the baffling addition of a baby. I hadn't completely grown up yet, but I was a mother now and would have to hurry up.

No one could have warned me about all of the fears that I would soon discover came along with being a mother. I never truly understood the depth and meaning of fear until Jaim was born. He was so little that I thought I might drop him or break his tiny fragile bones. I worried that I would fall asleep while breast-feeding him in bed and accidentally smother him, waking up to a cold and lifeless baby beside me. When I put him down for a nap, I'd panic – *Is he still breathing?* I checked the rise and fall of his chest, hawk-like and constantly. I feared that someday he would wonder where his father was, or feel pain over the fact that he was gone. Feared that he would hold me responsible and resent me. Feared that it was my duty to provide him with everything he needed to feel safe and secure. What if I didn't have what it would take to give it to him?

As the days and nights went on, we found a rhythm together. I became more confident holding him, even trying out new moves to rock and soothe him. I was becoming a nappy-changing queen and my nipples finally toughened up enough so I didn't tear up in pain every time I fed him. It was hard work – the hardest I had ever done – and a kind of work that no one could have ever prepared me for. From time to time I wondered if it would have been easier if I wasn't single. But then again, there were moments when being on my own made it easier. When Jaim cried in the night for food or a nappy change there was no rolling over in bed, elbowing a snoring man beside me and making sleep-deprived requests like, 'Honey, it's your turn. Can you change and feed him?' Because it was *always* my turn. But I often imagined the luxury.

I was single, but I was not completely alone. My mom had taken on the part-time role of stand-in partner. From bathing to changing and feeding to burping, there wasn't anything she wouldn't do. And she loved Jaim with every ounce of her heart, which helped me relax, knowing that he was receiving more love than just mine. My father kept his distance. When he was actually around – on his days off and in the late evenings after he had returned from the restaurant – he made it clear that he didn't even want to touch the baby until he was strong enough to hold his head up on his own. Until then he would smile and coo playfully at him, which felt strange at first because I'd never witnessed my father doing something so soft and almost sweet to a human – only to animals. Though he refused to call Jaim by his first name. Instead, he referred to him by his middle name, Jeffery, which was his own name. I realized it was probably the name he had always hoped he would name his own boy, had he had one. Slowly he was softening to Jaim, realizing it wasn't traditional as he had hoped, but it still yielded him the same result: his family name would carry on now.

By day I had free range of my parents' house while they were both off at work, my father at the restaurant, my mother teaching at school. I tried to stay active with Jaim in my arms, so I'd tidy and clean and do other small and helpful projects around the house, as some token of thanks for the room and board that they were temporarily allowing me. But what I enjoyed most was having the kitchen all to myself. Occasionally I'd have a chance to do a little dinner prep to surprise Mom when she'd arrive home after a long day of work. In the evenings, my mother and I would sit at the dinner table, exhausted. We would linger over dinner, both enjoying the quiet while my dad was still at work and Jaim was upstairs asleep. Some nights I'd wrap a plate of leftovers and place it in the refrigerator, knowing my father would be home later, tired and most likely buzzed and would be rummaging through the fridge for an evening snack. It was mainly to serve as a quiet act of kindness to dull his impatience with me. He had been waiting for my return to the diner and to the busy line for weeks now. My absence meant he actually had to work, which kept him away from playing with his drinking buddies.

As the weeks passed, the kitchen was the place I looked forward to being most – though not at the diner. I was getting more agile in my parents' quiet, tidy home kitchen and was becoming fairly good at getting some real baking done during Jaim's naps or even with him strapped to my chest – a little flour on his head never hurt. On cool autumn days I'd bundle him up for walks down the old dirt road that I had walked and biked so many times as a kid and I'd fill the buggy with roadside apples along the way, sometimes turning the foraged fruit into a cinnamon-sweet crisp. Eventually I rediscovered an old pastry set my mother had given me a few years back, tucked away in the back of a drawer. It reminded me of the joy that piping icing and creams on cakes and tarts had once brought me. I got to thinking that maybe I could make a little spare cash while being at home with Jaim, whipping up fresh baked goods and delivering them. I put together a list of cookies, muffins, cakes and other treats I knew how to make well and created a menu: there were Nanny's molasses cookies, oatmeal lace, good old-fashioned chocolate chip and simple sugar. I could make muffins of any flavour with the simple batter I knew how to mix, adding fresh blueberries, strawberries, rhubarb or raspberries. There were cheesecakes and coffee cakes and chocolate cakes too and last but not least, carrot cakes. I made trifold menus on my mother's computer and printed them out with 'CAKES! COOKIES! PIES! & SCONES!' followed by our home phone number. I hung handfuls of the brochures on the bulletin board at my father's restaurant and sent a stack along with my mother to place in the teachers' lounge at her school. I found stacks of brown Kraft paper bakery boxes at a discount paper store in Bangor and had a custom rubber stamp made at the local copy centre. I stamped 'FLOUR CHILD' on each box and tied each with a piece of twine, delivering the trickle of orders that came floating in. The teachers at my mother's school proved to be my best clients – cakes for birthdays or retirements, muffins because it was Monday, cookies just because it was Friday. It would never be enough for me to make any sort of living, but it gave me just what I needed: a smidge of hope that I could be a mom and find work that made me happy.

* * *

But coming back to the line at the diner was inevitable. It was a place I was comfortable with, a world I was familiar with and it was an instant job that would put some cash in my pocket. I picked up weekend shifts, waiting tables and running the line while my mother helped with Jaim. She happily picked up the slack of parenting, giving me the chance make a little money in exchange for the peace of mind of knowing that she wouldn't have to be the one at the diner instead. But when the dead of winter rolled around again and the diner closed to let the snowdrifts fill the quiet parking lot, I started looking elsewhere for work. Nappies weren't cheap, I had student loan payments still flowing in from the college I had dropped out of – a monthly sting that made me feel less than. Plus, I couldn't stay at my parents' forever.

I found a part-time job working retail at a kitchen supply store in the little coastal town of Belfast just twenty minutes away. It was like a candy store, filled with the most delicious kitchen tools I had only seen on TV and cookbooks I had dreamed of owning. There were colourful arrays of KitchenAids; food processors in all different sizes; copper pots; big, beautiful roasting pans; and knife racks filled with the sharpest full-tang knives that made our plastic-handled knives at the diner look like children's toys. There was a full display of cast-iron enamelled pots in all different sizes and bright colours, each costing hundreds of dollars. I lusted after these items, making a registry in my mind, debating which colours and sizes I would choose, knowing my chances of ever owning a single one were slim. There were piles of baking sheets, Bundt and other cake tins and cookie cutters in every shape and size you could imagine. And all sorts of gadgets and machines like culinary torches that you would use to burn the sugary tops of crème brûlée, waffle-cone makers and countertop ice cream machines. On quiet Sunday afternoon shifts, I'd paw through the pages of every new cookbook I couldn't afford to buy in between checking out customers. I had a library at my fingertips of every great cook, from the simplest of dishes to the hautest of cuisines and there were even books about baby food. Alice Waters's *Chez Panisse Vegetables* and *Chez Panisse Fruit,* Suzanne Goin's *Sunday Suppers,* Ruth Reichl, Martha Stewart, Ina Garten, Skye Gyngell and Judy Rodgers. I devoured their wisdom, intrigued by the ingredients they chose and how they were paired. I would daydream about dishes – how I would make them, how I would serve them and how people would feel inside when they ate them.

When I discovered that there was a staff discount, I splurged and bought a baby food book. Determined to get my money's worth out of it, I put it to fast use. I steamed winter squash we had grown in our garden and pureed it in an old food processor of my father's, then pushed the puree through a fine-mesh sieve so it was silky and smooth. I played with all different flavours from apple to fresh spinach, carrot, pear and beetroot, using the fresh fruit purees to mix into the vegetable flavours Jaim wasn't crazy about. Making baby food was simple and easy and it made me feel good that I was feeding Jaim the freshest food I could give him. Food made me feel loved when I was a kid and I wanted him to feel that too. I would make sure to tell him every single day that I loved him, to make up for every day I never heard the words myself. I would give him my best, my everything and with a few simple purees, I hoped he could taste just how very much I loved him.

10

SINGING FOR OUR
SUPPER

Working at the kitchen supply shop was the first real non-diner job
I had (minus the two short stints I tried to pull off working at other
restaurants after my dad and I had gotten into a heated argument.
He eventually lured me back). It was different, but at the same time
it was comfortable – an offshoot that kept me connected to food
(without the mess) and offered me a chance to grow in a setting
where I could be independent (without my dad as a boss). I was the
youngest of all of the women who worked there, but I could hold
my own. I was just as knowledgeable about many of the tools and
gadgets, thanks to my love of cooking and the fact that I had been
doing it almost all my life. If something was related to the kitchen,
learning about it seemed to come more naturally to me. I built
on my knowledge, picking up a nuanced understanding of the
countertop appliances, their intricate parts and how they worked.
The technical details got me thinking about the endless possibilities that exist in the kitchen. It got me thinking beyond the simple
diner fare that had been inked in my mind like a tattoo. I liked
the job well enough, but at the end of the week, the ten-dollars-
per-hour wage, minus the discounted store goods that I couldn't
resist, didn't leave much to speak of in my paycheck. It would never

be enough to support Jaim and I would have to find other ways to supplement it somehow.

I didn't have any bartending skills. And I had gotten pregnant just a month after my twenty-first birthday, so I didn't even have a lot of experience with booze. But I had certainly mixed a fair amount of vodka-tonics and popped the tops off hundreds of beer bottles for my dad and his friends, so how hard could bartending be? Either the catering company was severely desperate, or my simplistic skills were somehow enough to land me a gig working weekends, tending bar at weddings and art openings. I learned how to make a few simple cocktails and how to properly unfoil and uncork Champagne (I learned quickly after striking myself straight between the eyes with a cork how *not* to open a bottle of bubbly). It turned out to be good money, especially when party guests got loose and started throwing down tips with each drink. There were times when I was making as much in one night as I made in a full week working on the line of my dad's diner. But it wasn't just the money that I enjoyed about the job – the food that was coming out of the kitchen excited me. It was simple, straightforward and classic, but it had little twists that caught my interest. There were crab cakes with chili and lime-studded aioli; beef tenderloin with horseradish-laced crème fraîche; butternut squash lasagna with fried sage and creamy Parmesan sauce; marinated shrimp soaked in pickling spices, fresh lemon juice and spicy chilli flakes; and pecan pie spiked with bourbon and chocolate ganache. I'd get to sneak nibbles of the leftovers after the wedding cake had been cut and the bar had slowed down for the night. Sometimes a small tinfoil package even made its way home with me.

One late afternoon I was setting up the bar at the yacht club in Rockport, arranging glasses on a table with crisp white linens. I was stacking the emptied glass racks in the corner of the kitchen and I could feel the energy in the room wasn't as playful and bois-terous as it usually was during setup. I noticed a few members of the kitchen crew were circling around the wedding cake.

'It slid when I hit the brakes. Some asshole pulled out right in front of me on Route 1!' one of the crew members explained. The cake had slid into the back of a plastic cooler, leaving a gaping indent on one side, exposing the yellow cake and some lemon curd oozing out of the gash. There was panic in the air as the crew spun the cake around on its pedestal, scratching their heads and clench-ing their jaws, trying to come up with a miracle to fix the mess.

'Do you have any extra icing?' I asked from the outskirts of the circle. One of the kitchen cooks scurried over to one of the large coolers and started to rummage around, before pulling out a small clear plastic quart of buttercream and setting it on the table in front of me. It was almost solid from being in the cooler, so I picked it up and wrapped my hands around it to warm it back up.

'How about a cake spreader?' This time a couple of the cooks started digging through the boxes of utensils they had brought with them.

'No. No cake spreader.'

'Can I take a look?' I was given a nod to proceed. 'Here, hold this,' I said to one of the cooks, handing her the buttercream. 'Keep your hands on it. The warmth will soften it up.'

I dug through one of the plastic tubs of kitchen tools. There were countless whisks and metal spoons, peelers, cheap paring knives and tongs. No cake spreader. But at the very bottom was a small sandwich spreader with a wooden handle. It wasn't ideal but it would do the trick. I took a metal spoon too and ran it under warm water, dried it with a clean cloth and handed it to the cook who was warming the buttercream. 'See if you can stir it loose with this. Try to get it to move it around. Hope for smooth,' I instructed her. The warm spoon would help soften the butter in the icing that had solidified.

As she worked to bring the icing back to life, I got to work on the cake. I carefully pulled bits of crumbs from the crushed parts with my fingertips. Then, using the sandwich spreader, I gently scraped at the small streams of lemon curd that were seeping out of the gaping hole, essentially cleaning the wound. Then I used the crumblike pieces of cake that I had removed to stuff back into the hole to stop the flow of the curd. I took the mangled icing from around the gash and carefully spread it over the hole I had just filled with the salvaged crumbs. It was messy, but the dripping had stopped. There was hope. The small plastic tub of icing had smoothed out nicely and I took a few spoonfuls of it with the spreader, slathering it over the patched-up hole. I worked slowly to build out the indent with a bit more icing until it looked nice and full again, before dipping the spreader in a bit of water to smooth out the surface, conjuring up the practice I had playing with the cake-tip set my mother had given me years ago. It was almost as good as new. I heisted a couple of peonies from one of the floral arrangements, plucking a few petals and sprinkling them over the cake to conceal any blemishes that couldn't be perfectly repaired. Crisis had been averted and I was being seen in a new light by the cooks.

My kitchen ability didn't go unnoticed and my catering shifts quickly changed from bartending into helping with the food. I was plating cheese boards with tight clusters of Champagne grapes and crostini and garnishing finger food with edible flowers. It felt surprisingly refreshing to be back in the kitchen again and this time I was seeing it all through a different filter. It was as if a light went on in my brain: food didn't just have the ability to taste good, it could be beautiful too. Maybe all those lobster rolls dotted with nasturtiums weren't as frivolous as my father made them out to be. I realized that much of the joy and the freedom of cooking lay with creating that beauty.

* * *

At the end of the busy summer season, the catering company hosted its annual 'we survived the summer' staff party, renting out a small local restaurant for the night. It was designed to be celebratory, but I didn't really want to go. Most of the staff was young and around my age, but what did we really have in common? They were in their twenties, working this job as a summer gig, maybe home from college, maybe in need of a little extra cash. They weren't single parents; they weren't rushing home to a crying baby; and they wouldn't need to take pump breaks in the bathroom to express milk between the salad and main courses. They had their whole lives in front of them, to do as they pleased, go where they dreamed, work as they chose. They had the freedom that I craved. What could we possibly talk about over this dinner? But deep down I knew that overcoming my own insecurities would never happen by staying home. So begrudgingly and nervously, I went.

I managed to follow directions, find the address and park my car without a hitch. It felt strange – no baby in the backseat. I had not been out for an evening devoted to just enjoyment in who knows how long. The little bistro sat on a quiet street in the seaside town of Camden. It wasn't much to look at from the street at dusk, but I could see a cluster of bodies moving around inside and it seemed inviting. My insecurities left me feeling nervous – hesitant, even – about entering the room. I pulled on the handle of the front door and struggled a bit before the lock released and I was able to slowly push it open. Inside it was warm and cosy with smells of fresh bread and sautéed onions wafting from the tiny open kitchen. The lighting was soft and welcoming, a big arrangement of dried Oriental bittersweet branches adorned the bar and upbeat jazz tunes hummed in the background. Cheerful co-workers greeted one another with big hugs, trying not to spill the drinks in their hands as they embraced.

As dinner began, our communal group occupied each of the ten small tables, huddled together, chattering and laughing amid the flickering candlelight. I didn't know any of my dinner companions well, but I found myself so relaxed in this inviting space with a glass of red wine that my earlier anxieties had subsided. It felt so grown-up. It was true that few, if any, of these people could understand what it was like to be catapulted into adulthood and yet here they were, enjoying things that I found myself craving. Good music muffled by good conversation; moments to just laugh, sip wine and connect. It wasn't just that I had needed this momentary escape from changing nappies and bouncing a baby, or that it was more than getting drunk on cheap beer at the back of the diner. It just felt so real, so deeply satisfying.

The arrival of dessert signalled the end of this most perfect evening. The night had lasted for hours, but when it was over, it felt like it had only been the blink of an eye – the sign of a good dinner party. In front of me was a perfectly golden and lacquered slice of tarte tatin, a small dollop of whipped cream on the side. I lifted a flaky and fruit-filled spoonful to my mouth. My eyes closed involuntarily. Soft, sweet, caramelly, buttery, flaky, creamy – it was the best thing I had ever tasted in my life. Maybe it was the wine, maybe it was the craving to feel adult and alive. I was inspired, I was happy, I was high. Tonight was worth the pump-and-dump I'd have to accomplish later.

A week later, still buzzed from the memories of my night out, I couldn't stop thinking about that restaurant and the way it made me feel inside. I craved the joy, the warmth and the intimacy, not to mention the food, all over again. When I closed my eyes, I could still taste the tarte tatin on my tongue. It inspired me to apply for the serving position that had been posted on the door that evening, hoping I could conjure up all those good feelings again and again while bringing in some winter tips.

The bistro was no diner and I found that I had a few casual serving habits I'd need to break. I couldn't get away with my country-girl service of just slapping down a plate with a warm smile.

There were fine-dining rules that I had never heard of: always serve from the left, clear from the right. Never clear a plate prematurely. Wait until the entire table is done eating before clearing a course. Never ask someone, 'Are you still working on that?' Dining out isn't work, it's enjoyment. Never leave salt and pepper on the table during dessert. I wasn't used to serving courses, or resetting appropriate silverware, knowing the difference between a salad fork, a dinner fork and a dessert fork.

It wasn't just the service that woke me up, the food did too. There was fresh bread made each day from a sourdough starter kept in a jar in a cool, dark cupboard – the antithesis of the commercial rolls at the diner that we kept in a warming drawer with a soup cup filled with water to make it steamy, keeping the buns moist and hot. There were the lovingly remembered tarte tatins, which I learned were made with quince that was fanned over puff pastry, dripping with rich caramelized sugar – a wild deviation from the graham cracker pies topped with whipped cream from a canister. There was the tender hanger steak, served nice and rare with a drizzle of pan juices and mounds of crispy potatoes tossed in garlic and herbs. It made me salivate every time I served it, as did the herbaceous aroma coming from the smoking-hot pans of Maine mussels with bouquets of herbs and a squeeze of lime.

But it wasn't all too-good-to-be-true romance. There were a few small prices to be paid for all the beauty and pleasure I found in the food. The chef never called me by name, just a pet name, Trixie, which sounded more like a cute stripper. And he wasn't shy about rubbing my waist or my ass or lower back while telling me that I did a good job. 'You are a rock star,' he'd say. He had a slew of quick, dirty retorts and jokes that he couldn't seem to control from spewing out of his mouth, when he wasn't swallowing a swig of tequila, making me feel gross or uncomfortable. After years of listening to my dad's crass friends and their dirty innuendos, I'd learned that sometimes it was easier and less embarrassing to just let their words roll off, take the money and be thankful for the job, but it wasn't easy.

I was waiting tables five nights a week and for the first time I was pulling in enough real money to afford a fridge full of food, nappies, a part-time babysitter who could take care of Jaim while I worked and a small place of my own. I had never lived on my own before, going from teenage years of living at home, to a college dorm with a roommate, to back home with Mom and Dad. So the apartment in an older house in Belfast was a really big deal for me. I had a living room with hardwood floors and a bay of old, uninsulated windows that let in lots of light. A kitchen with a black-and-white checkerboard floor, two and a half bathrooms, a washing machine and dryer and a couple of good-size bedrooms, one for each of us. I rolled fresh white paint over most of the walls, but I painted Jaim's room a soft and soothing pale yellow. I hung a framed watercolour of the Velveteen Rabbit I had painted for him while I was pregnant. I stuffed his shelves with books and placed a rocking chair and cosy rug in one corner next to a few baskets of toys. I made our house a home the best way I knew how – by leaving little touches here and there. I made bouquets of forced forsythia branches in a big vase that I placed on the mantle of the old fireplace, which had been bricked up. I put handwoven hand towels in the half-bath and filled a glass soap dispenser with fragrant clear soap. I sewed simple pillowcases to add a bit of flair to our beds and our couch and saved up to buy a few linen window treatments to hang on the street side of the apartment. I was proud of the self-made life I was pulling together, feeling that my direction had shifted from shameful to hopeful. I had made a promise to Jaim when he was born that I would dig us out of the hole I had dug for myself and start to build a better world for him. Now I was making good on that promise and I started the best way I knew how: by building a home.

11

SAWDUST AND
SHINY FLOORS

Tom was becoming sort of a regular at the bistro. He'd occasionally pop in on bustling weekday evenings for a few glasses of wine and a snack at the bar and more frequently on the weekends for gin-laced cocktails followed by a rare steak with frîtes – and more wine. He'd sometimes show up with friends, but most often alone. And he'd always find a way to engage with me, even if I wasn't his server. He was inquisitive, striking up casual conversations and able to extract simple information like what days I worked, where I lived, what kind of car I drove and what kind of music I liked. He wasn't very tall, no taller than me for sure. He wore men's clogs that even gave him a few inches that weren't really his. He had a thick head of sandy blond hair, which I imagined was lucky at his age of mid- to late-forties. He was kind enough and had an easy laugh – one that stood out in a room. I'd hear it ringing out above the chatter and loud music that filled the dining room every night. *That laugh – he's here again.* I would often hear him before I even saw him, like an alert saying, 'Get ready.'

One night he lingered at the bar a little longer, sipping especially slowly on the final cocktail special Chip the bartender had shaken up for him and chatting it up with the few other remaining

Camden bar flies. I was across the dining room, wiping down the now-empty tables and collecting the burned-out candles. I could feel his gaze on me as I moved around the room. I looked up and his eyes were locked with mine. I smiled politely, a bit uncomfortably, and diverted my attention back to setting tables, but I could feel him, still holding on to me with his eyes. His gaze was bewildering; I felt no clear attraction to him, but was he attracted to me? It was all so confusing. I wanted to shrug the whole thing off, give it no attention, avoid the discomfort I was feeling. I looked up again and was startled to see him standing right in front of me.

'Oh! Hi!' I jumped.

'I didn't mean to startle you.' He chuckled. 'I just wanted to say goodnight and thanks for the nice dinner. It was nice to see you again.' He laughed again.

'Nice to see you too,' I said, as I had said to every other customer that night. 'Thanks for coming in. Have a good night.'

He smiled one last time, turned and left. I continued tidying and couldn't help feeling strange and uncomfortable over our interaction, like I couldn't tell if he was coming on to me or was just a nice guy who was my dad's age. I wrote him off as harmless and jokingly convinced myself that if I was ever cornered by him I could take him if my life depended on it.

After the floor had been swept, the cash-up completed, tips divvied and glasses and silver polished and ready for tomorrow's dinner service, we gathered as a staff around the back corner table for a casual family meal of leftover bits from the evening's service. There were scraps of rare hanger steak, some root vegetable puree, cold Brussels sprouts and some overdressed mustardy leaves of lettuce. I made my plate and just as I sat down with a small tumbler of white wine, the phone rang. We all paused, looking at one another to see who would do us all the favour of getting up to answer it, waiting to see who would fold first. It kept ringing.

'Don't get up. I got it,' I said, cracking. I made my way through the small kitchen to where the phone was cradled near the bar and answered.

'Good evening, thank you for calling Francine—'

'Erin?'

'Yes—' A chuckle came through the receiver and I knew it was him.

'It's Tom. Hey, I think I might have left my wallet there. Can you tell me if you see it?' Although highly coincidental, it seemed convincing enough to me. I didn't want to believe there was any kind of premeditated plan behind what could really just have been a simple mistake. I could feel the inevitable questions creeping into my brain – *Was he trying to get my attention? Was he attracted to me?* I didn't feel an ounce of attraction or interest in him and I was nervous just thinking about how I would tell him as much if it came to it. So denial felt like a more comfortable place to hide my uncomfortable feelings.

I told him I'd look; put him on hold. I yelled to Chip to ask if he'd seen it, who yelled back between bites that it was on top of the cash register. I relayed this to Tom.

'Awesome,' he responded. 'Hey, I remember you telling me you lived in Belfast. Any chance you'd be coming this way tonight? Maybe you could drop it by?'

I paused. The request was reasonable – I did live in Belfast, which was almost a thirty-minute drive away, making it completely inconvenient for him to drive back down here and home again. And it *was* on my way. But the idea of delivering the wallet to his house left a feeling of unexplained unease within me. Stop it, Erin, I told myself. He's harmless. I opened the wallet and looked at his license. There it was, his uncomfortable gaze, looking right at me. His live breath on the other end of the line. He was five foot six inches, about 73 kg, brown hair, blue eyes and twenty-one years my elder. He seemed taller in real life, but maybe it was the men's clogs he wore, which I found strange. He wasn't extremely attractive, but he was kind and his address confirmed he lived only a few streets over from my apartment. I convinced the voice in my brain again that he was harmless. What's he possibly gonna do to you? Don't be stubborn. Do the guy a favour and drop off his damn wallet.

'Well, I've got about another thirty minutes or so here, but I could drop it off to you in about an hour?'

'That would be great. I'm in the yellow house on Pearl Street. It's the apartment over the garage. I'll be waiting up. I look forward to seeing you again. Thanks so much, Erin.' He chuckled.

'It's no problem, Tom,' I said, concealing my uncertainty about whether this was a good idea. 'I'll see you in a bit.' I hung up the phone and went back to my cold dinner. 'I'll just drop that wallet off to Tom tonight. It's not far from my house,' I announced to my group of curious coworkers as I chugged my little glass of white wine.

'Watch out he doesn't jump your cute young bones!' One of the other waitresses giggled.

'He's harmless,' I told her, I told myself. I was irritated. 'Is there any more fucking wine?'

I tossed the weathered brown leather wallet onto the passenger seat. I felt it staring at me the whole ride home. I argued with myself in my mind; argued with the wallet sitting next to me.

What do you really want?

When you look at me like that, I feel hot and uncomfortable.

Don't flatter yourself, he's not that into you. Nobody is.

What's the big fucking deal? Shut up and drive!

I had a thirty-minute drive to keep convincing myself that his intentions were innocent, that he was harmless, that I wasn't a fool and that he was in no way attracted to me. I couldn't be talked into believing that some guy would give me any sort of sexual attention because at my core, all I could see was a young single mother, some sort of a delinquent, some mess of a girl no one would ever choose to love. There were a million less complex and more attractive options out there. I passed the street to my apartment and took a drive by it to check in from afar. I could see that the light in Jaim's bedroom window was off, which told me he was sound asleep and the flicker from the television emitting a glow from the living room, which meant Amy, the sitter, was fine too, patiently awaiting my return from work. I took a left onto Pearl Street and slowed my car, looking for the yellow house. I reached for the wallet beside me and looked inside again, confirming the address.

There it was, with the lights on in the apartment above the garage. He was waiting for me. I parked on the shoulder of the road and kept the engine running so it was obvious I was only stopping by for a quick drop-off. I walked up the steps to the porch and knocked on the door. I waited, no answer, I knocked again. Still no answer. I knew he was home: The lights were on and I could hear music faintly from behind the door. Oh well, I tried. I turned and started back to my car. Just then the door swung open.

'Hey! You made it.' He was standing in the doorway with a huge smile on his face. I stared at him for a moment. 'Thanks so much for bringing that by.'

'Oh, it's no problem – I mean, I live right here, so not out of the way. It made sense. It wasn't any trouble at all.' I stopped myself from continuing to explain why it truly wasn't a problem.

'Why don't you come in? I have some wine here if you'd like a glass.'

'Oh, no thank you – my car is running and I've got to get home to my son. I've got a babysitter waiting.' I pushed the wallet into his hands before immediately turning and walking quickly back to my car. 'Sorry to run! I'm sure I'll see you around town some-time. Hope you enjoyed your dinner tonight. Have a good night, Tom.' I didn't give him an opportunity to respond. Or if he did,

I had walked away so quickly that I couldn't hear him. I pulled the driver's door shut and pulled away. I was home in less than two minutes. I sat in my car for a moment pondering, What would have happened if I had gone inside? I felt a little self-centred, assuming he was attracted to me.

I reached into my coat pocket, pulled out the small wad of evening tips and counted out fifty dollars to have at the ready for the sitter. Twenty-three years old, a single mom to a less-than-two-year-old boy, a waitress, a girl going nowhere. To me there was nothing attractive about that at all.

I kept running into Tom more often. It was a small town, one where you were bound to run into people. We'd see each other on the street, in line at the Belfast Co-op getting coffee, around at the Hannaford supermarket and of course at the restaurant. He kept coming in, sipping on his gin cocktails, ordering rare steak with frîtes, looking at me. As time went on, I got used to it, got more comfortable with him. I didn't get the sense that he wanted to hurt me, or even that he was interested in me – maybe just a distant middle-aged man's wish that he could date a twenty-something, but nothing he spent too much time thinking about. He came in once with a woman and her daughter and I gathered from the conversation that the woman was his girlfriend. I felt relief, like it confirmed that all of my doubts were now verified bullshit. He was just an older, nice-enough guy who was looking for nothing and had no intentions of 'jumping my cute young bones'. Now when he came into the restaurant, I could wait on him with ease, laugh with him and converse comfortably when I ran into him at the Co-op – because he was just a nice guy. We were acquaintances now. It was maybe even safe to say that we were becoming friends. And when he invited me for a casual dinner at his apartment one Sunday night, I said yes – because that's what friends do.

Amy arrived right on time to babysit for the evening. I blew Jaim a quiet kiss from the kitchen so as to not make a grand 'Hey, Mom is leaving!' gesture. He was playing contentedly with his wooden trains on the living room floor, oblivious to my departure.

'I won't be too late. And I'll be just down the road if you need anything.' I made my way on foot only a few streets over before arriving at the yellow house on Pearl Street again. This time when I knocked, he answered immediately. The door flung open and there he was in his socks, a dish towel in his hand and his gaze.

I stepped inside his one-room apartment. It was remarkably clean, with bright wood floors that were so glossy it was as if they had just been freshly waxed. There was an extra-large Oriental rug, a comfortable-looking set of rattan furniture, a few antique-looking side tables and an oversize modern painting of a giant matchstick on the wall. Through the air wafted the smooth sounds of Césaria Évora singing Cape Verdean jazz over a little Bose CD player on the desk. The place was so organized, so grown-up – not what I had expected for a guy living on his own. Not guys my age, anyway. It reminded me how much older he was. Twenty-one years older. I took my shoes off and placed them neatly next to his, which were lined up in a tidy row. I looked down at my ragged socks, regretting that I hadn't put on a better pair.

Across the room was a small open kitchen with a thick butcher-board island with a flickering candlestick, two wineglasses and a bottle of white wine resting neatly on top.

'I'm just finishing up a bit of prep for dinner. Come have a seat and relax.'

I slid my way slowly across the shiny floor in my sad pair of worn-out socks and pulled up a barstool at the island. Tom resumed his prep, moving between the stove and island, chatting, chopping. He worked a pan over a low flame, then paused for a moment to uncork the wine bottle before going back to swirling the pan. In between he chopped a bit of red onion on a cutting board. He filled my wineglass with a tall pour and pushed it slowly across the countertop in my direction. 'Cheers,' he said without raising a glass, just looking me in the eye. I started to feel the uneasiness again. His blue eyes slanted when he smiled, which reminded me of my father's eyes. He was twice my age, old enough to be my father. But unlike my father, he seemed kind. I was attracted to his clean, adult-like apartment. I was attracted to the jazz he was playing over the Bose speakers. I was attracted to the vinaigrette he was making from scratch with shallots and balsamic vinegar.

'Cheers,' I said back. 'Thanks for the invite.' I took a big, long swig. 'Can I help you with anything?' I inquired politely, hoping he'd give me a job because I'd feel more comfortable doing something in the kitchen. He just shook his head and chuckled, turning back to the stove to tend to a pan in which he was preparing Parmesan crisps. He paused again to pour another big dose of wine into his glass and raised it to his lips, keeping his eyes on mine before putting it down and reaching for a large chef's knife to continue making a salad.

'So, where's your son tonight? How old is he again?' He was trying to make small talk.

'He'll be two in September. He's with the babysitter at my apartment. He really loves Amy. She's so good with him. He spends a lot of time with my parents, too. They live out in Freedom. But it was just easier for me to have Amy stay with him since I'd be so close tonight. Saved me a trip driving out there and back.' I was rambling.

'Freedom? Is that where you grew up?'

'Unfortunately.' I laughed. 'But now I'm living in the big city of Belfast,' I added. He laughed too.

'What's so wrong with Freedom?'

'Besides the fact that there's nothing there except a general store, gas station, tractor store and a diner?' This of course made him laugh again.

'Hey, the diner isn't bad,' he said. 'I've been there.'

'Really? That's my dad's restaurant. I basically grew up at that place. You eat there?'

'I ate there once – it was pretty good for what it is!'

'When did you go there?' I asked, partially for the small talk, but partially because I wanted to know if our paths had crossed before.

'Oh, jeez. It was years ago. I took my daughter and met a friend of mine there for breakfast. Well, I say breakfast, but my friend had prime rib.'

In that moment I realized that I had met Tom before. Long before the bistro in Camden, long before he looked at me long and hard, I waited on him one Saturday morning long ago at my dad's diner. I remembered it so clearly because of who he joined for breakfast that day. He was with Don Fox, who came in every Saturday morning around nine. He came in at nine because he knew that the prime rib special for Saturday lunch went in the oven early that morning around seven and he knew that it was a slow-cooked four-hour roast. He knew that if he got there around nine, he could ask my grandfather, who was running the breakfast line at the time, to slice off the first piece of prime rib while it was still roasting in the oven, ensuring that it would be very, very rare, if not raw. Don Fox came like clockwork every Saturday morning for his super-rare prime rib breakfast and positioned himself on the same barstool, where he would devour the entire cut of beef in one sitting. It was so big that the giant steak would hang off the edge of the plate so you'd have to walk slowly while serving it in order not to spill the sauce it was served with. As soon as we saw his bright red truck with vanity plates pull in, we got to work on his steak, a side salad with French dressing, an order of peas and an orange soda. He always left a $5.00 tip, which was a lot considering the average breakfast plate cost $3.95 and a cup of coffee was 90 cents. It was a big tip for the breakfast shift and one that we all fought over. And this one Saturday, I won. I got to wait on Don, but strangely, he didn't sit at the counter this time. Instead he sat in one of the side booths against the wall.

'Morning, Don. Everything okay?' I asked after he slid into the booth.

'Oh yeah, everything's great. I'm just meeting a couple of friends of mine. How are you doing this morning? You look real nice!' he said flirtatiously with his big white smile.

Meeting friends? Trifecta!!! I thought. I just might make fifteen bucks off this one table, which would even make it worth putting up with Don's inappropriate comments this morning. I was seventeen years old and on my way to having a real good Saturday shift. I grabbed Don's orange soda and delivered it to him with a big red plastic tumbler filled with ice and a straw. I was so sidetracked by the thought of a big tip that I forgot that he didn't take a cup or ice or a straw. He just popped open the can of Crush right in front of me and started guzzling it. His hair was a mess of salty blond flowing curls. He was wearing shorts and hiking sandals even though it was November. I never saw him wear a pair of trousers, or closed-toe shoes, for that matter, even in the dead of winter. He'd just keep his truck running in the lot with the heat blasting, then make an elegant dash from the truck to the front door and vice versa. It was ridiculous.

When Don's breakfast companions arrived, I was surprised to see that they weren't what I'd envisioned. It wasn't a couple of dudes joining him, or a husband-and-wife duo. Just a man and his young daughter. I didn't know Don knew anyone with kids, or liked kids for that matter. He didn't have any of his own, so it was a strange sight to see him dining with one. The little girl was six or seven years old with hair so blond it was almost white and eyebrows to match. She ordered the French toast. Her dad ordered eggs over easy with bacon, home fries and wheat toast. Her dad was Tom. And six years later I would meet him again, divorced now, at a restaurant in Camden. He would make me feel strange and uncomfortable, but he would oddly become some version of a friend and I was now having dinner with him in his apartment, just the two of us this very moment. I couldn't help wondering if there were other instances where our paths had crossed in life, or if this was a strange sign that we were meant to collide.

He had made a salad with half-decent greens and tossed it in a bowl with a bit of avocado and the dressing and Parmesan crisps he'd made. I finished my wine and he poured me more. He was diligent in making sure my glass stayed full. I felt relaxed now, again looking around Tom's immaculate apartment, savouring the wine, savouring the sounds coming from the stereo, savouring the relaxed meal without a two-year-old. I couldn't remember the last time anyone had made me a real sit-down meal with candlelight and wine and conversation, because nobody ever had. This was new and it began to feel delicious and sophisticated. I was loosening up; our conversation began to flow. We talked about kids; we talked about food and restaurants. We picked at our salads, sipped the wine and volleyed questions back and forth. We never spoke about his girlfriend.

'I just realized I don't even know what you do for a living,' I said with a relaxed giggle. I knew he drove a truck, because it was sitting in the yard. I knew he was friends with Don Fox, who owned a local gravel pit, so I imagined he might work for the city, maybe ploughing the streets or driving some giant piece of equipment around. He just struck me as that kind of guy.

'I build boats,' he said, a bit humbly.

'Boats? Oh wow, I wouldn't have guessed that! What kind of boats?' I asked, knowing nothing about boats. Tom reached for the wine and poured the last bit of the first bottle into my glass.

'Drink up; we can go for a walk and I'll show you.' I said nothing but grinned with genuine interest. I was feeling confident; I was feeling calm. I tipped the wine into my mouth, swallowed and paused to look at Tom again before I slid my way over to him at the front door where he was holding my coat with his outstretched arms. Could I be ever so slightly attracted to him? Or was I just attracted to the candles, the vinaigrette and the waxed floors?

We walked down the hill toward the centre of town, laughing, joking and chatting the entire way. We reached Main Street and continued down the pavement, heading toward the base of the street where it eventually dead-ended with the bay. But before we reached it, Tom grabbed at my hand and veered, pulling me between a few parked cars and into the front door of Rollie's, a local downtown bar.

'Shouldn't we make a quick stop?' he asked rhetorically. He guided me into the long barroom and down along the row of half-empty stools before stopping near the end and ushering me onto one of the wooden swivel seats before taking a seat beside me. I had been to this bar before, many times. Not as an adult, but as a kid, with my father and my sister. My father would take us there on occasion and give us a ten-dollar roll of quarters and set us loose on the old Pac-Man machine while he sat at the bar swigging beers. When we were hungry he'd give us dimes to buy pretzel sticks and the bartender would squeeze us fresh orange juice from the oranges they had on hand intended for screwdrivers. I hadn't been back here since.

Tom ordered himself a gin and tonic, then paused for me to make my order. The truth was, I hadn't been to a bar since I had been of legal drinking age and didn't have the faintest idea of what I should order. But I could envision my dad, bellied up to this very bar as he had done a hundred times before, with a vodka cozily cupped in his hand. I didn't drink vodka, but I did that night. I sucked down the entire pint glass full of the clear liquor and juice with a squeeze of lime over ice.

'She'll have another.' He raised his finger to the bartender. And I did. After I had sucked every last drop though my straw, he paid the bill. He scribbled his signature on the receipt in front of him, tossed the pen aside and grabbed my hand, pulling me off the barstool and toward the front door. It was very late now and the streets were dark and quiet. The air was crisp and I could see our breath when we laughed. I crossed my arms, clutching myself to keep my warmth in. Tom walked shoulder to shoulder next to me as we walked farther down toward the bay before taking the last side street and stumbling a little further. He stopped in front of a garage-like building, pulled a set of keys from his pocket and fiddled with the lock before opening the door and inviting me inside. It was pitch-black, but warm and smelling of fresh wood shavings. The warmth felt so good that I felt my body immediately relax. I stood in the darkness and took a few deep breaths of the sweet and woody scents. I could feel the room was huge, even in the darkness, by the way the sound of Tom's keys jingling in his hands bounced off the walls as he fumbled for the light switch. He flicked on the fluorescent lights, which blinded me for a split second and when my vision came back, I was standing beneath the bow of an enormous wooden boat. The hull was magnificent, like the beautiful stomach of a whale, wrapped with wide ribbons of variegated veneers of wood. I had never seen anything like it before. The raw, naked beauty was sobering and I approached it with an outstretched hand to touch it, cautiously, as if it were a giant live animal. I walked slowly along the length of the boat, stroking its underbelly, feeling its every curve and grain. Tom followed behind me without saying a word for several minutes. Then his silence broke and he began to tell me about the boat this would one day be and the labour of love he had put into it.

'Come take a look from the top,' he said, taking my hand and leading me up a makeshift staircase to a narrow work balcony that ran around the perimeter of the massive boat. From the second tier of the shop, we stood looking down over the immense hull. From up here it was an empty wooden shell. 'Sometimes I come here alone and just do this,' he said as he slipped his shoes off and stepped gingerly on the edge of the hull before lowering his body and sliding down the inside curved wall into the empty belly of the boat. 'Come on,' he coaxed with his hand reaching up toward me, signalling for me to join him. I slipped off my shoes and slid down just as he had. We lay beside each other, without speaking, between the wooden ribs of the hull, taking in the fragrant smell of fresh wood. I closed my eyes, letting my hands roam around me, exploring the grains of the wood and crumbling fresh shavings between my fingertips. I was drunk on vodka and wine and I was high on this feeling of something new. I was in love with the smell and in love with the idea of this massive piece of wooden art, art that would someday be floating in the ocean just outside and that Tom had built it with his own two hands, from scratch. His hand grazed mine and we intertwined our fingers. I was starting to feel dizzy, from the booze, from sliding down the hull, from lying down and closing my eyes, from my evolving feelings for Tom lying just beside me. The room was hot, partially on purpose to let the veneers cure, partially because I had drunk too much, but mostly because I realized I was feeling something for Tom now.

'I need to get some air,' I said as I let go of his hand and started to crawl my way out of the boat.

We stumbled back up the street toward our respective apartments, stopping at his place one last time. I was drunk on booze, high on the smells and feel of the boat shop and thinking in my haze that I might even be attracted to this guy. I had relaxed into the idea of him, not caring about his age, not caring about his height, not caring about his laugh or his clogs that made him a few inches taller. I was in strange new uncharted territory as I found myself in Tom's bedroom that night, a place I had had no intention of ever being. It was confusing, jarring, awkward and vaguely exciting all at once. It felt foreign, out of order and out of control. I didn't remember walking home, but I woke up in my own bed the next morning, knowing everything had changed.

12

AMARANTH AND FRIED CHICKEN

In the light of day, everything was different, but we kept quietly pretending it wasn't. Tom didn't stop coming to the restaurant; in fact, he kept coming more often. But neither of us was admitting to the world what was going on behind closed doors. I treated him like a normal patron to keep up the image that he was. Secretly I'd pour him extra glasses of wine – on the house – and slip a song onto the playlist that reminded us of our night together. The more he came around, the more chances we had to see each other and test the electricity that had ignited between us. We didn't stop bumping into each other around town, either; we even planned for it to happen, seemingly organically, secretly not. We had crossed over and through into a very grey area. There was no denying what had happened between us, but it was challenging to dissect what was really going on. Were we just friends? Were we lovers? Would we keep seeing each other? Or was this just a minor fling?

There were reasons I kept the night to myself. It was partly because I didn't know where it was going, but mostly because something about it still felt wrong. He was significantly older and even though I was an adult, a tiny speck from deep inside of me screamed that this was wholly inappropriate. But I muffled the voice of reason. I muffled the fact that he had a girlfriend. I muffled everything that was telling me that this was wrong because there were too many things about it all that I liked – the idea of someone caring for me, of someone with a career, someone with a nice apartment. And frankly, the inappropriateness was its own kind of spark, tempting me with the forbidden and exciting me even more.

Our evenings together were becoming frequent and regular, even though Tom had another girlfriend. When he could feel my hesitation or pullback, he'd start making promises that he would break it off with the other woman. But not before he took her to Florida one last time, for a trip he argued he'd planned with her for a long time.

'Erin, they are first-class tickets. I can't just give them up and not go. I already broke it off with her, but it would be stupid of me to waste the money I already spent.' Our relationship was so fresh that I felt guilty about even questioning him. We had only been seeing each other for about a month, so what place did I have telling him what to do?

He went on that trip. He spent a lot of time drinking and swimming and lounging by the pool with her. He had a real good buzz on the few times I spoke with him, when he managed to sneak off and call me. He'd whisper into the phone, explain that he was drinking so heavily because he was on vacation and just having a good time and maybe dulling the challenge of breaking it off with her. He admitted to picking fights with her so it would solidify that they were unhappy together. 'Don't worry, it's over. We are flying home on different flights. It's just us now. You and me.'

Was I some sort of victor? I had won Tom's full and undivided attention. But I didn't feel like I was just fighting for his affection, I felt like I was fighting for a life – a life that I had felt robbed of when I got pregnant. A life that I wanted to build, for myself but most of all for Jaim. I starting dreaming about the world I could start making for us, all of us, now. It had a clean home with nice furniture – a white slip-covered couch with fancy cushions, an oversize Oriental rug and maybe some nice artwork on the walls. I dreamed of a fridge stocked with all our favourite foods and ingredients that I could cook into beautiful meals. Organic chickens that I could slather with butter and stuff with garlic and fragrant herbs, big bowls of fresh fruit that you could grab as you liked, fancy organic juice boxes, lots of snacks like the French-style yogurts that come in pretty glass jars and even some of those expensive nut butters with the oil on top. Most of all, there would be stability and love. I owed Jaim all this and I was going to get it for him, no matter what.

Even with the other woman out of the picture, Tom and I continued to keep our relationship private. He had broken it off with her, but that didn't change the fact that he was twice my age – nearly the same age as my father. And the dirtiness I felt from the cheating didn't wear off even though the cheating was over. Tom would suggest I duck down in the passenger side of his truck, keeping a low profile when we'd ride around town together. I didn't question it, because deep down it did feel like I was doing something wrong. When we went out, we'd leave town so we wouldn't be recognized by someone we knew. He'd take me to Portland on the weekends, where we'd stay in the nicest hotel in town and go to the best restaurants. Fore Street for oysters and wood-fired lamb; Bintliff's, now Bayside American Café, for the best corned-beef hash and poached eggs. The matter of our age gap felt diluted when we weren't around home, but sometimes we would be reminded of it even when we were away.

'You sure you're old enough to be here?' asked the head bartender at Fore Street one night as we sidled up to the bar for dinner. He didn't card me, but he made another offhanded comment about the fact that I was Tom's daughter. It was harmless and it made Tom and me laugh. I figured if we could laugh about it then maybe it wasn't so bad.

Keeping up the illusion that there was nothing between us took energy and it was getting old. We were growing closer and more comfortable together. I had been casually bringing Jaim around Tom and Jaim was picking up on the familiarity too, calling him by name. I knew it was just a matter of time before he would squeal and drop the name 'Tom' to my parents and the cat would be out of the bag. I was tired of hiding when we drove around town, tired of lying to my friends and family, tired of keeping this relationship a secret and tired of feeling like I was doing something wrong when deep down all I wanted was to make a good life. I was a grown-ass woman making a grown-ass choice to be with Tom, whether or not that choice was the right one.

I had spent the night with Tom, so Jaim had spent the night with my parents. I drove out to Freedom to fetch him late that Sunday morning. It was unusually warm for a June morning and my mom and I sat on the back deck under the patio umbrella, trying to keep cool. She offered me a cup of coffee and I politely declined. It was too hot and I was already sweating inside thinking about how I was going to tell her that I was in a relationship with a man twice my age and that I had been hiding it for almost four months now. I had been lying to her about where I was going when I was with him all those times she would help me out with Jaim. I was lying like a teenager up to no good. I was lying because deep down inside, I *did* feel like I was doing something wrong. There were other reasons for my reluctance in being honest about this relationship, but I didn't want to admit the truths to anyone, least of all myself.

We sat in the shade and watched my father slowly drive his tractor across the field with Jaim on his lap.

'Did you guys have a nice night?' I asked my mother.

'We had a great time. Your dad made chop suey and we camped out down in the cabin last night.' She was referring to the small screened-in cabin sitting on my parents' property, where my sister and I would occasionally 'camp' over the summer, feeling rugged and adventurous without electricity or running water for a night. 'How was your night?'

'It was fine,' I said quickly to avoid going into the details of what I had really been up to. I knew I had to just jump in at the deep end and tell her. But I didn't even want to dip my toe in. I had to just be out with it. Be fucking out with it!

'Mom, I've met someone and I'm in love.'

'I know,' she said without skipping a beat. 'Tom.'

'What?! How could you possibly know?' I said, confused but relieved.

'Remember that time Tom ran into you, me and Jaim when we were having breakfast at Chase's on Mother's Day?' she asked.

Sure I remembered. Tom and I had planned that. He knew exactly where I would be and we played it off like it was a total run-in. I had introduced him to my mother as a friend, just a guy who came into the restaurant where I waitressed. I invited him to join us for a cup of coffee. He did.

'I saw the way he looked at you that day.' She went on to tell me about another time. A time I had no idea about. She was out at a local Mexican restaurant having margaritas with some friends after work when Tom came in with Don Fox and sat at the bar. He recognized my mother and approached her, making a good casual effort to visit for a bit. 'Your father thought he was after me. Flirting, you know? But I didn't think that was it at all. He was asking an awful lot about you. I had a gut feeling it was all about you. A mother knows.' She paused. 'Plus Jaim has mentioned his name a few times.'

I was slightly embarrassed, but more relieved than anything. It was out. I had come clean to the most important person I needed to come clean to.

'How old is he anyway?' she asked.

I knew what she was thinking – he's as old as your father! And it was true. I'd braced myself for a flurry of reactions to the fact I was dating a man double my age; my father's shaking head of disapproval; my sister's rolling fits of laughter; the submissiveness of my friends and their faux-approval.

I shrugged with embarrassment, then responded with irritation: 'Does it really frigging matter?'

Amaranth was the very first boat Tom had ever built from scratch. He started it when he was in his early twenties, the year I was born. Twenty-four feet long, plank on frame, a beautiful gaff-rigged cutter. Tom met his ex-wife while he was framing it out in a makeshift shed in the woods of New Hampshire. They proclaimed its name to be *Amaranth,* in honour of a poem they both loved. Together they had two daughters and sailed with the little tow-headed babies all around Penobscot Bay. But as the girls grew older and his first marriage fizzled, so did *Amaranth*'s heyday. It retired to a storage shed where it sat hiding underneath a huge piece of clear plastic, covered in dust, not seeing the bay for years even though it was just a few hundred feet away. Its white-painted underbelly showed the signs of its thirst to hit the water, each wooden plank aching with long, dry cracks.

I had persuaded Tom to launch it that summer. How much fun we could have out on the water with it, how much life we could breathe back into it. He reluctantly agreed and launched it back into Penobscot Bay one balmy July morning. For days it sat tied up to the town docks, bobbing heavily as it took on water. We'd visit the landing two or three times a day to pump out all the seawater that was constantly filling its cavity, waiting for its wooden planks to swell back up enough to naturally resist the incoming water, so we could take it out for a sail. Tom moaned about the obnoxious maintenance of getting this boat seaworthy: 'I don't see the point of putting all of this effort into this boat, when we could easily and happily be out playing with other people's much nicer boats.'

I was surprised at how he behaved, as if it were worthless. To me this sweet boat represented a piece of him and of his past, a piece that was beautiful and important and not small or trivial at all. But I also understood that he did have access to much finer, much bigger boats that belonged to clients and friends. And that to him *Amaranth* represented a past that he didn't necessarily want to remember. To Tom this boat wasn't big or fancy enough to show off.

Though it seemed like it would never swell enough to fill the tiny gaps between each plank, it finally did. It eventually bobbed happy and proud against the town landing dock. I did my best to contain my excitement because Tom found it to be overly dramatic.

'Is she ready?' I asked as calmly as possible.

'Is this really what you want to do today?' he asked.

I made myself pause before answering so as to not come across as too eager and earnest.

'Come on – it'll be so much fun. It's a beautiful day. You get her ready and I'll go take care of the food.' I headed back up the ramp from the dock before he could turn me down.

It was July Fourth and a goddamn flawless and glorious day on Penobscot Bay. The sun was shining bright and hot and the breeze was blowing an ideal salty, sweet fifteen knots. Our plan was to sail little *Amaranth* a straight and perfect downwind shot from Belfast to Castine, just ten miles southeast across the bay. Tom worked tirelessly through the morning to prepare for our tiny voyage, prepping the rig, checking the lines and getting all the sails in place. Meanwhile I was busy provisioning. As I dreamed about how our day would go and our adventure would unfold, I planned the food we would eat:

Fried chicken. Served cold, crispy and juicy. Like Grace Kelly once served to Cary Grant in *To Catch a Thief,* that Alfred

Hitchcock movie I loved so much. We could eat it straight from the box, add a sprinkle of Maldon salt, or just hold it up in the air as the boat screamed through the waves to catch a bit of salty breeze before devouring it to the bone.

Fresh summer cherries. We would need something sweet after devouring the crunchy, salty chicken. And we could spit the pits overboard, throw our stems into the wind.

Champagne. Something bubbly and celebratory to wash it all down. Fancy, Veuve Clicquot. Splits so we could each suck on our own little bottle and wouldn't spill when the boat was heeled over.

I filled a vintage basket with my dreamy provisions and threw in a few linen napkins, some bottles of water and a few votives and a lighter, just in case. I packed a duffel bag with a bathing suit and toothbrush and all the other overnight things I might need, then stuffed the remaining space with a down comforter, one of my nicer flat sheets and a couple of red-and-white floral cushions, just for fun. I returned to the docks, making my way down the steep ramp now with my loot in tow. Tom popped up from down below and took one look at me with all my goods. He looked irritated at first, but then stopped himself with a smile before asking me what the hell I was doing.

'What are you doing with all that? We're just going out for a day sail.'

'You've seen *Gilligan's Island,* right?' I joked, knowing at his age he sure had and knowing I was way too young to be throwing that line out there. 'I'm prepared. Martha-fucking-Stewart prepared,' I told him with a flirtatious smile before hopping aboard and placing my cushions just so around the cockpit and heading below to stow my goods.

We set sail by early afternoon and hoisted the mainsail in the harbour just as we pushed off from the dock with no outboard motor to speak of. Tom was skilful and brilliant as he jumped between the tiller and sails, adjusting here and there, owning the boat, yelling commands for me to pull in a line or tie off to a cleat. The current was with us and the wind carried *Amaranth* with purpose and grace as we navigated through the mooring field to the open bay ahead. I scurried below to grab the provisions so we could have them tillerside when ready. Down inside the little boat the sounds of the water rushing were all around the outskirts of the hull. It was alive, like a giant beating heart and I could almost feel us being pushed through the wake of the harbour.

I made my way up the few steps between the galley and cockpit, gripping the handrail all the way just to keep some sort of balance as the boat started to heel over harder at an angle. Tom was holding the tiller steady with an intent gaze on the luffing sails before heading off a bit and creating a calm. We were at a good twenty degrees, tipped over far enough that water was almost coming over the low-side deck. The wind was rushing past us and the spray was picking up as our momentum carried *Amaranth* through the waves. I slid the basket into the crook of the lower side of the cockpit and hiked my body up to the high windward side of the boat and took a seat on the edge of the oak rail. It felt like I was flying through the salty waves in front of us. I loved it so fucking much.

Tom was to my left and what felt like below me from the angle of the heeled-over boat, pulling the tiller to make the sails fall happily into place before he hopped up onto the high side of the boat beside me. He was so confident, so calm, so focused, so at home, so at peace in this little boat he'd built from scratch – a light I had never seen him in. A light that I was crazy attracted to. I pulled one of the splits of Champagne from my picnic basket, removed the foil and carefully unwound the wire cage around the rim. I aimed the little bottle toward the sky and pushed the cork gently with my thumb before letting it pop and fly off into the waves beside us. The sound stole Tom's attention from the sails and he smiled as I handed him the little bottle of Champagne. I opened the second bottle for myself, in the same celebratory fashion. We paused, locked eyes, clinked bottles and toasted. Perched high on the rail, we sipped Champagne and sailed on to Castine. Tom's gaze went back to the sails, but I couldn't take my eyes off him. In this glorious moment, I loved him more than ever. I thought I could spend the rest of my life with him.

We were married on a chilly Wednesday afternoon in April. It was a plan hatched in haste. We had woken up on a Monday morning, after hosting Easter dinner with my family and lain in bed feeling a bit bold, maybe still a little drunk on the limoncello I had made. We casually sipped our coffees and made the decision to get married that week: *Let's just do it!*

There was no downplaying the seriousness of this relationship anymore. It had found its way to a new, undeniably real level the day Jaim piped up with this little, nearly four-year-old voice calling Tom Dad. He had heard Tom's girls call him that over and over again, the one night a week they were with him and picked up the term for himself. It was real now, not a game we could play or a fling we could just keep casually engaging in for years. What Tom and I were doing held more weight than I had realized and the weight of this one word, 'Dad,' woke me up to the reality of what I was doing. Every decision I was making was impacting Jaim. As his mother, every big and little decision I made was shaping his world. This fling had become something greater and the responsible thing to do was to make it real, make it everlasting, make it right. Jaim liked Tom well enough and Tom was kind enough to Jaim. Tom wasn't keen on watching Jaim if I had to work and would prefer to send him off to my parents for the weekend and have me all to himself, but it didn't seem unfair or abnormal. I wanted us to work, the three of us, a patched-together modern family. I wanted to end my fears of Jaim missing out on the father figure I so desperately believed he needed and deserved.

Tom had asked me to marry him the summer before. He led me down to the docks late one Saturday night after I arrived home from working a catering gig. We boarded the now-complete boat he had introduced me to two years earlier, on our first night together, the night that still made me feel nauseated every time I thought of vodka and cranberry juice. He brought me down below into the finished space and perched me on what was now a mahogany navigation station. It was the very same spot we had slid down into when this boat was but a shell of raw wood. He got down on his knee and asked me to marry him, slipping an antique diamond ring on my finger. He admitted his contemplation over the ring and told me how he had left the jewellery shop empty-handed, then walked around the corner to a downtown bar. He downed two gin martinis before returning with a boost of confidence. I said yes. We had decided to get married, but we had made no decisions about actually doing it until now. There was something about the idea of marriage that made me feel like I could check off a big box, completing a task that Jaim's childhood was in need of.

We met at City Hall on our lunch hour and filed the paperwork for a marriage licence, which much to my surprise was quick and easy – the way I imagined a hasty Vegas wedding could be. We called a local lawyer and asked him to meet us and marry us. Check. We also needed two witnesses, so I called my parents the night before and asked them. Check.

'Can you come over tomorrow?' I had asked my mother.

'Yeah, sure. What's up?'

'We're getting married!'

She was silent for a moment before she nervously chuckled and said okay. My father, on the other hand, hadn't hesitated at the news. Tom had grown on him enough because they had one thing in common: drinking. A cocktail or two always managed to keep the mood between them jovial and light. They cracked jokes about being father and son, even though they were practically the same age.

I wore the only thing in my closet that was clean and unwrinkled, a plain green J. Crew dress that fell just above my knees. My hair was still slightly wet from the quick shower I had taken beforehand (so quick I didn't even think to give my legs a fresh shave). I had nightmares when I was younger about my wedding day and in them I was constantly feeling rushed and unprepared. In these dreams I always had wet hair when I walked down the aisle.

But this was real life, where it felt like the only time to get married was wedged between obligations and have-tos. I was unprepared, but this was it. My eyebrows weren't perfectly plucked and the only mascara I had on hand was old and dried up, so fuck it! I threw the expired tube in the bin, scraped the bottom of my lip gloss to slather my lips and brushed what remained of my cracked compact of blush on my cheeks for a pop of colour. I slipped on the only pair of heels that I owned and carefully made my way down the old, railing-less staircase of the house we were renting together from friends on Union Street. I rarely wore heels this high and moved nervously down each tread, step by step, gripping the wall the entire descent until I reached the bottom. I felt relief when I touched down on the landing, thankful I had managed not to stumble and fall, thankful I hadn't broken any bones today, of all days, because *oh my God!* this was my wedding day.

We congregated in the light-filled living room of the house, which had a slivered view of the bay in the distance. There were Tom and me, my mother, my father and five-year-old Jaim, who excitedly bounced around the room in his only pair of khakis – mostly because his grandparents were there on a most unexpected Wednesday afternoon. The haste of the whole thing was as undeniable as the absence of friends and close family members – my sister, Tom's girls, or anyone from Tom's side, for that matter.

My parents sat on the living room couch, while Jaim wriggled back and forth between their laps. Tom and I stood in front of the corner windows while our lawyer stood between us, reciting generic vows from a few sheets of white computer paper. I could feel a well of tears brimming up in my eyes. They dripped quietly down my cheeks on that weekday afternoon, in my green dress, with my damp hair, in the living room of a house we were renting. I was nervous with the haste of it all, but I was happy, because maybe I wasn't a fuckup and maybe I had had a baby when I was young and maybe he had no father, but maybe today I had corrected the very problem I felt responsible for.

Everything the lawyer was saying was blurred by my tears and running nose, which was now dripping as heavily as my tears. When the phone rang, he broke from his readings, adding to the depth of the imperfection of this day.

'Hey, Mom! Answer it!' Jaim squealed as he jumped off his grandfather's lap, making his way toward the phone as though he was going to answer it himself.

'Shh, shh! No!' I whispered. We all stood, paused and let the phone ring. Four full rings, then finally silence.

'Well, they weren't calling you, Tom, to tell you not to go through with it,' our lawyer joked. We all laughed nervously and it cleared my head enough to hear his final words to us: 'I now pronounce you man and wife.' I wiped my nose and brushed my tears aside before we kissed. And just like that, we were married.

There was no wedding feast to follow, no dancing, no cake. Hell, we didn't even exchange rings. Instead we sat around the kitchen table sipping Veuve Clicquot out of mismatched cups that my mother had had the foresight to pick up at the supermarket en route to our house. Tom and I had hatched a plan to drive to Boston for the night for a quick honeymoon while my parents would watch Jaim. We called my sister and a few friends on the drive to tell them what we had just done, then called around to the fanciest restaurants to see if they had any last-minute availability. After dinner we made our way to one of the nicer hotels in town. Tom passed out, drunk on gin, without even a kiss goodnight.

13

VINALHAVEN

Tom and I eventually bought the house we were married in. We jokingly referred to the house as 'Vinalhaven', like the island not far out to sea from us, because it had vinyl siding and it was a haven for us, with that sliver of an ocean view. It had a bedroom for Jaim and a big garden to play in, plus enough space for me to build a few beds. We even had shiny wood floors, a white slip-covered couch and a couple of fancy cushions that our friends had left behind. I was living the dream of a normal life, a dream that was even further cemented that following November when our petition to have Jaim adopted by Tom went through. It was official: a dad for Jaim. I felt I had finally righted all my wrongs and was finally on the path to living a good life. But what was perhaps most vindicating is that my father gave his blessing for Jaim to take Tom's last name, even though it meant not carrying on his own family name. His lack of protest symbolized his happiness for me and the pleasure he took in my building a normal, traditional life for his grandson, Jaim French.

In our new house we made the best of memories. Jaim learned to ride a bike and sold eggs from my parents' farm to passersby, just as I had when I was his age. He lost teeth and the tooth fairy came. We had countless birthday parties and Easter-egg hunts in the garden. I spent endless hours planting tulip bulbs in autumn and adding hydrangea bushes in the summer as I could afford them. On our anniversary I added a small magnolia bush. I mowed with our hand-me-down push mower, keeping the little lawn trim and tidy. Jaim and I raked giant piles of leaves in autumn to jump into. On snowy days, we shovelled, built snowmen and forged sled runs, then came into the warm house to make cookies. I stuffed stockings and trimmed trees. I waited each spring for the giant forsythia out back to bloom, signalling that warmer weather was on the way and that it was time to pick high-bush blueberries, strawberries and rhubarb ripe and ready from the garden. From our window we would watch the fog rolling in and out and sailboats scooting across the bay. We hosted friends for dinner in the garden on warm summer nights. I'd set an outdoor table, line the garden with mason jars filled with candles, grill lamb chops on a Weber grill next to the table and garnish salads with wild pansies that had grown rogue in cracks in the garden path while Billie Holiday played over an outdoor speaker. I felt lucky and thankful and relieved that I had made it and everything was going to be all right.

I cooked a lot at home and was enjoying the role of being responsible for our family meals. I cooked for us, I cooked for friends and I was always game to throw together last-minute dinner parties for Tom's out-of-town clients. What better way to woo potential business than with a bellyful of a heartfelt meal after visiting the boat shop. It made me feel relevant in my marriage too. Tom enjoyed showing off the beautiful food and he enjoyed showing off his young wife. The food and I were luxuries in his mind – luxuries that he increasingly took for granted.

It wasn't long into our marriage before Tom started to come home from work later and later. The table would be set, the candles would be burning, the music would be playing and the chicken would be roasted, resting on its platter ready to carve. But there would be no sign of Tom. I'd call, no answer. I'd text, no answer. It started to become a pattern, and one I was growing deeply frustrated with. Where was he and why was he avoiding my calls? Why wasn't he running home after work each day, looking forward to being in this house that I had made a home for him? Each time he'd arrive home late, I'd ask him where he had been. 'At the shop,' was always the answer. I believed him at first, but after a while, I began to wonder. So one evening, instead of pacing the kitchen floor stewing over where he was, I got in the car to go find out. I drove down to the boat shop to find the parking lot empty, the door locked and the lights off. His workdays started early, which meant they ended early too. By 3:30 P.M. (which the guys around the shop often referred to as beer-thirty), the crew had usually clocked out and headed back home to their families. So where was Tom?

I considered going back home, letting Tom's behaviour slide. For the first time in what felt like my whole life, I had built something so solid. Perfect, even. Did I want to start to unravel it now? But this particular night, I wasn't so eager to just head back, tail between my legs. It was one of the two nights a week that Tom's girls from his previous marriage were there. They were thirteen and sixteen and between the challenge of adjusting to a new woman in their dad's life and the fact that it was someone barely old enough to be their mother, adjusting to being their stepmom had been difficult. I figured I could maybe just be their friend, even though I wasn't sure they wanted that either. But I was doing my best to hold this family together and I'd be damned if Tom was going to ruin it for all of us. I would have thought that on the nights the girls spent with us, which were fewer and farther between, Tom would have made an extra effort to be there for them. If Tom valued the fraction of time that he got to spend with them, with Jaim, with me – I expected that he'd be home. Yet it appeared that there was something else more important going on in his world.

I put the car in drive, weaving slowly down each street, looking for a sign of him. It didn't take long before I spotted his car, parked around the corner from one of the local bars. Through the window I could see his figure perched on a barstool. He was surrounded by a few other patrons and was tipping back a drink, chatting, laughing, not giving a damn in the world. I sat in my parked car across the street for a few minutes just watching him, trying to understand what he was doing, why he was there and why he was lying to me. I dialled his number from my cell and watched for his reaction. He pulled his phone from his pocket and looked at it for a moment, then placed it upside down on the bar and reached for his drink for another swig. He just sat there, so casually, so unaffected, so oblivious to the fact there were people at home waiting for him, counting on him. I was burning inside with a mixture of anger and sadness. It seemed he'd rather sit there on his stool, alone in that dark and dingy bar, surrounded by flashing TV screens and neon beer lights, sipping on his booze, than come home to us.

I followed him a few other times out of suspicion and the consistency was clear: he was going to bars. Not always the same bar, but a bar nonetheless. I had to assume that he had been out drinking all those times he'd made excuses for being late; he had been lying to me all along. I was angry, but more than that, I was embarrassed. And I couldn't bring myself to do anything about it because doing something about it would be admitting that I had married someone so very much like my father: I had married a drunk.

When we first got together, the drinking felt harmless. I passed it off as romantic – sharing bottles of wine over dinner, sipping pints of beer at lunch. Even the night he showed up at my parents' house to meet them for the first time he had put down a bunch of gin to 'calm his nerves'. It seemed oddly endearing, an understandable salve for meeting his girlfriend's parents, who were his age.

By dinner's end he was outside, sick in the bushes like a teenager. My mother gave me the eyes that had said, Are you sure about this one? I brushed all the warning signs aside. Instead I drank with him. When I drank with him, it made it feel more normal, like the booze-soaked dates we used to go on when our relationship was new and full of electricity. He would come home from work on a weekday and we would dip into a bottle of white wine while I'd glaze right over the fact he had already been to the bar and put down God knows how many drinks before he had even set foot through the front door. Sure, he often took three painkillers every morning before getting up, but he was productive at work. Sure, he had spent a night in jail not too long ago after being arrested for driving under the influence, but that was just bad luck – nothing other people in town weren't doing, too.

He lost his licence for a few months after he was caught drink-driving, which left me to do all the driving. I drove Tom to work, I drove his girls to school and on the weekend I drove him to mandatory substance-abuse meetings per his court order. He disliked the meetings and protested after each about how disgusted he was, how he wasn't 'like' those other drunks. I was complicit. I made excuses for him and I lied to his girls, telling them his car wasn't working or that he had to go to work early so I'd have to drive them today. I refused to admit the problems we were facing because I was too hung up with the idea of the life I was trying to build. I refused to admit he had a problem with alcohol because I didn't want to be in that kind of a marriage. So I foolishly chose to deny it for as long as I could. We were enabling each other and living a lie until our reality was nothing but fighting, bickering and drinking.

Over time, Tom's drinking increased. On a solo trip to Mexico to spread his father's ashes, he ended up in a strange hotel room after a night of drinking and he admitted to me that when he woke up in the morning he wasn't alone. He told me that he regretted his behaviour, emotionally punishing himself for it, but he was still out of control. And still I stayed. He was arrested twice – once for drink-driving and once for throwing me around the house while he was drunk. Despite the increasingly visible red flags, his first arrest caught me off guard. It was past midnight and he had yet to return home. I phoned him endlessly, each time getting his voice mail. Eventually I couldn't handle the uncertainty of what had happened to him anymore. I left Jaim in his bed, deeply asleep and drove the few blocks down the street to Tom's shop. I found his truck abandoned on the side of the road. Confused and terrified, I drove a little further hoping to find him. I flagged down a passing police car and told the officer about Tom's abandoned vehicle and the fact that I hadn't heard from him.

'Yeah, I booked him tonight for drinking and driving. He's sleeping it off up at the county jail. He'll be released tomorrow.'

My panic turned to embarrassment and anger. But he had never scared me so much as he did the night of his second arrest – the night his eyes turned black and vacant after a day full of pounding beer, wine and gin. I didn't know the man behind those eyes. I didn't know the man knocking me out of my chair, throwing me into furniture and wrapping his hands around my throat. I didn't know the man chasing me around the house as I frantically tried to get away from him long enough to find a phone to call for help while Jaim slept upstairs, thankfully oblivious. When the police arrived that night, I could feel Tom's resentment toward me spike. He had lost control. As he was escorted out of our house handcuffed, he shouted, slurring, trying to take me down with intimidation. He yelled my name over and over again with his threatening anger as he was shoved into the cruiser. 'Erin! Erin! Erin!' he kept repeating in a voice so violently angry that it was palpable in the air. I worried that the neighbours would see or hear what was happening because then our secret would be out: our marriage was a toxic waste. The event was a wake-up call for Tom – he never touched another drink again. But it was a wake-up call for me too. I finally had to admit to myself that the fairy tale I thought we were building was, in fact, a nightmare.

Leaving Tom wouldn't be easy. At first I stayed in the house with Jaim, while Tom was forced to stay away due to the automatic restraining order that the cops placed on him after he had gotten physical with me. After a few months the order went away and when it did, Tom wanted to come home. He was sober now, but I wasn't sure that I wanted him back. I had been struggling, fighting feelings of depression and feeling a financial pinch on top of it. I wasn't in a position to be on my own, pulling in only a small, seasonal salary from the catering company. I had left my full-time job at the bistro a few years back. I had grown tired of the chef's behaviour and relationships with women at the restaurant. I let his advances toward me go only so far and it appeared that he was treating me poorly as a result. The final straw was when he began a relationship with my younger sister. I was mortified that Nina got involved with him and it led me to walk out on the job. I had pulled her in and gotten her the job in the first place, giving her work that she so desperately needed at the time. It was a chance for us as sisters to work together in this tiny bistro and maybe work on our bigger problems and distant love for each other in the same stroke. It turned out to be short-lived. I looked out for her, warned her even about the chef's lecherous patterns with female employees. Nina apparently didn't care about the repercussions or the damage she could cause as a result of her actions. She also ended up getting my shifts and all the good cash tips that came along with it. I felt betrayed and ashamed to call her my sister. Quitting left a hole in my bank account and a gaping two-year tear in my relationship with Nina. I couldn't afford to pay the mortgage on my own nor could I afford to rent a place. I was lucky enough to have a friend who agreed to let me live in the small apartment above her garage while Tom and I pieced together our shattered marriage.

By day I was making wedding cakes, the irony not escaping me. By night I would take turns with Tom, who had assured me that he was done with the drinking, 'nesting', rotating where each of us slept. On nights I slept at home, he stayed at our friend's apartment and vice versa – an effort to avoid uprooting and upending Jaim from home. Where this separation was headed was still unclear.

Over the course of our four months of separation, Tom appeared to be working through a range of emotions. He wasn't just battling the sting of my leaving him, he was simultaneously trying to stay sober. He would unpredictably swing from being angry with me, threatening to take everything, bullying me to come home to him; and begging, pleading and promising me the world: 'What is it you want? A dog? A baby? A new car? I'll give you anything! Just come back.' He offered all the things he had vowed he would never do, like wear a wedding ring or get a dog, even though he had always been clear about how much he disliked animals – our clear differences on this causing hours upon hours of bickering over the years.

I couldn't keep up the separation for long. Fending Tom off was wearing me down and I didn't have the financial means to make a go of independence. I didn't have my family's support, either. My father had become increasingly vocal with his opinion, ordering me to obey and work things out. 'You get home to your husband and work it out. You made this bed. Now lie in it. Don't you be fucking selfish and don't you dare break up your boy's world. You fix it!' I didn't necessarily see staying with Tom as the best choice for all of us, but I also couldn't live with knowing that I made the choice to decimate Jaim's world once again. There was no choice; I would go back; I would lie in that bed; and I would try to fix my broken marriage.

14

LAYERS OF ANGST

To be successful in our marriage, we would need to make a hard, honest effort to love each other and lift each other up once again. But Tom had been too drunk to lift me up and now seemed far too comfortable with tearing me down. The excitement of our initial courtship was over now and all we had left was a stale and dysfunctional marriage. We weren't growing together; we were rotting side by side. Trust had been broken, honesty shattered. Being back in the same house with Tom made it hard to breathe sometimes. I felt trapped and it was filling me with anxiety. It started out with tightness in my chest. My lungs would compress, like a stack of bricks was sitting on my rib cage, each inhale feeling shorter and shorter, leaving me gasping for air. It would happen while I was riding in the car with him, or in the shower when I was all alone. It would happen at the dinner table, or in the middle of the day while prepping for catering gigs in the kitchen. Anxiety was creeping up inside me anytime it pleased. I had no way to predict when the feelings would come on and when they set in, it felt like I was being swallowed by something much bigger than me. I felt hopeless, uninspired, insecure and worthless. It was getting harder to get out of bed and harder to fall asleep. Our marriage was a mess and I was starting to mirror it inside and out.

Tom was going through his own transformation. He was sober now, clean and clear of alcohol, clean and clear of lying about where he had been and whom he had been with. He had to start anew, making new habits to replace his old bad ones. He was attending an AA meeting each morning and coming home straight after work in the afternoon, avoiding the urge to slide into one of the many local bars along the way. Booze was out of his life, but I could tell he was mourning the loss of the daily ritual. At 4:00 P.M. on the dot he'd start to get really irritable. The smallest things would make him fly off the handle and the tension that shrouded him got thicker the closer it was to cocktail time. He picked fights, throwing countless barbs in my direction and yelled at Jaim for small unreasonable things. Alcohol was a way to relax, a liquid able to wash away his stress. Without it, the tax of everyday life was constantly stewing and we were absorbing its harmful effects. There were times when I would encourage him to find a replacement, something to fill the gaping void that had been left by the absence of alcohol. 'Take a hot bath, go for a run, read a good book,' I told him on many occasions. 'It's not that easy,' he'd tell me. I'd come home sometimes to find him vacuuming the walls, or under the bed cleaning up tufts of dust, mopping madly, or organizing Jaim's Lego pieces in tiny bins by colour and size. Tom had always been neat – so neat we weren't allowed to have pets because he hated the thought of the mess they would make, but this was extreme and I worried he was becoming obsessive. He was uptight, irritable and depressed – which was just about all we had in common.

My depression had become undeniable and the clouds of anxiety were hovering over me like a thick fogbank every day now. It was affecting my work, my ability to be a present mother and my joy – as in, I *had* none anymore, just angst saddled with hopelessness. And I was still building wedding cakes for brides with fairy-tale-like dreams of what marriage should look like.

* * *

Sometimes I'd be midproject, slathering layers of lemon curd and stacking vanilla cakes before spackling on the first-layer crumb coat and I'd think, You've got no business putting your miserable hands all over someone's wedding cake. I often wondered if my marital misery was seeping into these virgin cakes, inflicting some kind of doom on the couple who would take the first bite. Could they taste how unhappy I was in my own marriage? Could they feel it in the piping around the edges? Could they see it in the same way my depression was becoming visible in my hollowed face and purple-ringed, sleep-deprived eyes? In the flecks of butter that I failed to beat well into the buttercream and the splotches where my shaky hand had slipped while trying to smooth it all out? I dotted the blemishes with soft flower petals, covering up the imperfections and hoping to hell no one else would be hurt when they sliced into the cake that was layered with all of my angst.

My doctor sat on a small wheeled stool, rolling back and forth between the table I was sitting on and the counter with his computer, entering in all sorts of data. My height, weight, blood pressure, temperature. He took inventory of all of my bodily complaints without once looking me in the eye. I rattled off everything that felt wrong with me: the tightening in my chest that was stealing my breath, the lack of sleep, the lack of joy, the lack of desire to get out of bed in the morning, the hopelessness, the restlessness, the grinding of my teeth at night, the rock-hard muscles in my shoulders and neck. He sat with his back to me, quietly typing away as I lay on the white crinkly paper in a hospital gown. He didn't speak except to ask me when all these feelings had started. As he pressed on my abdomen with both hands, pushing and poking, searching for I don't know what, I recounted for him the painful downfall of my marriage and the persistent day-to-day struggles. He moved his hands under my gown, rolling his cold fingers around each of my breasts, searching for lumps. Concluding that my symptoms were due to temporary circumstances, he scribbled a handful of prescriptions on a pad and handed me the small stack of paper, assuring me: 'This should do the trick to get you through this.' The appointment had taken all of fifteen minutes. I got dressed and left, wondering how in the hell the bits of paper in my back pocket could cure all my problems at home.

I wandered through the drugstore searching for the counter to hand in my fresh scripts. I hadn't been to any pharmacy counter since I'd picked up a prescription for acne cream nearly a decade ago. I'd never needed medication – hell, I didn't even take headache pills. I slid the white sheet of paper across the counter toward the clerk.

I spent the thirty-minute wait wandering the aisles of the Rite Aid, thumbing through the magazine rack and wasting time filling a small basket with an odd assortment of goods. Tampons and extra-whitening toothpastes, a bottle of nail polish I'd probably never use, a night cream that seemed like it was worth a try and a pack of peanut M&Ms. I sat in the waiting area with my basket, checked my blood pressure for free with an automated cuff and pondered why the pharmacy sold *booze* and *cigarettes*. No, wait, it was a *drug*store; I got it.

There were three white paper bags prepared for me, stapled shut, with a thick pile of paper attached loaded with warnings, side effects and far too much information to digest. It looked like a lot, but when I peeled the bags open and discarded the paper, all that was left were three small orange plastic containers with an assortment of pills. There was a bottle of Ambien that I was to take each night for sleep and a bottle of Zoloft to fight my depression and hopefully bring back my desire to get out of bed in the morning. And last but not least, a nice full bottle of Xanax that promised to put the air back in my lungs. Pills for morning, pills for afternoon, pills for evening – pills for everything that was making me uncomfortable. I stuffed the bottles into my purse, tucking them away for the moment I knew I'd need them.

It was a typical evening at home that night. Tom was his new on-time self. Like clockwork, as cocktail hour approached, his agitation grew. He was vacuuming the walls again, yelling at Jaim to clean up the Lego pieces from the floor of his room and shaming me for not folding the laundry. I had no problem throwing in a load of laundry each day, but the folding I frequently avoided. It drove Tom nuts to see heaps of clean clothes mounded in baskets, getting all wrinkly, and he let me know it. He was berating me for not taking my shoes off at the door, for not loading the dishwasher properly, for not putting the rubbish in the appropriate bin and for being 'too emotional'. He was scolding me as if I were a child and harping on every little imperfection he could find, making me feel naive and low. Along with his sobriety came his ability to nitpick the most insignificant of circumstances. Living with him had become like tiptoeing around broken glass, knowing that at any moment, even the slightest of moves could be wrong and you'd be punished with a splintering shard of reprimand. I couldn't do anything right, no matter how hard I tried. I could feel the bricks piling up on my chest, the bowling ball in my stomach, the vice constricting my lungs. But this time I had a weapon against it. As I sensed the feeling coming on, I reached into my purse and pulled out the bottle of Xanax from a zipped side pocket. I popped off the top and gently shook out one pill into the palm of my hand. I threw it into the back of my mouth, chased it with a few gulps of water and waited. It took all of fifteen minutes for the sweet high. It was as if a blanket of calm had wrapped itself around me. Tom kept vacuuming the walls and shouting nonsense at me, like: 'I told you there's a special cloth just for cleaning the television; don't use anything else!' But his words drowned in the soft 'I don't give a damn' haze that was shrouding me. He didn't bother me anymore. I felt untouchable; I could breathe and it felt divine. I had a weapon now, one that shielded me from his barbs all in one little convenient pill and I felt like I was finally starting to take back control of my life.

PART THREE

PROSPECT

15

THE TRIANGLE MADE
OF BRICKS

The former bank at 108 Main Street had been vacant for ages. The small three-story Gothic flatiron in downtown Belfast had been sitting dormant and dark on the market for nearly five years, waiting for someone to breathe new life into it – and waiting for a price drop too. I monitored the listing almost daily, driving by and fantasizing about what I would do if it were mine. On occasion I'd sit on the bench in Post Office Square, sipping coffee and staring up at the triangle made of bricks. I had painted the picture in my mind hundreds of times – I'd have a little café on the first floor, simple and sweet with intimate tables scattered throughout the room. There'd be a long zinc bar along the plate-glass window where you could look out at Main Street, sipping prosecco and nibbling on a cheese plate, a salad garnished with edible flowers, or maybe even an icy oyster or two. The tables had tiny vases filled with fresh-cut flowers and there'd be a few giant glass hurricanes with tall branches, like flowering forsythia or quince. Flickering candlesticks would reflect light off antique mirrors on the walls, while my playlist of upbeat jazz mixed with laid-back, acoustic songs echoed around the room. I'd serve hard-boiled quail eggs as bar snacks that you could peel-n-eat and dunk in a dust of celery salt. I'd invent cocktails with fresh-squeezed juices, swirling them with herb-infused syrups and good liquor. I could see it all in my mind so vividly that I felt electrified every time I thought about it. I knew in my bones that something special was supposed to happen in this space.

The top two floors of the building housed a large apartment that you could get to from the street level via a long wooden staircase that divided the downstairs space neatly in half. I envisioned the three of us living up there. Even though I had grown up in a restaurant and knew how the busy line could steal from a family and I still carried the pain of my father's emotional unavailability over all those years, I thought if we lived above the restaurant I could be close to my family all of the time. I wouldn't give Jaim the same life. I could be present, work and still be Mom. I could even run up between orders and tuck him into bed, I thought. The key was doing it all in this beautiful brick box. The odds were slim, but I couldn't seem to be bothered letting facts get in the way of this dream.

Turning thirty was an eye-opener for me. There was something about this particular number that forced a bit of pause and reflection upon the first three decades of my life. I started to think about what exactly I had accomplished in my thirty years on this earth and I started to belittle the few things on that list. Sure, I had graduated from high school. I had gotten accepted into college and moved to Boston. Then again, I had dropped out of college and moved back to the sticks, gotten pregnant and ditched at twenty-one and brought a baby boy into the world alone. I had been a waitress, a cook and a bartender – not exactly the pre-med track I had originally envisioned. And while I had gotten married, I was still struggling to keep my marriage on the rails. When I stopped to look back on my life and add it all up, I couldn't help questioning my value. My heart was burning for more in a way I couldn't deny but, at the same time, couldn't yet identify. I just felt a need to create something, make something from scratch with my own hands, share something. I had pored over ideas and outlets to release this pent-up energy and the common denominator in each and every one of my thoughts was undeniable: food. I had simple fantasies of turning an old Airstream caravan into an elevated food cart, serving fried fish baskets with homemade sauces (garnished with nasturtiums, of course). Like a fancier variation on my dad's own carnival-wagon days, when he used to travel around serving up fried food at country fairs for extra cash. Or maybe it was as elaborate as a full-blown restaurant in that dreamy downtown building I couldn't seem to stop thinking about. Either way, there was food involved.

Tom allowed me to dream about the building. The tables had turned since our fairly fresh marital stumble and for the first time in our relationship, he was eager to please me and to entertain my hopes and dreams. He could feel me slipping away and had become hopeful that he could spoil me into staying by dangling his contrived efforts in my face. So he'd try again to throw bait that might keep me on the line. *Tell me your dreams. You want that building? A restaurant?* He hoped that if he fed me the crumbs I had been craving that it would be enough to keep me. So, continuing to dream felt like the right thing to do. It kept a glimmer of goodness alive in our nearly dead marriage. Something fresh and new might be just what we needed to bring us back together.

Tom and I didn't have anywhere near the kind of money it would take to buy the building, let alone enough for a down payment to secure a mortgage. I would never be considered a serious buyer. The only chance I had of bringing my dreams to fruition was to make a creative plea to the out-of-state husband-and-wife owners and paint them the picture that had seared itself into my mind. I wrote a letter and made my pitch, inviting them to lunch at our house.

I composed a simple menu and prepared it with care and attention – warm pasta with fresh collard-green pesto, a salad of spicy mustard greens, tossed with a pink shallot vinaigrette and the last of the edible blossoms the frost hadn't yet killed. We sipped on a nice dry rosé (and a bottle of San Pellegrino for Tom) and made polite conversation. Then, before I served slices of French apple tart baked into a rich, buttery crust, I made my case. I recounted my doe-eyed dream of renting the upstairs apartment while I sought creative ways to secure a mortgage to buy the building outright. I told them that if they could just let me do that, then I would have a place to start slow, dabbling in dedicating my days to food. I would use the apartment kitchen to test recipes and experiment with dishes that might one day be served downstairs. I would spend each week hunting for new ingredients to play with and come Saturday evenings, I would convert the apartment living room into a dining room where I could invite friends over to sample my creations. I expressed just how deeply in love I was with the building and how hard I would work to be a good steward of the space.

They asked for some time to consider the proposal. A few agonizing weeks later, I received word of their decision. They had seen something in me that afternoon, something that reminded them of their own daughter. It was the same way their daughter had pleaded with them many years ago about the same building, with a passionate excitement burning in her heart, too. They helped her buy the building so she could open a small coffee shop that she would pour her heart into, serving baked goods, homemade ice creams and the first espresso that the town of Belfast had ever seen. In the end it hadn't worked out for her and maybe it wouldn't for me either, but just because dreams sometimes get crushed doesn't mean we should stop dreaming. My passionate prayer had been enough to overturn all their logic. And so, they offered me the place to lease. With a modest rent and a few minor conditions, it was mine, all mine. I had a blank slate.

The old wooden staircase that led up to the second-floor apartment creaked with each step I took. It was dark and smelled like a dusty antique store, which I liked. At the top of the staircase I pushed aside the heavy velvet curtain that shielded the apartment from the cold of the stairwell to reveal the empty living room. I soaked up my reality as I slowly paced around the room, taking in all the details that I had dreamed about for years. One by one I folded back the old wooden shutters and flung open the tall windows, letting light into spaces that had been dark for so long. The smell of cold November salt air trickled into the room along with the soft murmur of the city buzz below. It brought the space to life. The place was dripping with character, with its hardwood floors, high ceilings, thick period mouldings and doors with frosted glass and heavy hardware. But as much as I wanted to call this home, for now it would serve as my workshop, where I would create something to share with the world. It would start with a secret supper club.

The kitchen in the back corner of the apartment was humble yet elegant. The ceiling was high, which lent ample space to the wall of towering white-painted cabinets and cupboards. There was a sink, an old dishwasher and a basic refrigerator; plus butcher-block and copper-lined countertops and one small cupboard that I would eventually stuff full with an array of pantry goods like bottles of fine Kalamata olive oil, assorted vinegars (rice wine, apple cider and simple white), dried beans and grains, pickles and preserves and jars of local honey. Last but not least, there was an old four-burner GE electric range sitting between two large windows that poured warm light into sun-kissed space. It wasn't a professional range by any stretch, but I trusted it to do for me what I needed.

I begged Tom for the small contribution of helping me move in a large wooden island he had built at the shop from scrap mahogany and oak leftover from a project years before. It was the same island that had sat in his apartment that very first night I had gone to his place all those years ago. The one we sat around eating salad with Parmesan crisps and slugging down white wine. A night that was confusing, yet had become a pivotal point in our relationship.

A relationship that was still confusing, more layered and complex now than way back when. Part of me wanted to include this piece in the space because it felt like a small acknowledgment of the part of me that was trying to hold on to the thread that still cherished our past. Another part of me just needed a goddamn countertop and I felt like Tom owed it to me to invest in me and my dreams. A small token in replacement for all the apologies I never received from him. I filled its shelves with dishes and plates that I had collected from flea markets and estate sales over the years and moved in a borrowed ice cream maker along with my KitchenAid, blender and food processor, as well as other small appliances and utensils I had accrued from my days of working in the kitchen supply store just down the street. It was a comfort to see that all those years of spending most of my paycheck on kitchen items and cookbooks might finally prove to be a wise investment.

Tom and I built four beautiful tabletops from more scrap wood from the shop, using galvanized trestles for legs to save money. He was giving me his time, his energy and the use of the machines of his shop to bring this little dream of mine to life. It was a rare and hopeful moment as we milled the wood together and as the smell of the fresh shavings filled the air, I could feel a fragment of goodness existing between us. I bought mismatched vintage tableware from the secondhand shop across the street for a dollar apiece and spent a few afternoon hours polishing each spoon, knife and fork back to as good as new. I found a bolt of inexpensive fabric from an odd-lot store that looked like a natural linen and made napkins and table runners using my grandmother's sewing machine. I visited every antique and vintage shop in a thirty-mile radius, amassing mismatched floral dinner and salad plates, soup bowls and platters; and borrowed an inherited set of green Depression glass that belonged to my mother's mother. I found glassware and stemware at off-price discount stores, filling a bookshelf-turned-bar in the living-room-turned-dining-room. I threw down an oversize rug for a touch of homey softness, hung a few photos on the wall and placed a floor lamp in the corner with a low-wattage bulb for some soft mood lighting. My mother donated an old chalkboard from her teaching days that I would hang on the wall in the entry where guests would arrive and use to scribble the evening's menu. Below the chalkboard was a small shelf with a stack of envelopes, a pen and a clear glass jar where guests could leave donations toward the food costs for the night.

Once the dining room and kitchen began to take shape, it wasn't long before I could really start cooking in the place. When I wasn't scouring for plates and glassware, I was busy seeking out produce. One thing I was convinced of was that I couldn't make good food without good ingredients. So I visited the farmer's market each Friday, sampling goods, taking notes and getting an understanding for the variety of produce that was available and who the people were that were selling it. I paid attention to the labels at the food co-op, recording the names of farms, their locations and whether they grew the nicest greens or just so-so ones. I sought out fishermen and cheesemongers and made farm visits. And when I was done I compiled a list of all of the people from my tight radius who produced things that excited me. There were Polly and Prentice from Villageside Farm and their most perfect heads of baby lettuce, still glistening with droplets of water. Ken and Adrienne with their rainbow assortment of beetroots. Kyffin from Morrill Century Farm with the best eggs, rich and bright with strong yolks that stood up to a good poach and Debbie Hahn, whose cheeses blew my mind with their complexity and perfection. Every time I discovered a new source for ingredients, I felt lucky to call Maine home. I had food to cook and a place to cook in. Now all I needed was a name. Something simple and easy to remember. Something that would draw people into the second-floor apartment of an unknown.

* * *

The first Saturday of December was cold and snowy, but it seemed as good a date as any to kick off my first secret supper. I had emailed invites to a group of friends, hoping to get just twenty-four interested souls to join in for my experimental dinner. I offered a five-course meal in exchange for pay-as-you-please donations; wine was Bring Your Own. The response was underwhelming. I received a mixed bag of replies, from polite declines to radio silence to questions like 'Why would we pay you to come to dinner at your house?' I began to wonder if I was making a terrible mistake, if maybe this idea that had been burning a hole in my belly was not such a great one after all. But with a bit of persistence (and begging), I managed to wrangle sixteen guests, including my parents and husband. It wouldn't be enough people to fill the homemade tables we had just built, but it would be enough to make a respectable go of it. I staged a cosy spot for eight-year-old Jaim on the third floor, complete with a movie, a stack of books, a bag of crackers, a few juice pouches and a box of macaroni cheese in the pantry that I could whip up in a flash for him. It was a test to see if we could make a go of Mom working in the kitchen while keeping him happy, fed and entertained with only a staircase between us.

With the cold and snow swirling around the quiet winter streets of Belfast, I cranked up the heat in anticipation of the arrival of my dinner guests. I wanted them to feel warm and cosy when they ascended the creaky wooden staircase, while they inhaled delicious smells wafting from the kitchen. I put a borrowed set of teacups on the radiator to warm in time for coffee service at the end of the meal. I set each table with a linen runner and the napkins I had made, the vintage plates and mismatched silver, a few flickering candles and a vase of wheatgrass that I had forced to grow the week before, lending a wispy pop of bright green colour. I dimmed the lights to a soft glow and turned on a playlist I had made, filled with my favourite Miles Davis riffs. I flicked on the light at the bottom of the apartment porch as a welcoming sign and began to scribble the evening's menu on the chalkboard, moments before the handful of guests would trickle in with bottles of wine tucked under their arms. Any good menu would headline with the name of the restaurant. I knew that. It was no different from when I was a girl and used to invent menus for my mother with hand-scribbled offerings for the evening. The place always had a name and this place was no different. So what would I call this little rogue supper club that I was concocting in my home kitchen, quietly tucked away on the second floor of my apartment, with no sign or great announcements to help anyone find it? I pondered for but the briefest moment, feeling the simple name take shape with the chalk in my hand. At the top I wrote '*Welcome to The Lost Kitchen*'.

Tonight we would feast on briny oysters with a red-onion-and-beetroot mignonette and a bite of apple-cider-and-Calvados sorbet to cleanse the palate. A simple salad of spicy local rocket tossed with crunchy fennel and sweet fall fruits would be served just before a plate of line-caught Maine cod. I'd sear the fish skin-side down in cast-iron pans on the old electric range to get it nice and brown and crunchy before finishing it in the small oven with lots of good butter. I'd serve the flaky fish on a smear of potato-and-parsnip mash with roasted pickled beetroot and sautéed Tuscan kale on the side, a drizzle of the buttery pan juices and a squeeze of lemon for good measure. Once the plates were cleared, I would bring out platters of local cheese that I had picked up at the market the day before, alongside tiny squares of honeycomb and toasts, in European fashion. And last but not least, there would be thick slices of a caramelized pear-and-cornmeal upside-down cake accompanied by a scoop of tangy crème fraîche ice cream. A cafetière of strong coffee would circulate the room and be served in the teacups that had been warming on the radiator, thick local cream and lumps of raw sugar to go with them.

* * *

As I moved around pouring coffee and clearing empty plates, I took in the happy chatter that billowed around the warm room. Everyone was having the most wonderful time, laughing, drinking wine and licking their dessert plates clean. I could *feel* the joy pumping into me like a shot of endorphins, something I'd sorely needed. I had made this moment come to life from nothing but dreams.

After everyone had departed, it took me hours to wash all the dishes and clean up the beautiful mess we had made. Jaim had gone home with my parents, excited for an overnight with 'Nana' and 'Buppa'. Tom had left along with the other dinner guests. I tingled with disappointment that he hadn't even offered to stay behind and help clean up. He had just waltzed out like a buzzed guest. I had been craving his approval, maybe a moment together to recount the successes of the evening, but didn't even get as much as a nod or a good-bye wave. I stopped myself from letting it spoil my evening because I was still enjoying the high too much. I drank from a half glass of leftover white wine between dipping my hands into the sudsy warm dish water, recalling each course and the smiles on everyone's faces. I had found some bliss and I couldn't wait to find it again next weekend. I could feel myself coming alive.

Week after week I was turning out suppers on Saturday nights, now filling the room to capacity. The second dinner had filled more easily than the first, booking up moments after making the announcement. And by the third dinner, word-of-mouth had spread far enough that half of the people in my apartment were complete strangers whom I was meeting for the first time. Each week the light at the bottom of the stairs would flick on at 6:00 P.M., the door would open and a steady stream of dinner guests would climb the staircase. The small donations that people left in paper envelopes helped me recoup the hefty cost of food and pay for the aid of my teenage stepdaughter and a good friend of mine who helped serve the dishes I was pumping out of my tiny apartment kitchen. As the dinners raged on, I could feel that my cooking was starting to take on a life of its own. I had a blank slate every week to cook whatever I pleased. From rope-grown mussels and local lamb lollipops, to seared Maine scallops and thick filets of local halibut, to savoury sorbets with citrus and Pernod or cider and star anise, I was cooking the kind of food that I'd daydreamed about while leafing through cookbooks in the kitchen supply store. I visualized these dishes, imagined their flavours and then taught myself how to make them. I took small chickens and taught myself how to make an 'airline' cut, using my boning knife to bone out the breasts but keep a drumette attached. I brined the pieces overnight in a water bath of sugar, salt and bay leaf before roasting them off in the oven slathered with butter and surrounded by clusters of sweet grapes. I taught myself to shuck oysters and broke into dozens of them each week to get good practice before plating them on a bed of cold seaweed and beach rocks that I harvested from the bay. I dressed them with a tiny spoonful of finely diced shallots with vinegar and black pepper and some chopped cucumber and fresh dill.

On one level, my movements in the kitchen felt rote, choreographed by years spent on the line at the diner. The slow waltz between counter and stove was one that had been etched into my DNA. It was a comfort to have a tether to something so familiar as I pushed myself further and further from what I already knew. I wasn't just working on technique, I was working on my identity as a cook. I hadn't fallen back on food as a safety net because I believed it to be the only skill I had ever really learned; it was becoming my absolute passion. I understood then, in perfect clarity, what drove my father to do what he did all those years, even at the expense of his family. But while feeding people was a driving force, it wasn't in spite of my family, it was *for* them. And for the first time in so very long, it was something for me, too.

* * *

After months and months filled with dinners, my skills were improving, my cooking was getting better and along with it, my confidence was slowly growing. I had a following of nearly five hundred people who had dined in my little apartment and were eager to do so again. I started to wonder if I might have it in me to open a real restaurant. That I wasn't formally trained and had no savings were just two among a million other reasons why I shouldn't even consider entering such a risky business. But I also believed that if I wanted it enough, there was no way I would fail. I couldn't run an illegal supper club in my apartment forever. I'd eventually get found out and busted for not having the right licenses and inspections. So the question was: What's next?

16

THE CLINKING OF GLASSES, THE FLICKER OF CANDLES

Tom and I were in desperate need of a diversion, something exciting and positive to throw our focus toward, instead of wallowing in our endless loop of fights. We needed a project where we could build something together, something to give us hope that we could reconnect and ignite some love and trust between us. For the first time in our relationship, Tom seemed, occasionally, eager to help me live out my dreams instead of his. I didn't know how long it would last, so I took him up on every kind offer he put on the table. He had never apologized for all the ways his drinking had harmed me, or the lying, cheating or abuse. Instead I accepted his willingness to help me as a symbol of his sincere remorse. I knew, deep down, that he believed that getting me to stick around would ultimately serve him and that his motivations weren't purely selfless, but I took his help all the same.

'What are you, *nuts*?!' my father exclaimed after I shared with him my plan to open a restaurant. 'You don't get it, Erin. Belfast doesn't want a place like that. People want real food. It will never work; it's too *groovy*.' It was the same thing he told me when I would try to sneak edible flowers onto the lobster rolls at the diner. I wondered if he truly believed that, or if he just didn't believe in me enough. Or maybe he was pissed that I didn't want to just take over the diner from him, giving him relief and retirement. Either way, he would have no part in helping me.

He wasn't the only one who doubted me: almost everyone did and they weren't shy about telling me so. From my father to my grandfather, my aunt Rhoda to the mayor, the neighbours to my mother's co-workers, people just couldn't keep themselves from vocalizing their skepticism. For those whose lives had been rooted in Belfast, they were convinced that an 'upscale' restaurant was dead in the water. Even Tom had his doubts, but his freedom to discuss them was muzzled by the fear that I might just up and leave him. He knew that feeding me this opportunity might be the only way he could continue to hold on to me. And he loved the idea of acquiring more property. To me the building was a space to bring a hope of mine to life; for him it was a prime piece of real estate at the centre of town to claim as his. As little business as I had opening a restaurant, I knew I had no business not to. I also had the support of my mom, who, while never one to share a firm opinion, would never lose faith in me. I'd start slow and simple, using my Yankee intuition and frugal sensibilities. The space below the apartment was small enough to feel intimate and not overwhelm a novice in the kitchen, but large enough to fill with just enough tables to turn a profit and maybe, just maybe, liberate me from my past, bring some sort of purpose to my life and heal my marriage. Like I said, I could dream big.

Renting the quaint second-floor apartment on a month-to-month basis could only last so long. The building had been up for sale for years and it was only a matter of time before some out-of-towner would come along and snag it, kicking this local girl to the curb. I had dreamed about buying the place since the day the For Sale sign went in the window, but it was a dream far out of reach of my bank account. I didn't have the means, but I had will and endless hope. It would take a few years, a few price drops and a rough business plan to get closer. It would take some begging, some borrowing and massive amounts of pondering and planning, but I was eventually on the path to making the Lost Kitchen a permanent fixture. Tom helped me talk a local bank into lending to us – leveraging everything we could. My grandfather – who had been so clear with me that this was a dead-end, go-nowhere dream – couldn't deny the sparkle in my eyes when I talked about my big plans and lent me some savings that he held at a local bank as collateral to get a loan so we could buy the triangle made of bricks. We closed on a warm spring day. As Tom and I sat on an old banquette in the space that I envisioned would one day be the dining room, I was dazed with disbelief that we had actually pulled it off. Even with the shades closed, shielding us from Main Street and the busy pavement just on the other side of the large plate-glass window, the warm afternoon light couldn't help peeking through all the cracks, bathing the room in soft light. I could sense how divine this room would feel in the early evening, the last of the sunlight casting intricate designs on the walls as it set behind the buildings across the street. I could see the tables scattered around the room with fresh wooden tops that Tom and I would mill from raw boards at the shop. I could see the candles flickering from the little bits of ocean breeze that would find its way through the front screen door. We would build that bar of zinc, which would weather a bit with each drink that was served on it, giving it an aged patina like it had been there for a hundred years. And flowers – so many flowers. Apple blossoms in the spring, sunflowers in the summer and scraggly twigs with red berries come fall. I could see it more than ever as I stood in the space that we now owned. The dream that was once so distant was becoming a reality.

I immediately started work on the place, ripping out the out-dated kitchen, discarding old, bulky equipment while salvaging the bits that were still useful. There were baking trays and a few pots, some metal utensils and an old Hobart dishwasher that still had a glimmer of life left in it. I made a seemingly endless list of things I would need to get the kitchen up and running and ready for inspection – a three-bay stainless-steel sink, counters, shelving and refrigeration. The stove was a home range with four electric burners, which, while fine for twenty-four people at a supper club, wouldn't cut it for full-blown service. But there was no gas hookup and no land that came with the postage-stamp-size lot the building sat on to put one in, so electric it would have to be. I had neither the budget nor the space for a walk-in refrigerator, so I'd make do with a single stand-up unit. I would change the menu each evening and bring in fresh produce each morning to keep the refrigeration needs to a minimum. There was painting to be done, tile work, plumbing and electrical. I would pitch in every way I could to help keep the costs down, rolling fresh coats of paint onto the walls and building out simple drum-shade light fixtures to hang over the bar. I found an old cast-iron enamelled sink at my parents' house that had once been in the bathroom of our farmhouse but, after a renovation in the nineties, had been buried in a heap of junk and old chicken wire. It was the sink I used to scrub my hands in as a little girl and the sink at which I said my very first word ('Horsey!') as I washed up and looked out the bathroom window across the pasture outside. It would do just fine as a handwashing sink and with a quick scrub of scouring powder, it looked, to me, almost as good as new. Tom hated the sink with a passion. He hated it because it was old and worn, because it had separate cold and hot spouts and because it had a constant drip that couldn't be repaired without replacing the antique fixtures. He fought me on it, giving me dirty looks and trying to talk me into using a different fixture instead, something shiny and new. But it was perfectly imperfect, exactly the way I wanted things to be. With a resolve that surprised us both, I put my foot down: the sink was installed.

I was shrouded by the opinions of others on every detail you could imagine. From what colour to paint the walls, to what kind of chairs I should choose, to whether the barstools should be made of wood or metal or have backs or not, to what kind of food should be on the menu. There were opinions on signage and lighting and tile choices and even the sheen of the urethane on the floor. There were so many opinions that sometimes they clouded my own. In my moments of doubt I lacked the courage to think I knew better and I let others tell me otherwise. It was in my nature – as an individual, as a woman and as the daughter of my non-confrontational mother – to want to please. I wanted people to love this place as much as I did and I wanted that love to translate into every corner. But when I looked at the space in the light of day after the first coat of dull antique green paint went on along with dissonant greyed lavender trim, I realized that if I kept shutting out my own voice and letting everyone else's in, the place would just become a hodge-podge of what everyone else thought this place should be, instead of what I knew it *could* be.

I had made the mistake of taking the suggestion of some hot-headed, know-it-all guy I barely knew about what colour I should paint the walls and now the restaurant looked like a gentlemen's smoking room, the gloomy colours evoking depressing feelings inside me. I had had a clear vision all along of how I knew this space could look and feel, so why wasn't I trusting myself to follow that intuition? I went to the store that day, bought two gallons of paint and stayed up through the night rolling and brushing on the colour that I had picked out on my own – a wrought-iron charcoal for the walls, a soft white for the tall wainscoting and for the baseboards, a tin-grey shade that looked perfect against the golden warmth of the newly polished wood floors.

* * *

More determined than ever, I hid my lingering feelings of self-doubt deep inside by pouring myself into the finishing details. I bought a handsaw from the local hardware store, borrowed Tom's truck from the shop and drove to the outskirts of town to hack down a handful of baby birch trees, using their slender stalks to fill big glass vases, then arranging bright bunches of red berries for autumnal floral displays. I once again used my grandmother's sewing machine to turn bolts of linen into simple napkins, as well as aprons for the cooks and servers. I hung the antique mirrors that I picked up for a song at the flea market, adjusting their positions just so and filled glass candleholders with votives. I polished up the mismatched silverware to make it shine and scrubbed the growing collection of vintage plates, eager to give them a new life in my tiny kitchen. I displayed baskets of fruit on the bar that would be turned into the often-dreamed-about herb-infused cocktails and boiled the imagined speckled quail eggs to serve in bowls with celery salt for dipping. I checked the speakers for clarity and position and made a tape mark to denote the perfect volume – not too loud, not too soft. I played with the lighting, replacing bright bulbs with low-watt Edison bulbs and making notches on the dimmer so the servers would know exactly where to leave the switch. In the kitchen I used spare shelving that wasn't already filled with pots and pans to stack my growing collection of cookbooks that I had purchased over the years. On the wall I tacked up a row of large wooden letters that had been left behind from the former bakery, spelling out 'From Scratch' in bold white lettering. I hung a paper towel holder over my beloved old sink, added a glass bottle of hand soap that smelled like sweet herbes de Provence and smiled as I watched its familiar drip *tap! tap! tap!* Fresh produce deliveries started to roll in, the refrigerator and the bar were stocked and it began to feel real. I began to curate a crew to fill the shifts, sifting through applications and holding informal interviews in order to build a team that felt more like a group of friends than co-workers.

I was excited to have a few familiar faces from my catering days sign on to join me and was encouraged by the number of other people who wanted to work for me, too. The team came together organically and as we all felt our way toward opening, we became an extension of family for one another. We genuinely enjoyed the work and each other's company – with the exception of my sister, who had picked up a few bartending shifts and always found a way to pick a good fight with me. We had managed to reconcile after some time, but our tensions were still clearly running high after our falling-out all of those years ago. I knew that working together might be short-winded, but at least we were speaking and able to be in the same room together. It was a step.

Not surprisingly, as the opening day grew closer, the tension also grew. There was a mortgage to pay and loans to keep up with and my bank account was dry. I had been hemorrhaging every penny for months trying to get the place up and going and I desperately needed money to start coming in soon if I wasn't going to default before I even opened. There were countless sleepless nights – worrying about the money, worrying about the restaurant working – so much worrying – but I still had a stash of Xanax to calm me down if wild panic threatened to steal my breath away. I was in it now and there was no turning back; it was time to dig in, dig deep. And no pill could put as much breath back in my lungs as peeling back the signage I had designed on my laptop could, exposing the frosted letters on the front door: The Lost Kitchen.

Found.

17

PHYSICAL, MENTAL, EMOTIONAL

The doors opened on an October evening and the guests flooded in, from the loyal supper clubbers who had been following for months, to those who had heard of the restaurant thanks to the buzz the supper club had generated, to those who were just eager to see what was going on in the old flatiron building that had been dark and vacant for so many years. It was an instant hit and even more beautiful in reality than I had imagined. To ease into things, I kept the menu small, serving lots of small plates and starters plus four main courses each night that changed daily. I was pumping out meal after meal from the tiny kitchen in the back, from cheese boards to pans of piping-hot mussels and fried squash blossoms, to pork burgers topped with slabs of blue cheese and slices of late season heirloom tomato, to nice rare lamb chops, fish dishes, thick flaky cuts of halibut and big organic rib-eye steaks slathered with whipped herb butter. The kitchen was humming five nights a week, testing my limits, pushing my boundaries. I had gone into this experiment with mediocre skills that I had taught myself. I had run the line of my father's greasy spoon diner, I had waited tables at a fine-dining restaurant, I had worked as a bartender and in the kitchen of a catering company. But that's it. I had never run my own restaurant before; I had never been a boss to anyone. I'd have to keep my lingering imperfections and insecurities to myself and lean on my spots of confidence for strength. I'd have to grow and learn. I didn't know how to properly sharpen a knife or what the hell a sous-chef did. So I made it up the best way I knew how. And what I did have was instinct – how to tell if a steak was done with the simple touch of my finger, how to perfectly whip fresh cream, how to dress a salad just so. In a way I'd been preparing for this my whole life. I had been told over and over again by friends, family and strangers that a restaurant like this in the town of Belfast would never work. I proved them wrong and I knew it the evening I watched my grandfather, with his 'old Belfast' ways and his this-will-never-work stance, sip happily on a whiskey in the waning evening light of my dining room with a big organic rib eye in front of him. The dining room alive and bursting at the seams with patrons around him. At the end of the night, with a good whiskey buzz, he grabbed me and gave me a big squeeze, the smell of his Old Spice aftershave rubbing off on me as he pressed his cheek against mine. He was beaming with pride. 'Well, baby girl, I guess you knew. You did it.' It was the first and last dinner he would ever have in that dining room. He died that spring, leaving my heart broken but full, knowing that I made him proud before I lost him.

There was some gratification when the naysayers went silent, which meant that they knew I was proving them wrong. My dad still bitched – mostly about the beer list and how it was lacking a good American Budweiser – but there were a few occasions when I'd see him sitting at my 'groovy' bar with an Absolut, tonic and lime in his hands, laughing with strangers. I realized that he might be secretly holding an ounce or two of pride for me inside that hard heart. As I watched him enjoying himself in the space I created out of dreams, it was like an even bigger dream come true: in this moment *I* was responsible for the joy he was feeling.

In the kitchen I was vulnerable. It was like ripping my heart out, preparing it with care and then serving it on a platter to strangers. They could do with it as they pleased, slicing it into tiny bits to chew and spit out, pick apart, judge, hate or send back. The pain of such disapproval was sometimes enough to weigh heavy on my mind for weeks, the feelings of failure and self-loathing, all over a simple dish. There were the inevitable send-backs and criticisms, especially on extremely busy nights when I was maniacally running around, trying to get all the orders out as quickly as they were coming in. There were times when, after service, I'd retreat to the basement just to sit on a case of wine in the dark and cry it out. Eventually I would learn that I had to stop letting my heart get nicked every time I screwed up a dish. I had to remind myself that I was only human, that it was only dinner and that there was little that a free glass of wine and dessert wouldn't cure. I learned to take my failings and learn from them: how can I get a better sear on that steak? I should warm the plates next time instead of placing hot food on a cool surface. I need to work on my timing so the chicken dish won't get dried out. It forced me to school myself hard.

And then there were the moments when I'd put my heart on a plate and it would touch someone. There were the moments when I would peer into the dining room from the kitchen when a plate had been delivered, using the reactions of complete stranger to know if I had failed or succeeded. I'd watch them take the first bite, close their eyes and smile with delight. To witness that utter enjoyment from something I had made with my two hands and placed on a simple white plate was better than any drug. As I got my footing in the kitchen, I began to see that more and more. The send-backs dwindled. Then there was the night a gentleman stormed into the kitchen and yelled: 'Who *did* this?!' The entire kitchen crew stopped what we were doing, fearfully staring wide-eyed at the man. All that went through my head as I timidly raised my hand was, *Oh shit oh shit oh shit*. He bounded toward me and gave me a huge squeeze and a peck on the cheek. '*Oh my God! It's fabulous!*' he squealed before all but skipping back into the dining room. And there was the time a table requested me in the dining room, one of the servers relaying the message that, 'They want to see the chef.' Well, shit, I wasn't a chef – I was just a girl who cooks. Plus, I figured that the only reason a table wants to see 'the chef' is because 'the chef' has fucked up their meal. I nervously approached the table of four. I could feel a complaint coming on and was processing how best to react, what I could send them as an apology.

'Are you the chef?' one of the women asked. I was unsure of how to respond but realized it would be quicker and less confusing if I didn't take time to explain that I wasn't a chef, that I hadn't been to culinary school and that I had no business wearing a white coat. So instead I just said, 'Yes. I am.'

'My father would like a word with you,' she explained. I turned my attention to the elderly man at the table as he reached his hands out to me, grabbing mine and holding them softly cupped between his. His hands were soft, cool relief on my skin, which had been scorched by the hot stove all night.

'I'm eighty-nine years old,' he said slowly, 'and I haven't had fish that good since my mother made it for me.' His eyes teared up with happiness. I blushed, could feel my heart swelling, tears welling. I always knew that food held this kind of power – that something as simple as a piece of flaky halibut served with a silky puree of parsnips, lightly dressed rocket leaves, a squeeze of lemon and a spicy nasturtium blossom could evoke a memory and make an emotional impact. And now I wielded that power.

The kitchen was also physically demanding. For sixteen hours a day I'd be on my feet, moving constantly, running up and down the stairs between the basement, where we kept dry goods and storage, to the kitchen. Every waking hour was devoted to the restaurant, my scattered duties as a mom the only reason I'd leave. I'd wake by 7:00 A.M. to get the now nine-year-old Jaim up and going, feed him a warm breakfast, pack his lunch and walk him to the primary school before heading back down the hill to the restaurant for a full morning and afternoon of prep in anticipation of a full evening of dinners ahead. There were orders to place, orders to receive, floral arrangements to tend to, banking, bookkeeping and baking. There were ducks to be parted out, then cured in salt and spices overnight, mussels and oysters to be rinsed and scrubbed clean. Lettuces to be washed and huge sides of fish to be broken down and portioned. By 3:00 P.M. I'd give myself one break to run back up to the school and grab Jaim. The quick escape from the place did me good. I'd return with Jaim in tow and set him up in the dining room to do homework and feed him scraps of upside-down cakes with a big glass of milk as an afternoon treat. By 4:00 P.M. Tom would be returning from work and would shuffle Jaim upstairs for the night, just as the waitstaff was arriving to set the dining room for service. At that point I would have been on my feet for eight hours and there were eight more to go before I could stop for the day.

Daytime prep was a cinch compared to the pace of the evening. At 4:30 P.M. a small group of people would form a line on the pavement to try to grab the bar seats that were first come, first serve. My heart would start to pound, my chest would tighten and I would feel the pressure. One Xanax, a glass of wine and fifteen minutes later I could breathe again. The flurry of tickets would start streaming in just after 5:00 P.M. and my electric stove would soon be covered with cast-iron pans. Sure, I had help in the kitchen, two sets of helpful hands manning the cheese boards, salads and desserts and such, but I couldn't help having my hands in everything, tweaking the plating, making sure dishes weren't overdressed or underseasoned. The responsibility for the success of every dish that left that kitchen was on my shoulders and it was one I took most seriously. I would bounce from cooktop to oven to fryer to sink, pausing here and there to garnish a plate with a sprinkle of bee balm or microgreens before yelling: 'Hot food, please!' It would go on for hours, the tickets never dying down until nine o'clock. Tom would sneak downstairs after putting Jaim down for the night, just as the line had quieted and I could finally sit for the first time all day. But not before Jonah, the bartender, came in with a glass of prosecco in hand and an order from Tom, who would be sitting at the bar sipping a nonalcoholic beer that he had poured into a frosty glass to make it look like he was having a drink. It almost felt like he didn't want people to think he was sober. He was going to AA meetings but had never admitted to me that he was an alcoholic, maybe because that would mean admitting fault or actually apologizing for all the ways his drinking had hurt me. But I had stopped holding my breath waiting. The prosecco was a sympathy offering, since Jonah knew that I'd have to cook one more meal before taking a well-deserved break. It was also out of hopefulness that it would dull the piercing look I'd give him for bringing in another order.

Jonah could see how tiring the long days were for me – everyone did. Well, apparently everyone except Tom. He appeared to have no problem with coming in just after the kitchen had closed and ordering a starter and salad followed by a nice big main course for me to prepare for him. He'd sit at the bar or on occasion take a table with out-of-town clients, showing off *his* restaurant. I couldn't help feeling like a servant to him. Maybe he liked me serving him – I'd been a waitress when we'd first met. I suspect it made him feel more comfortable, like he was in control. He seemed oblivious to the long hours I was putting in and the amount of pressure I was under to make this place fly, or he knew and just didn't care. And when he had finished his last bite of the three-course meal that I prepared for him and soaked up every last drop of nonalcoholic beer from his glass, he'd leave his dishes on the counter, no tip for the staff who had waited on him and make his way upstairs without a good-bye or even thanks. He'd take a hot shower and curl up in our warm bed while I finished scrubbing down the kitchen, cashing out and lugging the day's rubbish from the basement to the curb. Around midnight I'd make my way upstairs and take a hot shower of my own – the most anticipated part of my day, when I'd wash away the grease and the stress. But my resentment of Tom wasn't washing away. It was growing and the bigger it grew the deeper I buried it. I'd wash down an antidepressant, an Ambien and a muscle relaxer with a glass of white wine and crawl into bed. Relying on the pills and the booze to see me through the day was becoming a problem, but my clouded mind just whispered, This is survival, keep going. So tomorrow I'd do it all over again.

On Sunday mornings I could sleep in a bit since the restaurant was closed. It wasn't a day off; it was a day to recover, to rest, eat my first real meal in days and get my body ready for another busy week. I'd wake up feeling like a truck had run me over, bruising all my bones and muscles. I would spend an hour or so soaking my aching body in the bathtub and digging the week out from underneath my fingernails. My arms were covered in burns, signs of my novice moves in the kitchen. I dabbed the wounds with antiseptic, then slathered my skin with triple antibiotic ointment – to heal faster – before wrapping my arms in gauze for the day. I also took those moments to clear my mind, which had been just as battered as my body. I was cooking with local and seasonal produce, which meant having to constantly keep up with its daily arrival, changing the menu to do it justice, needing to invent new and interesting combinations for every night of service – in time to print the menus and let the ink dry. Then there was the pressure of actually executing these ideas, plus getting the meals out in a timely manner and making the best plates I possibly could. There was the pressure of running the scheduling, making sure that all the shifts were covered, from bar, to hostess, to waitstaff, to kitchen and dishwasher.

If someone was sick, it made an already challenging day that much more so, having to scramble for someone to fill the void. And at the end of the day, I was still a mother to a son who needed me. Wife to a husband, too. But there was too much riding on this thing now to let the stress crack me. So I would pop another Xanax, take another hit of wine and get through it.

Tom seemed to turn a blind eye to the depression and anxiety I had been battling over the past few years. He dismissed my fatigue as weakness and my tears as stress – or just being 'dramatic' and 'emotional'. He said nothing about all the weight I was losing, perhaps finding my slender and bony figure some sort of bonus. I was around food for sixteen hours a day and it was in my face, in my nose and in my mind. When I was asleep, it was in my dreams. As far as my stomach was concerned, I had been fed, over and over and over again. I was too busy to make time to eat and my body had stopped giving me cues to be hungry, so I had stopped eating. Sometimes the only thing I'd have in my stomach was a Xanax and a few glasses of wine. The burns on my arms were lasting reminders of the splatters of hot grease flying up from the blazing skillets because I foolishly didn't know to pat dry the fillets of fish before throwing them into a hot pan. My fingers and hands were nicked all over with cuts from dull knives and misfires on the mandoline. My feet ached and my back and shoulders were stiff with pain. There were times when all I wished was that Tom would just feed me a meal – takeout, even – something, anything. I just wanted some sort of a gesture, some sign that he was looking out for me and that he cared whether I was okay. I wanted him to root me on, lift me up and tell me that all this hard work was worth it. I wanted him to be proud of me. I was starving for his approval and my heart was already emaciated from the very same feelings my father had failed to feed me. I kept quiet and kept working, burying it all deeper and deeper. Whining about it would only have revealed my weakness and I didn't want to be weak.

While the restaurant was thriving downstairs, our marriage was slowly crumbling upstairs. The cracks and weaknesses in our relationship were making our interactions brittle and hostile. My resentment of Tom grew every day he didn't lift a finger, every day he treated me like a waitress, every time he looked past my bony body and my sunken eyes and put in another order for mussels and a medium-rare steak. I continued drowning my frustrations, stress, depression and anxiety in my stash of prescription drugs, sometimes taking more than four times the prescribed amount and topping it off with a few glasses of wine. Eventually it got to the point where even the Xanax couldn't numb me anymore. But with one quick trip to my doctor, I got a bottle of Klonopin to throw into the mix. It didn't make the sixteen-hour work days any shorter and it didn't make my stomach tell me I was hungry, but it was a fresh new high that would wash over me with a calmness that made everything going on in my life seem bearable. It made me want to drink more. Two glasses of wine turned into three and sometimes even four by the time midnight had rolled around. It wasn't uncommon for me to start the shift with a drink in hand, a glass of wine or sometimes a cocktail special that Jonah had made for me to give him notes on. I'd use whatever alcohol was handed to me to wash down a few pills. It had become a ritual, a means of survival. It was becoming my way of life.

18

KICKING, CLAWING, FALLING

The Saturday-evening hum had finally come to a quiet halt at the restaurant. No more clinking of glasses, no more laughter, no more chatter. The stove had been scrubbed down with a thick, soapy lather; the cash-up completed; the dining room swept; the last candle snuffed; and the staff clocked out and departed. It was just me and the last of the echoing tunes from the evening's playlist bouncing around the dining room. I walked over to the bar and ran my fingers along a row of red wine bottles resting on the counter. The unsold pours that I hated to see go to waste. There was maybe a glass or so remaining in each bottle and it would do just fine to top off my already glowing buzz. The wine would be no good come Tuesday and the frugal Yankee in me was wicked good at persuading myself to consume the leftovers, not leaving a drop to be wasted. The intensified alcohol cravings that the drugs gave me coaxed, *Take another drink, babe*. I grabbed a bottle, pulled the loose cork from the rim and raised it to my lips, swigging sweet currant sips as if it were water, gulp after gulp, until there was nothing left. I was drunk on wine, high on prescription meds, but mostly feeling free and high from a successful Saturday night at the restaurant and the thoughts of a lazy Sunday ahead of me.

I grabbed another partial bottle, tucked it under my arm and took a seat in the corner of the room to take in the sight of the empty dining room. I sat, sipping and staring at the space. Over the last few hours I had pumped out sixty-eight dinners, dozens of appetizers and sold out of every homemade dessert from that tiny kitchen in the back. I was elated that not a dish had been sent back, felt warm all over from the joy I saw on people's faces as they had sat leisurely in the dining room that had become so nice and cosy over the course of the evening. The tables Tom and I had built by hand, the chairs that I deliberated over (too hard, too soft, just right), the dark grey paint I had laboured over all those late nights until the shade looked just right, the old wooden floors that I had sanded and varnished on my hands and knees, the antique mirrors on the wall with the reflection of one forgotten candle still quietly flickering on the verge of going out. Every bead of sweat that went into this space felt so well spent. After more than a year, I still pinched myself over the reality that the place was working. I had pulled it off. This giant and nearly impossible dream had come to life and it was a success. And I was drunk-buzzed-high-proud and thankful about it all. All the hard work, the muscle aches, the burns, the cuts, the anxiety, the self-doubt – it all disappeared into the waning flickering light of the room.

The sound of the side door opening and closing was followed by the sound of footsteps with a purpose. Tom appeared in the dining room to find me sitting at the corner table with the wine bottle in my hand. His anger and disapproval became more palpable the closer he came to me. I could see that he was burning mad from the squint of his eyes. What was his problem? I had fed him a nice dinner tonight at the bar, had handed over the day's earnings from the drawer to him. He seemed to enjoy the feeling of the cash in his hands. I could feel his disapproval enter the room, like I was a disobedient child. I could feel my body start to bristle, just waiting for him to come down on me, belittle me in this – yes, buzzed, but – rare happy and proud moment I had stolen for myself.

Tom had sat upstairs in the apartment, listening to the bustle of a busy, successful evening at the restaurant. There was a crowd below and he would always make an appearance. He would shower, shave and dress, putting on a pressed button-up shirt and his best pair of polished leather shoes, knowing there was a full house below to greet him. A bit miffed that the bar was full, leaving no space for him to sit for his dinner, he mingled with a few familiar faces and a frosted glass of non-alcoholic beer that Jonah handed him while he waited for space to clear. He inserted stories of boats he was working on, fancy clients he was tending to and elite regattas he had sailed in over the summer. From the kitchen I could hear spurts of his signature laugh over the music bouncing around the room, the clinking of glasses and the bustling conversation. But, more and more frequently, the customers didn't seem to care so much about boats or fancy clients or regattas: quite a restaurant your girl has, Tom! She sure has done it! You must be some proud of your wife and her success! We saw the piece in the *Globe*! Love that she opened a place like this right here in little old Belfast! Do you think she'll open more restaurants? What will she do next?! Tom's laughs had dissipated, his mood turned to a sober irritation. He would respond 'It's *our* restaurant' between the clench of his jaw before snagging a vacant seat at the bar and eating in angry silence. There was wind in my sails now and I was getting a lot of newfound attention. Attention from customers, attention from foodie-fans, even attention from other men who were sniffing around, picking up on the clear scent of our unhappy marriage. I did nothing to stop it, even though I could tell that he hated it. In fact, I ate it all up. From the patrons, the fans and even the men, because I wasn't getting an ounce from my husband. I had visualized other realities, lusted even at the thought of being with someone else besides Tom. Someone who would feed me, love me, lift me up.

'Shut the music off and get upstairs. Now!' he barked. 'Enough is enough.' I wondered if he could tell how much I had been drinking.

'Why? I'm not bothering anyone.'

'You are bothering *me*! Shut it down now.' I didn't move, so he kept going. '*Now*. Shut it down and get upstairs!'

'No. Leave me be.' I could feel a sharp shift in my mood, almost like a snap, as the words left my mouth. My peaceful contentment was dissipating into agitation. Anger. My heart was pounding, my blood pressure rising. Tom's efforts to control me and shut me down had been gnawing at my insides for years, but it had only led to anxiety, worry. Tonight it was rage. I felt the fuse pop inside me.

'Shut the fucking music off *now*!' He looked at me with his best version of authoritative disapproval. It reminded me of the many times my father had looked at me with the same face.

'No,' I said quietly through my clenched jaw.

Tom made a beeline for the stereo, grabbing the iPod that was connected to the speakers, ripping the cable from the device. 'Party's over,' he growled before walking out the door. His footsteps pounding up the staircase to the apartment rumbled through to where I sat below. I followed him, flying up the staircase in a fit. I found Tom at the top of the landing, waiting for me. He just stood there with a smirk on his face. My heart pounding, my fists tight. We stood, staring each other down in motionless anger, waiting to see who would make the first move. Keeping his eyes locked on mine, without a word he raised his hand, the iPod in it and threw it across the living room floor. I lunged, pushing him into the wall behind him. He pushed back. We began tumbling down the length of the hall, shoving each other against the wall. I clawed, kicked, screamed and wailed. I felt like a wild animal.

The strength that came out of me was one I had never known before, coming from a deep place of fury that felt like it had been seething in me for longer than I could comprehend. I was somehow, miraculously, stronger than he was, releasing that unknown power as if I were fighting for my life. It went on for what felt like hours but was really just minutes. I collapsed to the floor with fatigue, panting, wincing and trying hard to catch my breath. Tom stood above me doing the same. We just stopped. Separately we retreated to our bedroom and crawled into bed. Not a word was spoken. I lay silent in the foetal position with my back toward Tom, still trying to catch my breath and slow my heart rate before I passed out and slept a deep intoxicated sleep, hoping to wake and find this had all been a gigantic nightmare. Jaim slept in the bedroom just next to ours and never woke to hear the commotion that erupted in our house that night. I'd never been more grateful that he was a deep sleeper, that he would be spared the disgusting truth of what Tom and I had become together. Just as he had been able to sleep through fireworks as a baby, he slept through all the screaming matches and domestic explosions over the years.

No matter how deeply I slept, it didn't erase the reality that last night wasn't just a bad dream. In the sobering light of day the scratch marks I had made on Tom's face were still raw. We moved about our Sunday morning with an eerie stillness, both of us knowing that there was a darkness hanging over us, but neither of us sure what to do about it. I had attacked Tom like an animal that had been caged for years, releasing pent-up energy, resentment and frustrations that had been festering and become wild. Humans didn't behave like that, I told myself. I was disgusted and ashamed of what I had become, but at the same time my anger and animosity held me back from feeling completely apologetic about it. I didn't want to live like this any longer, but at the same time I didn't know how to escape the mess I had made for myself. Filled with confusion, I left. I left Jaim playing contently with Lego on the floor of his bedroom and Tom sitting quietly in the living room with my fingerenail scratches on his face. I wanted to get away from him, I wanted to get away from myself. I wanted to run, I wanted to hide.

Without a single idea of what I would do or where I would go, I just had to get out of that apartment. I drove, going nowhere. I spent hours hiding out in the dusty booth of a flea market, picking out dinged-up plates, hiding from the reality that was waiting for me at home – that my life had become unmanageable and that I had become a monster that needed to be faced. I was hiding from myself and the embarrassment that I had become. When I returned early that evening, I poured a few Xanax into my hand and swallowed them in anticipation of what waited for me. I told Tom I wanted to leave. He was silent. The silence between us lasted through the night, but it broke the next afternoon when I ascended the apartment staircase to find Tom sitting in the living room with my mother and Aunt Rhoda sitting emotionless by his side. This was Tom's 'divine intervention'.

I questioned them, asking what they were doing there, knowing the anwer full well. My life had come undone and there was no way to hide it anymore. There were marks on Tom's face to prove it. I was embarrassed and ashamed for my family to see the details of my rotting life. My marriage had been sick for years and I had been tirelessly trying to keep up with it, using the antidepressants, antianxiety pills, mood stabilizers and booze to manage it. Each time I would visit my doctor, he'd give me a new drug to take away the pain. Now I couldn't get through a day without them – *lots* of them. Each one making me want to drink more than the last and yet not a single one of them was able to fix my dead-end marriage. I was even self-medicating now, doubling my own doses because nothing seemed to be working. The pills could never right all the wrongs, turn the lies into truths, replenish real trust, or erase the hurtful words that were spoken. We had become a toxic mess together. We had come to the end of our road.

I was out of control and couldn't help feeling Tom took some sort of pleasure in it. It became clear to me that he had painted a lopsided picture of my addiction to Mom and Rhoda, a picture that only involved his out-of-control wife, a pill-popping alcoholic who was a world of a problem. It felt unjust to cast all the blame and dysfunction on me, after all these years, omitting his own role in our marital breakdown. The scrutiny and open takedown in front of my family filled me with shame and anger. I felt vilified and on trial, with no defence. I hoped in my heart that my mother wouldn't believe that this was all my fault, that I had taken this marriage and my family to this burning point on my own. She knew Tom wasn't lily-white, she knew he held a heavy hand in this, but it wasn't in her to speak up if she disagreed with a man. Tom had seen her act this way with my father many times over the years. He must have known she would stand behind him sheepishly, like the soft lamb that she was.

I was ready to be done pretending, but I felt that Tom was going to hold on to the lie, or at least keep his grasp on me, for as long as he could. Tom presented me with two choices: I could either go to rehab right now, where a bed waited for me, get better and then come home to him, or he would file a protection-from-abuse order against me for what had happened between us the previous night. We had been through this before and both knew what would transpire after a protection order was filed. He knew that the very same thing that had happened to him years ago would happen to me if he pulled the trigger. Just like the night Tom had taken his very last drink, the night when his eyes went black and vacant and he lost control. When they took him away that night, they booked him at the county jail and he was banned from being within five hundred feet of me and along with that, he was banned from being within the same distance of Jaim. If he put an order on me, I'd lose my kid, I'd lose my house and I'd lose my business. The thought of it made me sick to my stomach. But if I went to rehab for a month, I would also be leaving Jaim and the restaurant would be forced to close in my absence. It was a loss either way and Tom had all the power. I was slipping away. He had to have felt it. Maybe I had to lose it, really lose it, if he was going to have the chance to gain back whatever control he felt he was losing. He had given me an ultimatum with two dead-ends. I couldn't bear the thought of him holding the keys to my future, writing my history into chapters that I didn't want to be written. I felt I would rather die and I said as much. And the moment I said it out loud was the moment complete control was lost. I could feel my heart rate climbing and my chest tightening, wild anxiety seeping in. I was backed into a corner and trapped. I needed my pills, lots of them – all of them, maybe. The whole fucking bottle. I wanted to drown out my reality so hard. I wanted to drown out the fear-filled faces of my family, my humiliation, my self-hatred. I lost it, right then and there, in front of my mother, in front of my aunt, in front of Tom, who was ready to pounce. Tom pinned me down, batting the plastic prescription bottle from my hand, pills scattering across the apartment floor while waiting for the police to arrive with the ambulance he had called to take me away before Jaim came home from school.

I was involuntarily committed to a psych ward for two days. I spent them in lockdown in a tiny room, bedridden with shock, grief and the kind of profound embarrassment and shame that would make it difficult ever to admit that this had happened. I knew that this was what rock bottom felt like. I starved myself in punishment, in honour of my self-hatred. For two days I tossed and turned in my bed, listening to the screams and moans of other patients reverberating from the rooms surrounding me. Sometimes if their screams became too wild, I could hear the nurses as they swarmed the patient before sedating them. Screams of *'Don't-fucking-touch-me!'* followed by fast silence, then deep-slumbering snores. I couldn't wait to get the hell out and yet I feared more than ever what awaited me at home. Upon my release I would discover that the last two days of my life were just a taste of the storm that was brewing that would take me to my knees. This wasn't rock bottom; this was just a taste of it.

I couldn't call my parents to pick me up upon my release. The shame inside me was so deep that I couldn't bring myself to dial their number, see their faces, see their gross disappointment in me. I called Jonah instead; he had, to the surprise of many, been sober for over fifteen years. In his early twenties he had been running with a band and had become addicted to drugs and alcohol, living an out-of-control life. You'd never guess it now – he had a wife, two children and was steady and reliable. The only stain from those wild days was the giant tattoo of a cross on his back that the staff would occasionally catch a glimpse of while he was changing into his ironed shirt before dinner service. Still, I was embarrassed to show him, an employee, a moment of such personal weakness. At the same time, I felt he wouldn't judge me. There were few people I could think of who would do the same. Our relationship was almost sibling-like, or what I imagined a good solid sibling relationship could be like, unlike my relationship with my own sister. I could lean on him in this time of weakness, confusion and need.

The ride home from the hospital in Rockland to Belfast was dark and fairly quiet. I sat contemplating what my world would look like upon my return and not wanting to share too many dark details with Jonah from the days that had already passed. The landscape of my home life had been slowly crumbling for a while, but had accelerated recently into an avalanche of shit. Jonah dropped me just down the street from my apartment and I lay low in a hotel room for a few days while waiting for the storm of my and Tom's demise to slow down. Jaim was safely hunkered down with my parents, protected from the dysfunction of both of his parents. Tom dangled the option of making it all better – if I would just come home and promise him I would stay with him, he wouldn't make things worse for me. The promise was one I could not keep and the consequences were beyond my ability to fathom.

Tom and I were playing a game and he was holding all the cards. When I refused to fold and give him a promise to stay in this marriage that had died years ago, I felt sure that he would do everything in his power to take every chip on the table. And he did go big and all-in. He filed for a protection order and for full custody of Jaim, arguing to the courts that I was an unfit mother because I had been committed for two days. I had no chance of fighting him, the stigma of an involuntary admittance to a psych ward would be a stain I could never scrub away. He was awarded temporary full custody and in that moment I felt like I had been sentenced to death. I had lost my only child. The simultaneous protection order he filed kept me at a distance of five hundred feet, which he hadn't thought through, not realizing he would be the one who would have to vacate our home since it was directly over my place of business. He was angered that I was given temporary control of the building, to live and carry on with work, without him. He retreated with Jaim to a friend's vacant apartment. And while I felt a new strange sensation of lightness that I had broken away from Tom, I also felt an overpowering force of darkness from the gaping hole that had been left now that my son was gone. Tom had snatched Jaim away from me in a manner that only felt designed to be cruel. He requested that the court deny visits and he controlled all communication, often prohibiting phone calls or simple check-ins. But his relationship with my parents had now eroded, too, after he began to deny them access to their grandchild as well. Our family had been robbed of a member and there was a heap of pain and anger to fuel the growing fire. It felt like some twisted legal form of kidnapping: The forced radio silence from my own kid made my blood boil, made me tremble with electric currents of angst and sadness all through my body. I was filled with a mix of emotions – anger, frustration, heartache, rage and humiliation. I was devastated and struggled to search for reasons to keep living. Tom apparently wanted me to hurt and he knew where to punch me to destroy me. 'If you leave me, I'll eviscerate you!' echoed over and over in my mind so clearly that I could almost smell the gin he had on his breath when he told me so. He had told me years before that he would eviscerate me if I ever left him. I had always wondered what exactly he had meant by it, what exactly he thought he would do to me. All I could picture were the frigid February afternoons when my father would take my sister and me ice fishing on Freedom Pond, the diner closed for the deep months of winter. He'd set thin wooden traps over a handful of holes he had drilled through the thick ice with his auger. Bright orange flags would fling up when a fish was biting and a glistening pickerel would be reeled up from the icy chute, flailing about in fear. He'd pull a pair of pliers from the pocket of his green wool trousers and snip the hook from the bloody lip of the fish while it continued to thrash and squirm in his hands, until he used the back end of the pliers to whack it over the head. Then he'd take his jackknife from his other pocket and lay the fish out on the snow-covered ice, running the blade from the base of the tail all the way up the length of the belly to the base of its jaw. He'd pull out the guts from the abdomen with his bare fingers and throw the bloody contents out onto the snow before dipping the freshly killed fish back in the icy hole to rinse it clean. That was eviscerating. Being deprived of my son felt like I had been gutted too.

I threw myself into the restaurant to hide from my painful reality. Over the five months that followed, the sixteen-hour days carried on, but now they were even heavier with emotional weight and legal fights. As the weeks rolled on, I took more pills and drank more booze to fill the void, to mask the pain. To drown myself, really. My checked-out doctor upped my doses, doubled my anti-depressants and threw in a new mood stabilizer. Without a second thought he prescribed more and more pills to lift me up, calm me down and knock me out. Pink ones, blue ones, orange and white ones. Round ones and oblong ones. A handful for the morning, another handful for the afternoon and another for the evening. I supplied the full bar to wash it all down.

Somehow, miraculously, the restaurant was unfazed. It kept thriving, its demand and popularity increasing day by day, though a not-insignificant amount of stress and pressure came with that too. As the weeks rolled into months, all the meds I was downing started to anesthetize me from just about everything. My depression had severed my ability to care. I couldn't feel anymore. I slept with a handful of strangers and had my first one-night stand. Though I was so numbed out by the meds that I couldn't orgasm if I tried. I hated myself, I hated my body, I hated my life. I couldn't recognize the woman I had become. When someone commits suicide, people often wonder: *How could they do that to their family? To their children? How selfish.* I saw it in my darkness. I could see now that they could do it without remorse because they felt nothing, because they were so blind and sick with depression that they couldn't see or understand what they were doing. A good person in a bad place can do things she'd never imagine. Spring was approaching now, which meant summer would follow, which meant the busy season at the restaurant hadn't even begun. If I was struggling to get through life in March, July and August would likely do me in. I'd be dead soon; I was sure of it. It was only a matter of time and part of me couldn't wait.

19

NINETEEN STEPS

There were nineteen steps to the bottom of the old apartment staircase. I stood at the top, teetering for a moment, hesitation clouding the front of my mind. My rolling suitcase in my right hand was the only thing holding me upright, keeping me from tumbling down the flight of stairs. At the bottom of the steps was the front door. I knew that if I left, Tom could try to take everything. I knew that if I stayed, I would die. So I had to take the chance and move forward, ready and willing for rehab. I turned and looked over my shoulder. My mother was behind me, standing motionless with her jaw firmly clenched.

'Let's go,' she said, with a firmness that was uncharacteristic for her. Her face was tired and pale. She had been living with me for the weeks since Tom had moved out, taking Jaim with him and the suicidal thoughts had moved in. I told her so much one night, begging her to sit on my hands to keep me from hurting myself. She stayed with me, rationing the bottles of prescription drugs I had become addicted to and managing my mood swings and night thrashes. I was growing more ill by the day, pouring myself into keeping the restaurant afloat downstairs, crashing at the end of service into an emotional heap upstairs. Toast and peanut butter became the only things I could manage to keep down, but even those would end up passing through me like water. My insides felt like they were shutting down on me, torn up over losing custody of Jaim and from the bottle of wine I was using each day to wash down the handfuls of pills that were supposed to manage my deep emotional pain.

My mother rarely displayed sadness. Even at her own mother's funeral, I never saw her shed a single tear. Faced with my father's barbs and rants, she never yelled back or showed her pain. She had always had a silent strength. But I stood here at the top of these steps, ready to leave everything behind, because the night before I saw her weep with sadness and fear for the very first time in my life. The sight of this stoic woman with tears streaming down her face awoke something inside me that I had shoved deep down in my haze of depression. I saw with clarity that I was the cause of her immense pain and distress. It was all my fucking fault. I felt heart-broken and cruel because I had inflicted every ounce of agony I saw on her face. I had wounded the one woman who had loved me, raised me, raised me up. Those nineteen steps below me were the only way I could ease her pain. She'd put down a few thousand dollars of her hard-earned savings as a down payment for rehab that would hopefully save her daughter.

'It's time,' she reminded me, without blinking. She was right. It was time for me go. And it was time for her to rest. The time was now. This marriage was going in the shitter and a divorce would ensure my loss of insurance benefits under Tom's policy. And we worried that the longer we waited, the greater the chance that Tom would shut off my access just the same. I'd be out of pocket for a lengthy and costly rehab stay and there was no way in hell I could afford that. The time was now, because my body and mind were shutting down.

The depression had become so deep and sprawling that it had swallowed up my feelings. I stood on the top step feeling numb and broken all at once. It was in the numb moments of emptiness that I didn't care whether I lived or died, as well as in the moments of rage and anger over what my life had caved into. I spent most hours wishing I wasn't alive and right now was no different. I didn't care if I fell down the flight of stairs in front of me. I began to move forward down the old wooden staircase step by step, my suitcase pounded loudly as I toted it carelessly behind me. I could feel my mother trailing close behind and I sent her quiet messages from my mind in hopes that she would catch them as she descended: Don't abandon me. Don't give up on me. I'm broken, but I'm in here somewhere. I don't want to hurt anymore. I don't want to hurt you anymore. My God, I'm so sorry.

Before I knew it, I was through the front door and dumped onto the cold, dark, early-morning streets of the little coastal town that had become the epicentre of my demise. I turned to lock the door one last time. It was the very same key that had given me so much excitement for life just a few years back. I remembered the moment when I first turned that lock. I remembered the smell of the stairwell the first time I ascended it and how much I liked that endearing old, musty scent. I remembered the bright empty rooms and the joy I would breathe into the old space. I had rotted in this beautiful building that was built on dreams that had turned into illusions.

I handed the key to my mother before I climbed into the passenger side of my aunt Rhoda's car, knowing there was a good chance I could lose everything behind that door without me there to guard it. That didn't change the fact that I needed to go. If anything, so my mom could have her first good night's sleep once I was under professional care, someone else's suicide watch. I could see the relief in her face as Rhoda and I pulled onto Route 3 and headed south to the airport.

My aunt Rhoda and I had an atypical relationship. She was my father's youngest sister and had never really been around when I was growing up. She and my dad had a falling-out when I was just a baby. I had only spent a handful of moments with her when I was younger and was in my early twenties before I spent any real time with her. In a way that made our relationship more like two friends than niece and aunt. It was a rather large commitment she had made to bring me all the way to rehab and I wondered if she might be helping me with this journey to make up for lost time that we could never regain.

Rhoda kept my prescriptions in her purse by request of my mother. As rehab started feeling more imminent, I started craving them more. I managed to talk her into feeding me an extra Xanax and buying me a few beers at the airport to wash it down. She made peace with the fact that her mission was to get me on the plane and through the front door of the rehab facility, not to keep me sober while getting there. If a few drinks and an extra Xanax did the trick and kept me calmly moving forward, so be it. She knew it would be my last buzz for a good long while, which also spared her any guilt. On the plane my cravings for booze persisted. I apparently wanted to get drunk and drown out my reality. I could see the drink cart making its way painfully slowly up the aisle. While I waited, I pondered the mathematics over what drink I could order that would get me drunkest. My dad used to drink beer when he knew he wanted to drink all day. He drank vodka when he wanted to get the job done.

'What can I getcha?' the flight attendant asked Rhoda and me.

'We need a couple of strong cocktails. Vodka. With some juice?'

Rhoda had given up on trying to control my consumption. She knew that in a few short hours it wouldn't matter anymore and if she couldn't beat me, she'd join me for a friendly drink. The flight attendant handed us each a plastic cup with ice and a concoction of juices and a nip of vodka to mix in.

'It's my special; orange juice, pineapple and a splash of cranberry,' she explained with a smile. I couldn't help remembering the last time I had vodka with juice, sitting on the barstool at Rollie's with Tom the first night we went out together.

'Can you make it a double?' I asked before she handed us each another nip with a wink.

'Where you ladies headed? You look like you're in for a good time!'

Rhoda and I looked at each other, knowing we couldn't very well tell her the truth. I tried to imagine her reaction if I blurted out, 'Rehab!'

'Girls' weekend,' Rhoda said. 'Just a much-needed girls' weekend.'

I tipped my plastic cup toward hers, extending a sarcastic toast. 'Cheers to that.'

When I got to the bottom of the cup, I started to suck on every last round cube making sure I got every drop of alcohol. I needed more. I unclasped my seat belt and excused myself to the lavatory. I needed an excuse to visit the back of the plane to see if I could talk the flight attendant into making us another round. It was its own kind of buzz when I got back to my seat to see that she had obliged. As we sat sipping our drinks, the plane began to jolt in the air and Rhoda grabbed her armrest in reflex, her knuckles whitening. I grabbed my drink. It scared me that death had stopped scaring me. I could hear myself involuntarily think: Sure, let the damn plane plummet to the ground in flames; I don't care. Through the thick fog, we landed just fine.

I arrived on a dark, damp April night at the all-female rehab facility. Rhoda and I were received by a chaperone and escorted to the locked dormitory that I would call home for the weeks to come. There was a doorbell adjacent to the thick glass door to alert the team inside that I was here. With a loud buzz, the door opened and I stepped into the glass vestibule. Another locked door stood in front of me, the door behind me now closed, locked. There was no going back. I didn't feel nervous, maybe because I was still buzzed from the airplane booze. A stern-faced nurse with glasses approached the door in front of me, waved the badge around her neck over a keypad and typed in a code. Another loud buzz and the door was open.

'Here she is,' said the chaperone.

'You can say your good-byes here and follow me,' said the nurse as she continued walking down the hall, expecting me to follow. Rhoda and I embraced in one last hug. It was promising how much love and gratitude I felt toward her in that moment. Somewhere, deep inside, I was still alive.

'Don't forget, it's girls' weekend,' I joked with her. 'Whoop it up for me tonight.' She laughed through her tears before turning and waiting to be buzzed out through the big glass door.

It was nearing midnight now and there wasn't anyone else in the halls besides the nurse and me. I paused for a moment to take in the sobering new surroundings: a couple of lumpy couches and an empty coffee table (no magazines, out of fear that they would trigger any of the girls with body-image issues). The floors were carpeted in a soft mint green and the walls a pale yellow – colours that were supposed to evoke feelings of calm, balance and optimism. The smell was sterile yet lived-in, laced with hints of cheap coffee. I turned to follow the nurse down the hallway. She led me into a small, windowless exam room and shut the door. There was another nurse inside seated at a desk, scribbling on a sheet of paper. She didn't look me in the eye and never said a word.

I placed all my belongings on the stainless-steel table as the nurse with glasses instructed. She requested that I remove all my clothing as she handed me a white-and-blue-dotted hospital gown. I took the gown from her outstretched arm and waited for her and the other nurse to leave the room so that I could change. They didn't budge. The nurse at the desk sat with her head down still scribbling and the nurse with the glasses stood cross-armed, staring me down impatiently.

'Look, it's late and this is going to take some time. Don't resist and make this take longer than it has to. Remove your clothes.' She looked me in the eyes for the first time. I realized then that neither of them was going to leave the room. This wasn't like a regular trip to the doctor's office, when they hand you a gown and give you three to five civilized minutes of privacy to strip down and politely stack your folded underwear and clothes on a chair in the corner.

'Let's not do this the hard way.' My buzz was coming down hard and I could feel from the sharpness in her voice that she meant business.

I began removing my clothes, piece by piece, folding each item and placing it neatly on the chair beside me. 'All of it,' she said, as she saw me hesitate to take off my bra and underwear. I put on the hospital gown first, trying to remove the remaining articles discreetly, shimmying my underwear down to my ankles, snaking my bra through an armhole. I tied a fast bow behind my back in an attempt to keep the gown closed and maintain some modesty. The nurse measured my height, took my weight, checked my blood pressure, took my temperature and breathalyzed me. She dictated to the nurse who was still at the desk.

'Five feet five inches. One hundred eight pounds. One twenty-eight over seventy-six. Ninety-eight point seven. Point one six.'

She examined my eyes; she looked in my ears; and she drew three vials of blood from my right arm, after two painful failed tries from my left. Then she stabbed that arm again for a TB test. When it was time for a urine sample, she followed me into the bathroom, handed me a cup and hovered over me, watching me out of the corner of her eye as I squatted to give her a sample. She announced that I wasn't pregnant, which was a relief given my slight promiscuity over the past few months.

The exam room was cold and the lights were bright. Exhaustion was setting in from a combination of the day of travel and my impending hangover. I figured we must be close to done, but then she positioned herself behind me and I could feel her breath as she untied the knot at the top of my gown, letting the johnny fall to the floor. I stood there in the cold and overlit room, naked and frozen in fear and shame.

'Raise your arms please,' she said, emotionless. I did as she asked and let out an uncomfortable and involuntary giggle. I trembled with shock as she began to scan the surface of my skin with her fingertips, starting with my left hand. She moved up to my wrist and forearm and paused, rubbing the surface gently with her gloved hand. My hands, wrists and forearms were littered with elongated red splotches and remnants of old scars. She paused at each mark, rubbing it slightly, taking note of its shape and size. I knew what she was thinking. She analyzed them as if they had been self-inflicted. She was charging me as a self-mutilator, assuming they were scars from a few botched suicide attempts. She pointed to the marks and stated, 'Note here, here, here and here.' The nurse behind the desk made small x marks on a piece of paper with a human figure outline, noting my dings and scratches like I was a rental car being taken out for a few weeks. I didn't tell her what the marks really were – burns I had gotten over the years from scorching hot pans, fresh-from-the-oven baking sheets and Fryolator explosions. Some from when I was twelve years old and some from just last week. If she knew me, really knew me, she would know that these marks indicated choosing life, not the alternative. Besides, I had already decided that if I were going to take myself out, it would be with pills. I had envisioned my suicide often and had firmly resolved that a bottle of pills would be the polite way to do it. There would be no mess and it would be far more peaceful to go out on a giant high. I had made one attempt already with a full bottle of Klonopin, but quickly forced myself to vomit, feeling like I wasn't quite ready. Because deep, deep down I didn't want to die, I just wanted all the emotional pain to go away and the clouds greying my mind to lift. I just didn't know how to make that happen.

The nurse with the glasses ran her fingers up my arm, over my shoulder, down the left side of my back and my legs and made her way back up the right side. She came to my right arm and again paused: 'Here and here.' More burns, more false judgments. She moved to my front and I lost it. Tears began streaming down my cheeks. I began to shake and whimper. I pulled my arms back in toward my body, an innate reaction to protect myself.

'Arms out!' she barked. I closed my eyes because I couldn't bear to look at her. I could feel her with my eyes closed. Her hands ran up and down my naked body, her breath over my bare skin, over my breasts, between my thighs, across my abdomen. She finished, finding just a few marks of interest that weren't really that interesting after all. Satisfied, she handed me a tissue and let me dress.

I had become so consumed with the exam that I hadn't even noticed that my duffel bag had been overturned on the counter, all of its contents combed over and divided into two piles: 'allowed' and 'not allowed.' The acceptable clothing and personal items had been stuffed into a clear plastic bag with my name written in black Sharpie. I was handed the bag and escorted to my room. The light was low and my eyes were bleary with tears, but I could make out two other beds with sleeping figures tucked into each.

'This one is yours,' said the nurse, pointing to an empty bed.

I crawled under the starchy sheets, curled into a catatonic foetal position, closed my eyes and went to sleep.

I stayed in that bed for thirty-two hours. I slept in small increments, tucked into a ball, wishing more than anything that I weren't there and that this weren't happening. Nurses would come in and out throughout the day and night, saying my name, attempting to rouse me. I would ignore them, keeping my back turned to them, pretending to be asleep even if I truly wasn't. I wanted to sleep it off like a bad dream, but the sounds of slamming doors, shouting girls and the occasional violent burst of bulimic gags coming from the bathroom across the hall kept reminding me of the hell I was in. After thirty-two hours with no food, I had to give in and pull myself out of bed, plus I hadn't peed since my urine test. I was dehydrated and my head pounded (probably from withdrawal); my shoulders and neck were stiff from lying in the same position for so long. A bit of food will do you good, I told myself.

I had been here less than forty-eight hours, which meant I was still in the 'red zone'. I wasn't allowed to make or receive phone calls and I wasn't allowed to leave the lodge to go to the cafeteria, which meant dining in the small lounge room just across from the nurses' station. Eventually I'd graduate and get to eat in the cafeteria with everyone else, but today I would be confined to a small table in the kitchenette. Lunch arrived in a Styrofoam box wrapped in plastic. Inside, a soggy peanut-butter-and-jelly sandwich, a bag of crisps and a mealy Granny Smith apple. I tried not to make eye contact with any of the other women who also sat around the small table. I was feeling self-conscious, knowing my face had to look like shit from all the tears I'd shed over the past few days. I couldn't be sure because there were no mirrors allowed (even the mirrors in my makeup compacts were meticulously removed by staff upon check-in), but my eyes felt swollen. Bits of conversation floated by, but I made no effort to engage. Some of the girls played simple word games. They were childish in nature and asked about simplistic things like 'What is your favourite colour?' Or 'What Disney character would you most want to be?'

We all picked at our lunches like birds, me because I was bummed out about the food, but the others for other reasons, namely eating disorders. The awkward conversations continued. I was feeling increasingly annoyed by the dumb-sounding games, but I recognized that my waning patience level was probably due to low blood sugar, intense cravings for a chemical pick-me-up and the simple fact that I didn't want to be there. As I kept listening to their games, I noticed patterns. I realized the games they were playing weren't silly or pointless. They were mind games – they helped them not to focus on the food in front of them.

I realized I had been making snap judgments about the other women there: this one reeks of stale cigarettes and is nervously chewing gum, twitching her leg and biting her nails. Probably an addict. Is she strangely quiet? Does she have sunken eyes, swollen cheeks and constantly do things with her hands like knit or play crossword puzzles or sudoku? She's probably got an eating disorder. I didn't think I belonged with this sad and sorry bunch. But the truth was I did. I was the bony blonde with puffy eyes, sitting with my head in my hands. I was the depressed girl with the prescription-drug and alcohol addiction.

At the end of the meal the boxes were examined by a nurse and the results were recorded. It was expected that all the contents be consumed. If not, you lost 'points', which you could use to buy things like deodorant or nail polish from the campus store.

'You can do it! You can do it!' chant a few of the girls in support of another who was working hard to choke down the remaining bread in her box.

We ended each meal with:

'My food was ____.'
'I'm feeling ____.'
'I'm thankful for ____.'

My answers were:

Shit
Pissed
Nothing

At 5:45 A.M., a nurse entered our room, as she would every morning. The jingle from her set of keys was like an alarm clock as she unlocked our bathroom for thirty minutes. It was just enough time for me and my roommates to each squeeze in a lukewarm shower and a quick brush of the teeth before the door would be locked again until evening. I had raging night sweats the night before from my alcohol withdrawal and made sure I was the first one out of bed so that I could get the first shot at a shower. The small plastic stall awoke feelings of claustrophobia as the showerhead let out a light spray of barely warm water. There was no chance of a luxurious hot shower because this place was clearly designed to remind you that you were in hell. The towels they provided us were the size of hand towels and were made of scratchy cotton. A towel any bigger could be tied into a suicide tool if a girl was desperate enough. I used the small piece of cloth like a chamois, patting myself down, spending a little extra time drying my hair. Hair dryers weren't allowed because they had cords and cords could be made into self-harm tools. I barely had enough time to brush my teeth before one of my roommates was banging on the door for her ten minutes. I quickly got dressed and made my way down to the kitchen area to see if I could get my hands on a cup of coffee.

A small line of anxious women had formed in the kitchen. Caffeine was the only non-prescribed drug for miles around and the line had formed before the first pot of the morning was even brewed. The only line that was longer was the line for morning meds when we'd get pumped full of the drugs our doctors had prescribed to cheer us up or calm us down. It was a big commercial coffeemaker, not much different from the one my dad had at the diner, designed to pump pot after pot into the bulbous glass carafes with plastic handles. We all stood swaying, watching, waiting impatiently for the last drop to fall into the pot before swarming it with our white Styrofoam cups. By the time I got to it, the pot was empty. I picked up the glass urn to confirm there wasn't another drop left. The room had gone silent as the women lined the walls, drinking the scalding-hot coffee as fast as they could.

'Are you gonna make another pot?' a woman standing behind me asked as I realized another line had formed behind me. 'It doesn't make itself, you know. It'll be seven-thirty A.M. and turn to decaf before you know it.'

'Yeah, sorry. I'm new.' I felt warm with embarrassment.

'I can tell. How long did you stay in bed?' she asked.

'I don't know. Thirty or so hours, I guess. How'd you know?'

'Puffy eyes. Don't worry, the first few days are the hardest. I musta slept for thirty-six hours when I first got here. It's normal.' Then she gestured to the other women in the room. 'Don't worry, they all looked like shit too when they first got here.'

It was the first bit of warmth I'd felt since my last hug with Rhoda.

'There are a few tricks around here that you'll want to learn fast. First, coffee. This ain't no Starbucks, okay? It's watered-down weak shit, so we improvise.' She slid out the metal piece that held the coffee filter and paused. 'Don't throw the grounds out. If you want a semi-good or not-shit cup of coffee, keep the dregs and add a new packet on top. It will give it just a little more kick.' She dumped the bag of fresh grounds on top of the still-steaming just-used ones and flicked the switch to Brew. 'When it's all you got, you make do.'

'Why don't you just put two bags of fresh coffee in? Why use the old grounds?' I couldn't understand the logic. She sniffed and cut her small laugh short, trying not to embarrass me further. She could tell I was new and fragile.

'You see those bags of coffee right there?' She pointed to three individual bags of ground coffee that sat in a basket on the counter. I nodded. 'Those are one pot each and that's all we get for the entire day. You can't just throw two bags away on one pot! Girls around here would lose whatever's left of their minds. It's not an all-you-can-drink coffee bar. When it's gone, it's gone until five forty-five A.M. tomorrow morning.'

I nodded obediently.

'Here,' she said as she poured the fresh batch of hot double-run coffee into my cup. 'I'm Anna.'

'I'm Erin,' I said as I looked at her with humble gratitude.

'Drink up, Erin, because it turns to straight decaf in an hour and a half.' She tipped the hot coffee into her throat before leaving the room.

In the time it took to make a pot of coffee, Anna had opened my eyes to realize that in here, fucked-up was the norm. All the other women in this room had slept for a solid day and cried their eyes out too. They were fighting pain and demons of their very own. Everyone in this room was hurting, just like me. I reached for a creamer from a jar on the counter and tore the top off, pouring it into my coffee. It curdled in the cup, bits of chunky white cream surfacing to the top of my cup. Fuck, I thought, before dumping out the hot liquid into the sink and going to the back of the line, starting all over again.

20

SEVENTY-TWO

Forty-eight hours in the place had already felt like a lifetime. Sure, I had lain in bed for most of it, lethargic and catatonic, which was maybe the reason time seemed to move so slowly. But I was coming to now, moving around, eating again and sucking down cup after little plastic cup of water to satisfy my outrageous feelings of dehydration. I had been unable to communicate with my family and friends in the outside world since my arrival, having agreed to a forty-eight-hour window of 'phone sobriety' in an effort to help me commit and acclimate to my new surroundings. Once the window had passed, I would be awarded phone privileges that were anything but free. We were permitted to use the phone in twenty-minute increments at randomly scattered times throughout the day in a shared telephone room. Phone/Smoke Break was the most popular scheduled programme in the lodge. When the clock would hit 10:00 A.M., streams of women would move herd-like either to the fenced-in smoke area on the back deck for a quick puff or to the phone room to call home. The small room was covered in warm yellow paint and had eight telephones lining two long desks on either side. Each phone had a corresponding black fake leather chair on wheels, a box of tissues and a pump bottle of antibacterial gel. I signed in on the whiteboard on the wall, scribbling my name and the time with a fading dry-erase marker. I questioned whether or not I should use the privilege, realizing I was nervous about what might have transpired at home in the time I had been gone. If only I could call Jaim, hear his sweet voice and chat about simplicities and normalcies like what he was working on at school and what he'd been eating for lunch. There would be no such luck. Tom was still forbidding contact and, quite frankly, my embarrassment over where I was deterred me from dialling him just the same. Jaim didn't need to hear from his mother while she was in a state of near-incarceration. I couldn't help feeling like a criminal and that, maybe, shielding him from his own mother while I trudged through these dark days was best.

I had left the restaurant to run on limited cylinders, spending the week leading up to my admission into rehab planning a pared-down spring menu. The practiced crew I had left behind was more than capable of managing the place without me. The hope was that the customers would never even notice that I was gone or catch wind of the fact that my life beyond the stove was crumbling. I had organized a local jazz trio to come in each night and play a set or two for tips. I cooked up a big batch of duck confit before my departure, curing the legs in salt, garlic and spices before slow-cooking them in rendered duck fat in a low oven for hours and hours until tender. Stored submerged in the cooled fat, they would last for weeks and simply needed to be dropped into a hot fryer upon order to crisp up the skin and warm the succulent meat before accompanying a side of organic frites, tossed with herbes de Provence and fresh garlic. I taught the other cooks in the kitchen how to make my spinach salad, the one that reminded me of my mother, with a warm bacon vinaigrette, buttery fried croutons and a soft poached egg. They would serve cheese boards that I had laid out in detail for them, with local cheeses, honey, jam, nuts and toast points. And there were our staples: oysters – available with an apple-and-shallot mignonette – and hard-boiled quail eggs. Diners could finish with a slice of rich chocolate tart or a luscious lemony semifreddo with hazelnut brittle, which I had shown them how to make hundreds of times. They had this and were ready to rally behind me, knowing I was in this place trying to get better. I was confident they had everything under control for the patch of time I needed to step away to heal. I was confident that in a month's time I'd be home, hopefully a new woman, ready to take on the busy summer season at the restaurant, ready to face the challenges of my marriage to Tom, which was destined for divorce court.

I sat facing the yellow wall staring at the line of phones that was quickly filling up with other anxious women. Most were calling home to their families, checking in with loved ones. In the wake of my rock bottom, I had managed to decimate the core of my family and embarrass the rest. The one smidge of 'family' that still felt somewhat unscathed from the mess I created was the restaurant. I wondered if I should just let it be, let them do their jobs back at the restaurant, continue to be confident that they had this because there was nothing I could do from all the way out here, even if something did go wrong. But the suspense was killing me. I needed to hear that everything *was* okay there and I was craving the sound of a familiar voice, too. I picked up and dialled. It was morning and the prep help would be in the kitchen by now. The sound on the receiving end made a few strange beeps before prompting a recorded operator's message. I hung up, figuring I must have dialled the wrong number. I dialled again. Again, three beeps and a recorded operator's voice. I tried once again, this time moving my fingers slowly over the keypad to make sure I got the numbers right: 'The number you dialled has been disconnected or is no longer in service. If you feel you have reached this recording in error, please check the number and try your call again,' it repeated over and over again. What the fuck? What the fuck? *What the fuck?!* I hit the switch hook a few times to get a fresh dial tone, this time dialling the number of one of the women I left in charge of the restaurant. The phone rang a few times before she answered.

'Hello . . . ,' she answered in a bleary, cold and cautious voice.

'It's me! What the hell is going on!? I just called the restaurant to talk to you guys and keep getting a message saying the line has been disconnected? Is everything okay?' I rushed with my questioning, hoping that the quick answer that everything was fine would follow.

'Erin, call your mother.' Her voice was emotionless, slow.

'Call my mother?' I couldn't imagine what my mother had to do with the phone being disconnected at the restaurant. 'Call my mother?' I repeated. 'What?' I could feel the frantic rush of blood beginning to flow through my body, my heart beating faster and faster as I began to realize that not only was something wrong, something was *very* wrong.

'Erin, call your mother,' she said again in her reserved voice. The line went dead. She hung up without even saying good-bye. I paused, clicked the receiver and dialled the line out to my mother. She answered after only a ring, as if she was expecting me.

'Hello?' she answered. With just that one word I could hear in her voice that she was holding the bad news that I feared in her possession. It was the first time we were speaking since she put me on a plane to rehab, but we skipped the normal questions that should have started this conversation – How are you? How was the flight? How are you feeling? How's it all going? What's the food like? I was already beginning to choke up, even before she told me what had happened, going through all of the possibilities in my mind, knowing that chances were it was the one I feared the most.

'Mom.' I let out a soft wincing cry, anticipating a blow to come. But by now, I knew what had happened. I waited through her moment of silence for a response.

'It's gone . . .' was all I could make out before I started to lose feeling in my body, numb all over and light-headed. I could hear the faint details echoing through the phone as my mother explained what Tom had done, but it was surreal and dreamlike and cloudy.

Tom had seized everything. Hours after my departure he had strutted into that triangular building made of bricks and fired all of the staff, changed the locks and taped a cardboard sign on the door with CLOSED spelled out in black marker. In one flip of a lock, everything I had spent years building was gone. The truth, I later discovered, was it had been his for the taking all along. I wasn't on the deed; I didn't have any legal ownership of the building; but the mortgage, on the other hand, was mine. It seemed to me like Tom had planned the whole thing out – maybe rehab wasn't about sending his wife away to get better. I thought back to the day we closed on the building and all of the heaps of paperwork that sat on the lawyer's desk, my eyes big and bright with excitement. I must have signed my name a hundred times . . . but it couldn't have been a mistake. I was on the mortgage, not the deed and it was hard not to believe that Tom had wanted it this way so when and if he ever needed to, he could take it all away from me in one easy and cowardly move. Now he had kicked me while I was at my lowest. He had locked me out of my dreams and along with them had taken every whisk, every spoon, every spatula and knife that I had worked all those hours for at the kitchen store. He had confiscated every table and chair, the zinc-lined bar. He had even robbed me of my grandmother's dishes. He had taken my child, he had taken my home, he had taken my business and he had drained all of our mutual bank accounts. He had taken it all.

'I have to go, Mom. I have to go.' I was struggling to catch my breath through my flux of heartache and hatred and rage. I hung up the phone and grabbed a handful of tissues from the box beside me to clean up my wet face. I got up from my seat, left the yellow room and walked over to the nurses' booth. I knocked wildly on the glass window to get the attention of the woman inside. She slid the door open, asking what I needed.

'Give me my seventy-two,' I said, my teeth and jaw clenching tighter and tighter. I was here voluntarily and the seventy-two was the form used to check yourself out. The catch was that you had to wait seventy-two hours to be released after signing it. I scribbled my signature at the bottom of the form and I walked down the hallway back toward my room, plotting my discharge. I would check myself out, I would fly home and I would kill Tom. I would kill him with the anger that was raging like wildfire through my body. I would kill him for all the lies that he had told me, the pain he had caused me and everything he had stolen from me. I wanted to strangle him with my bare hands. I wanted to feel what it felt like to squeeze every single last drop of air from his lungs and watch his face gasp with panic until his lying blue eyes turned grey and rolled back into his head. I wanted him to feel the pain and fear that he had made me feel.

I rolled into my bed with the murderous thoughts. If I killed Tom, they would know it was me. It was too easy. I'd spend my life in prison and if prison was anything like what I imagined, it would be even worse than rehab. Maybe I would just rather die. I started to play with that thought. I wished Tom had just killed me. He would eviscerate me, over and over and over again and if I survived, he would at least have the satisfaction of knowing that I would be left with nothing. My mind started to fill with dark thoughts: What good are you now, you lousy excuse of a woman? You are a disgrace to everyone who has ever known you. You lost your kid to a man who isn't even his father. What kind of a mother are you? You lost your home. You are jobless. You are a fucked-up pillhead. What do you have left to live for, you no-good-piece-of-shit girl? I deserved to be punished. Maybe even die.

It was almost as if a light switch had flipped off inside me. End it now, I thought. I pulled myself together, sat up slowly and walked over to my closet. I pulled a pair of sneakers from the bottom shelf and went back to my bed. Slowly I removed the laces from each shoe and tied them together. Surprised that they didn't confiscate them upon my arrival, I tried to tie a noose, but struggled with the knot, realizing that one of the many things I regretted about my marriage to my sailor husband was not paying better attention to him when learning how to tie a proper knot. I improvised and wrapped the long double lace around my neck twice. I lay down and I began to pull the laces tight with both hands until I could feel the taut tension on my throat, compressing my windpipe, constricting my breath. I pulled it even tighter and tied a simple knot in place. My head started to feel fuzzy. I felt surprisingly calm. In my blurry haze my mind wandered back to all my losses and failures, my self-loathing and how I hated Tom with all of my blackened soul. I had lost all reasons to live. My light-headedness gave way to a vision of Jaim. I could see him swinging on the playground swing set at the city park in jeans and a white T-shirt, pumping his legs and swinging so high with his little Converse sneakers. He was squealing with delight and begging for me.

'Mom! Look at me! Look at me, Mom! Can you see me, Mom? I'm going so high!'

I could see him and I could feel him. I could feel that bright and beautiful smile and the joy for living that he had. And I could feel that I did still have one thing left to fight for, left to live for. I pulled at the poorly tied knot around my neck, released the tension of the laces from my throat and gasped for a good breath. Killing myself with a pair of shoelaces wasn't the answer. I wouldn't kill myself. I wouldn't kill Tom, either. But I would divorce him and fight tooth and nail for the one and only thing in my life that mattered, my son.

The laces that I had wrapped around my neck had left an indentation that I could feel with my fingers. I threw the sneakers back into my closet wondering again how the lace-up shoes had made it into the 'acceptable' pile in the first place and exchanged them for a sweater that would cover the evidence of my weak moment. I retreated to my bed and remained there for the rest of the day and night. I forgave myself for becoming bedridden again, allowing myself to mourn the loss of these pieces of my life. Tomorrow I would wake early, take a lukewarm shower with a tiny towel and get in line for a crappy cup of coffee. I'd tear up my seventy-two and I would stay. I would inch forward to live because I had one small, sweet, kind and gentle ten-year-old reason to and that one reason alone was more than enough.

21

TIME TO GO, GIRL

A few weeks into rehab I started to feel the twinges of progress and saw gentle signs that things in my life might be starting to stabilize. I had worked myself into a daily routine and was taking the intense daily schedule seriously. I awoke early each morning to catch a quick lukewarm shower and I would make a point of making my bed, tucking the sheets in nice and tidy. My mother had always told me that a messy room was a telltale sign of a chaotic and depressed mind; the kind of mind I was working hard to get away from. I would make my way to the kitchen for a few cups of crappy double-run coffee before it was time to line up for morning meds, then breakfast, followed by a full day of group meetings, therapy sessions and medical exams. There was a rhythm and I was falling peacefully into it with a bit of radical acceptance. I was absorbing what I could and was hopeful it would help shape me back into a woman I could recognize again. The only way out was through.

Much of the day was dedicated to group sessions. It was rehab's version of open-mike night. It was here that we, the women confined to this space, would share stories. They weren't simple stories, they weren't easy stories, they weren't lyrical stories that made you feel good inside. They were the stories of our struggles, pain, weakness and fears. They were the ways we had been harmed, the harm we had caused and the ways our lives and the lives of others had been affected by it and fallen to hell. Stories of pain, abuse, grief and shame. There were stories from the time a woman went to a house party in college that seemed innocent enough, got drunk, passed out on a couch and woke up with a guy she didn't even know inside her – and how it made her hate herself, blame herself, cut herself and stuff herself with food instead of feelings. Stories from when someone experimented with drugs in high school because her boyfriend had convinced her it was cool. She got hooked, couldn't stop and got so high that one day she missed her grandmother's funeral, a woman she loved dearly. She quit the drugs then and there, but she punished herself for all the days that followed by gagging herself to the point of puking after most meals. Stories from when a girl had been adopted and struggled with her identity. She didn't know who she was or where she had come from and it pained her deeply. It had been eating her up inside to the point where she starting cutting herself to understand her blood.

The stories were different in detail, but at the core we were all the same. It didn't matter if we were cutting, taking pills, drinking until we blacked out, depriving ourselves of food or puking up our meals – we were looking for ways to deal with our pain. It was an awakening, forcing me even to wonder if I had been so very wrong about my seemingly fractured relationship with my sister, thinking all of these years we were so very different, but maybe at our cores we, too, were so much the same. Here in this place, without the drugs, the booze and the weapons we used to hurt ourselves, love and care were rediscovered. We were women; we were born nurturers. We reconnected with those powers we had in us all along. We offered tissues when we saw a tear, quiet hands on shoulders, strong words, long hugs. We got it; we got one another. We spilled our guts and supported one another when we fell apart afterward. For so long each of us had been quietly trying to mend ourselves, but what we discovered here was that we needed a village to lean on – to listen, to love and to remind us that we weren't alone.

I felt safe here; I let my guard down, I opened up and I talked. I shared my pain, I shared my grief and I discovered that I felt lighter than I had in a very long time. After weeks of easing this burden from my chest, I could smile on occasion, even laugh here and there. For the first time in my life I could be vulnerable and safe. No judgment, no turning of backs, no joy in my downfall, no punishment. I could cry without being ridiculed, without being told I was *emotional,* like Tom had said, or *weak,* like my father had. 'Get over it,' I heard from both of them, over and over and over again. I came here alone and found a group of women and together we were so much stronger. I could feel hope beginning to grow inside of me again and with it grew the certainty that I could rebuild a happier, healthier life.

It was late in April, a little more than two weeks after I'd first arrived, when a pair of social workers at the rehab facility asked me to join them on the back deck of the lodge. I felt privileged with the excuse to get outside for some fresh air, but I'd soon learn that the meeting was far from a reward. They explained that my insurance had run out. It had quit four days ago and I had no warning. Not only had it eaten up my mother's deposit money, I would now be financially responsible for the thousands of dollars that had accrued during the four-day lapse. The news was a bomb in my lap. I was given two choices: pay up now and continue to pay out of pocket for the pricey programme, or pack my bag and get out. I was fucked. I had thirty-four dollars in my personal savings account – all that was left after Tom had drained our joint accounts. If I stayed I would be engulfed by a tsunami of medical bills, which would take decades to dig out from. If I left I would be dumped onto the cold and unfamiliar streets of this Midwestern suburb with no transition plan and no flight for home booked. I was pissed off and panicked, knowing that neither option would end well.

I tried to keep it together as I challenged the set of vacant-eyed women who were reading me my patient rights, but it was a struggle. Just over two weeks ago I was on suicide watch and today they were going to kick me out because my insurance had run out and I didn't have the cash. It seemed careless, coldhearted and contrary to all the hard work I had been putting in to get better and stronger. My tears of frustration seemed lost on them – it made me feel that they really didn't care whether I lived and thrived or died. I went back to my room to pack my small bag of belongings, only to discover that they had already stripped the sheets in preparation for the new patient who would take my bed.

Sure, I wanted out. I wanted nothing more than to be free of the prison-like environment I had endured for the last two weeks. I wanted to be free of the locked doors that kept me away from fresh air. I wanted to take a piss when I pleased without someone hovering over me, enjoy a long hot shower with a towel that was big enough to wrap around my body, shave my legs and armpits with a fresh, sharp razor and have a good, strong cup of halfway decent coffee. But I wanted to stay because what I wanted more than anything was to finish what I had started. I wanted to keep working hard, to be clean and clear again, finally at peace with all of my angst, self-hatred and depression before I walked out that door. If they were giving me the boot now, it would all have been for nothing. During the time I'd spent in the rehab facility I had lost my home, my business and my kid. Everything was gone. All I had left was this programme and now that was being taken away too. All I wanted was to get the help and strength I needed to return to my nothing.

'Have you booked your flight yet?' asked an impatient nurse who was peeking into my room. I wiped the tears from my face and shook my head no.

'An hour ago you wouldn't even let me take a private pee. Now you're just going to open the door and let me walk out. Is this what

you do? Just push suicidal girls out of the door?' I asked her with
bewilderment. I had been blindsided not even ten minutes before
and they expected me to have a flight booked already? Was she serious? An hour ago I was on lockdown, not to be trusted to move
freely through the facility because – in their eyes – I wasn't yet
equipped to make good, healthy decisions. Now I was being asked
to leave for the nearest airport with no exit plan, no guidance, no
support whatsoever.

'Can you at least help me get a ride to the airport?' I sobbed
to the foot-tapping nurse. 'I don't have any money for a cab.' She
turned down the hallway to see what she could do for me. I zipped
up my bag and followed her with my rolling suitcase behind me.
I sat in the couch-filled common space and waited for the plastic
bag of contraband goods that had been confiscated from me upon
intake. Inside the bag was my cell phone. I powered it up to find
barely enough juice to make a call. I only needed one – to my mom.
I planned to call her on the way to the airport to let her know that
I had been discharged, that I was now in major fucking debt and
that I had to try and figure out how the hell I was going to pay for
plane fare home. I wasn't ruling out the possibility that I'd have to
stay at the airport for a good long time.

It always stirred the place up when a woman left abruptly, even
though it happened almost every day that I was there. The sudden
departures were hard because so many of us had formed friendships with one another, built sister-like trust from having shared
our sacred stories of deep pain. We leaned on one another for support and comfort in what were rock-bottom terrifying moments
in our lives. We shared an intimacy in a way that even our closest family members might not be capable of. We understood one
another when no one else could. I witnessed countless girls before
me be cut loose and forced out onto the streets because of insurance issues. In the snap of a finger they would be gone. I knew I'd
never see any of them again; after all, I didn't even know their last

names. I knew their deepest, darkest secrets and fears, but not their last names.

Some of the women began buzzing around me with concern when they saw my suitcase in tow, inquiring what the hell was going on. Hasty cards with contact info and words of courage and hope scribbled on them were stuffed into my coat pocket. We knew we would never see one another again, but the gesture didn't feel empty. I sat quietly on the couch, waiting for my ride to the airport, weeping and accepting soft pats on my back as passing women made peaceful attempts to console me.

The common area got a bit more frantic as a code was called out over the intercom and women started scattering toward their rooms. The code meant that a girl was losing her shit somewhere and help was being called in to deal with the situation. In moments like this, we were instructed to clear out and return quickly and quietly to our rooms while staff would work to defuse the emotional girl-bomb that was going off somewhere within the lodge. Inevitably a dramatic line of police cars and ambulances would follow, making their way to the lodge to whisk the problem woman away. Everyone couldn't help standing in the doorways of their rooms to see who was melting down and getting carted away this time. The hallways cleared out. I didn't have a room anymore and stood awkwardly with my roller case in hand before asking a nurse.

'Where should I go?'

'You stay right here,' she responded with a slow, calm voice – as if she was trying to defuse a bomb. Like clockwork, I could see the line of police cars and ambulances pulling up to the front door. A nurse beside the thick glass entrance door punched in the security code before letting in a steady stream of bodies in uniform. Police officers, ambulance attendants, backup nurses from the lodge next door. There were dozens of them, surrounding me like a raid, moving slowly as if I had dynamite strapped to my chest. *I was the emotional bomb-girl. I had said the magic word: 'suicidal'.*

They were here for *me*. It was all so wildly confusing until I realized they called a code, which inevitably provoked a scene ... it also resulted in another hospitalization, causing my insurance to kick in again. It was how the system worked and I was stuck in it like a prisoner. 'We can do this the easy way or the hard way. You choose,' one of them said. I stood motionless and stunned, surrounded by a team of uniforms and a stretcher. They threatened to use restraints if I gave them trouble. I tried to control the hysteria that was starting to take over me, fearing what they might do if I started to display how crazy and confused I was starting to feel inside. It felt like a bad dream inspired by a TV show; I half expected them to scream, 'Put your hands up!' I co-operated out of fear and was escorted by the swarm into the back of the silent ambulance before they closed the doors and drove me to an undisclosed location. From the back of the ambulance I couldn't see where we were going and they wouldn't tell me. I felt like a criminal and a hostage all at the same time, guilty yet terrified. I could feel myself starting to spiral down all over again, back into the chaos of square one where I had started. All the hard work I had done over the last few weeks for nothing.

They carted me off to a local emergency room, where I sat in a sterile, curtain-lined room for enough hours to fill up nearly an entire day. I was waiting, just racking up my medical bills. Over the span of time I was there, I saw three other women I recognized from the rehab centre who had been transferred as well. I wondered how many more there were. We were like pawns being moved around, seemingly based on our ability to pay. I didn't have insurance and was sent to a pricey bed in the local emergency room, meaning the bed at the rehab was available, including for private patients who were paying out of pocket. I felt trapped in an entire ecosystem, moving weakened women around to fill beds and make insurance claims. It seemed we were being held hostage, at the mercy of the broken mental health system. All I wanted now was to get out and be done with this godforsaken setup. I wanted to get to the airport and figure out how the hell I was going to get home. But I'd soon be informed that I wouldn't be going home anytime soon. Instead I would be transferred by an ambulance against my will to a psychiatric unit for an unknown amount of time.

The hospital ward they sent me to felt more like a prison than part of a healthcare system. I had been sentenced to do time in a locked unit, stripped of basic freedoms yet again. Stranded in the room for days, I felt trapped and became idle. I would only spend four days' actual time here, but the madness of it all made it feel like weeks in my head. I lost all my bearings while I was confined alone in that empty room. With no clock in sight, I struggled with time, which seemed to be moving at an excruciatingly slow speed now. The view from the small window would reveal only a continuous grey, cloudy sky, making it impossible to tell which direction I faced. With nothing else to do all day, I watched little bugs on the tree branches outside my window jump back and forth from bud to bud in what looked like a celebration of the blossoming of spring. I yearned to be home, planting my spring window boxes, forcing forsythia, gathering arrangements for the restaurant and helping Jaim clean the pavement with a broom and a hose. Those days were gone now.

On occasion I'd sprawl out on the cold tile floor to practise the handful of simple stretches I'd learned to try to calm myself from the flood of tears and hyperventilation. I was fed irregularly and when I did receive food, it was so inedible that I couldn't gag it down when I tried. I gobbled down the occasional fruit garnish and I rationed little packets of Saltines and digestives, eating them only when I truly felt like I was starving. Lying in that bed for hours and days, I felt hot and numb from the frustration of being held there against my will. I was captive for what felt like no good goddamn reason. I was growing impatient and brimming with worry that my mind would rot in this bed, or that I would turn truly mad. I thought it couldn't get any worse until my abdomen started to throb with oncoming menstrual pains. I called for a nurse for some tampons and maybe some Advil, but she just looked at me, scratched her head and said in a thick Midwestern accent, 'Oh-kay ... um ... lemme see about that, hon. I think all we got around this unit is pads.' I waited for what had to have been hours, but she never returned. I resorted to making thick wads of toilet paper and stuffing them in my underwear, then lying in a foetal position to try to crush the pain with my own body. I had been cut cold turkey off a handful of prescribed pills that I had been working for weeks to wean from slowly in rehab. I was beginning to withdraw from those drugs that only took me a moment to become addicted to and that were taking ages to wean from. If I managed to fall asleep, I'd awake with full-body sweats so intense that I'd have to change my clothes. By day my mind felt fuzzy and numb. My body pulsated as if there were electrical currents flowing through my veins. I could feel myself sinking lower and lower. After all the progress I had made over the past few weeks, I feared this setback could sink me again.

I phoned my mother a few times each day from a bank of communal phones. It was a setup like what I imagined a prison would have – all three of them side by side on a painted concrete wall with barely a foot of space between, lending no privacy for the painful calls that were being made on them. A dial tone would turn on at designated times throughout the day and would only remain on for twenty-five-minute intervals. If the phones were occupied by other patients for the entire twenty-five minutes, you'd miss your turn and have to wait hours for the next opportunity. Family members attempting to call in could become equally frustrated and were frequently unable to get through. The freedom to communicate with anyone on the outside was just another liberty that had been stripped away. I needed an advocate to help navigate this challenging system that was holding me hostage. I needed answers;

I needed help managing my now-fucked-up prescription regimen and the resulting withdrawal symptoms; I needed a decent meal and at the very least I needed an aspirin and a goddamn tampon. Luckily my mother received my cry for help and impulsively purchased a ticket, putting the expensive last-minute airline fee on her already burdened credit card and stuffing her pocket with a few rolls of change to pay for tolls for the rental car. I was weak and in the depths of despair and past the point of embarrassment and I needed someone with a clear head to help navigate this mess and maybe offer me a little love. I needed my mom and when she finally arrived, I was overcome with relief.

It took four days to be seen by a doctor, looked up and down, told that I was not a threat to myself or others and to be released into the care of my mother. Finally, free to go home in a rental car to the airport, I was reminded that I couldn't go home because I had no home. Thanks to the last four days, I had lost any strength I had gained during my time in rehab. I was suffering from prescription-drug withdrawal and had no reentry plan. I was too weak to be greeted by the giant shit storm and estranged husband that were waiting for me. And rural Maine had few resources to help me recover from this major tumbledown. My messed-up reality was waiting for me, ready or not.

At the airport I got the full pat-down and deep search through my one bag. I was used to it by now, but on the other side of security, a feeling of newness came over me: Freedom. People moving, rushing, walking, strolling, sitting and standing in line for food. People doing as they pleased, going places, no one watching over their every move. And drinking *coffee*. I made a beeline for the first Starbucks I saw, a roll of quarters that my mom had shared with me in my pocket. I ordered two double-shot cappuccinos, one for each hand. At the gate I sipped each of them like hot liquid drugs, relishing the delight of every last drop. I'd never take a good cup of coffee for granted ever again. In the bustling women's restroom next to the gate, I lined a toilet seat with a few pieces of toilet paper and sat down, taking a nice leisurely pee. I couldn't imagine I'd ever appreciated a pee as much as this one. As I scrubbed my hands in the sink with a good, warm, soapy lather, I took my time, enjoying the freedom of this moment. I looked up at my face in the tall restroom mirror. It was the first time I had seen myself in weeks. I barely recognized myself. My cheekbones protruded from the weight I had lost after days of eating only crackers; my eyes were still puffy from all the tears. I glanced at the reflections of the other women scrubbing their hands in the line of sinks on either side of me, applying makeup and fixing their hair in the mirror. I smiled slightly, realizing I was probably the only girl here savouring the normalcy and simple liberty of a glance in a mirror and an unattended piss in a public restroom. Even if that smidgen of appreciation was all that I had walked away with from this mess, it was something. And maybe it was good enough to build on.

PART FOUR

LIBERTY

22

A GREY DAY IN MAINE

The sky was thick with clouds of defeat on the day of my return. I had never known a spring day in Maine to feel as bleak, grey and hopeless as this one – as though the atmosphere were mirroring everything I felt inside. I was moving back to Freedom with nothing but a suitcase that contained a few pieces of clothing and some toiletries. It was all that was left of my life besides the heavy feelings of loss, embarrassment and self-doubt. The reality of my overturned life was becoming more real by the second as I approached my parents' house on Penney Road, sitting in the passenger seat of the car. I was still trying to kick the tremors that lingered from the prescription drugs, but I wasn't sure if I was trembling from withdrawal or from nervousness about the uncertainty that awaited me.

At the end of the mile-long dirt road was the farmhouse I had grown up in. My parents would take me in, giving me a safe haven of sorts. It was a bunker to hole up in while I prepared for the storm of my divorce. I'd stay in the small one-room cabin that sat on the edge of the farm pond, a short walk from the main house, to endure the messy hell while trying to reclaim and rebuild some sort of life. I'd be starting over from scratch. And even though I was home, I was lost.

Living in the shingled cabin nestled in the woods would give me a space of my own and my parents their own space, too. Living on top of one another in the small main farmhouse was not an option – there wasn't enough room under one roof for the pain and anger of three. The cabin was rustic and simple; there was an old enamel table with a couple of painted wooden chairs. A wall of single-paned windows overlooked the pond that I used to ice-skate on as a kid in winter and catch frogs by come spring. There was a full-size bed with an oak bed frame that once belonged to my great-grandmother and a cast-iron woodstove in one corner of the room, which would keep things toasty on damp spring days or cold autumn nights. There was no electricity, just a few oil lamps, a wrought-iron candelabra and some small glass votive candles sprinkled around the room. There was no toilet, just an ironstone chamber pot under the bed and a washstand with a ceramic bowl and jug for cleaning up. I could share the shower in the main house with my parents, but sparingly, as the old dug well was short and went dry easily – much like my father's patience for me. It was a little rough, but I was thankful nonetheless for the free roof over my head and the reassurance that there were warm bodies just a short hike away if I needed company.

The cabin had been sitting dormant over the winter and needed a bit of spring cleaning – a metaphor that didn't escape me. With a damp cloth I swatted at the corners of the room where big cobwebs had formed and wiped down the few pieces of furniture. I swept clouds of dust from the floor out onto the porch and opened the windows to let in the fresh air. I emptied the ashes from the stove and lit a fire using some scraps of wood left from last season to help cut the dampness in the spring air. I hadn't lived with wood-fired heat since my childhood. It took me a few tries to get it good and going. Eventually the sparks held, but when the smoke started to billow softly into the room, I realized that the damper had been closed for the season. I flipped it open and the flames instantly started to get a good draw. The room began to warm as the healthy fire picked up and the crackle and hum of the burning wood made the space start to feel more alive, as if there were another beating heart in the room. I made the bed with a set of floral flannel sheets and a patchwork quilt, tucking and folding the corners just as my mother had taught me when I was a girl. I filled a few glass bottles with water from the house to store on my bedside table, which I could warm in an enamel kettle over the wood fire and wash up with at bedtime. Over the next few days I spent hours making the small space feel more like home, including collecting a series of mismatched extension cords from around the farm to run a network of cords nearly a hundred yards long through the field from the barn. This gave me three outlets for a couple of lamps and a fan (though my father would fuck with me sometimes and pull the plug in the barn, turning the room pitch-black without warning – his idea of a joke). It was a glimmer of luxury for what would become my new home for God only knew how long. Outside, I trimmed the overgrown trees and bushes that had begun to encroach upon the little cabin over the seasons. I filled the window boxes with ferns and furry mosses that I had gathered from the adjacent woods.

I'd trudge up the hill to join my parents for coffee in the morning and dinner in the evening, the conversations over our kitchen table becoming patterned to end in arguments and frustration over my looming medical bills, mounting legal fees, the eminent repossession of my car or the painful ongoing custody battle against Tom. I was realizing that my entire family had fallen victim to this malignant divorce and that my parents had fallen ill from its effects as well. They were living and breathing my hell alongside me, torn up over all the name-calling, loss and emotion that had been swirling around us for the past few months. They too were sleeping like shit, feeling furious and broken all the time. They too had been torn away from Jaim and were aching deep inside from the loss. I began to worry that my divorce was killing them, literally breaking their hearts. It felt different from the last time I had put them through such emotional strain, the time I'd moved back to Freedom broke, single and pregnant. I had brought shame and disappointment into their lives and filled the house with stress, but it had ended with so much joy – a baby boy. The baby boy my father had begged me to abort but who ended up being the bright and soft spot in his twisted heart. He had eventually admitted, in tears, to that being the only time in his life that he was wrong. He couldn't imagine our lives without our beautiful boy and now it was a tragic reality that we had lost him. I wondered how much more they could endure without completely cracking alongside me.

My mother was her usual soft and supportive self. A retired primary school special-needs teacher, she had been trained in family crisis, but she was clouded by the proximity of this particular one. Compartmentalizing emotions was more challenging. She managed to keep up her pragmatic and organized side, always taking notes at doctor's appointments or meetings with lawyers, decoding the information into fragments that I could comprehend in my weakened emotional state. My mom believed that you couldn't get through a crisis alone. Just like when one of her kids melted down at school, it took a team to get the broken kid back on the rails. She saw this crisis as being no different, believing that this too would take the support of a village. She declared a 'crisis posse', composed of my aunt Rhoda and two of my closest confidants, Dave and Ivy. Dave and Ivy were my parents' age, retired and childless. We met through Tom years ago and we became fast friends. Ivy was a bit of a gastronome and took to me through our common love for good food and lots of wine. Dave was a born-and-bred Mainer, with soft, almost maternal qualities unlike any other – a real caregiver. When couples split, it is inevitable that friendships divide too, people picking one side or the other. For a while Dave and Ivy stood strong and steady by Tom's side, often making efforts to persuade me to go back to him. Tom was cunning and smart, filling their in-boxes with victim-laced tales of our breakup. He was convinced that his master-manipulator skills could weasel a way into

Dave's and Ivy's hearts and that they would lobby hard for me to go back to him. It almost worked. But the day Tom locked the doors to the restaurant with all my possessions and my kid inside, they saw through his bullshit. 'You don't kick a hurt pup when she's down,' Ivy told me. In that one click of the door, the changing of the locks, Tom had proved to Dave and Ivy that his efforts to get me into rehab weren't just so that I could 'get better'. I certainly felt like he had never cared about my well-being. Instead, it felt to me like he wanted me there, locked up, so that he could take control, like a hawk, attacking from the sky in a smart, planned moment. It seemed it had always been about control. Controlling me, controlling Jaim, controlling the business. The message on the whiteboard in the sterile phone room of the rehab centre made it clear one day, whose side Dave and Ivy had chosen. The message board read:

TO: Erin
FROM: Dave & Ivy
MESSAGE: 10:48 am DIVORCE THE MOTHERFUCKER.
Call us . . . xo

From that moment on their support was enormous and never-ending. They would claw, kick and fight too, to see me through this hellhole I had fallen into. They were like family, lending their love and support that was tender yet ready for battle. Not too dissimilar from the special bond I had with my own flesh-and-blood grandparents, who would have been right on the front line to see me through this war of injustices if they were both still alive.

My mother arranged weekly meetings for the five of us to gather and brainstorm how we were going to inch me forward. We would meet on the back deck of the farmhouse while Mom would serve little treats like fresh-baked popovers with butter and strawberry jam. It made everything feel so civilized, even though we all knew it wasn't. But instead of wallowing together, we talked about the whole mess as if it were a business. Together we compiled my blizzard of bills and we formed a plan for putting a dent in the mounting and overwhelming debt. We went to pawnshops to try to find the best cash deal for my engagement ring, for a small bit to put toward the impending legal bills surrounding my divorce. We sent ten dollars here and twenty dollars there, just to keep everyone I owed at bay. The small gestures showed good faith and kept the medical bills from going to collection.

Through each low moment, my sister remained absent. But I didn't mourn her lack of presence: I was used to our non-existent bond. Rooting me on wasn't her style. Our relationship was riddled with decades-old decay and drifting apart that had yet to be repaired. We were anything but sisters, not even friends, really. Our blond hair and the blood that bound us were the only things we had in common. If anything, her distance gave me peace from the anxiety I felt when she was around. I didn't have to worry about her judgments, her all-knowing opinions or what she might next say to put me down or embarrass me further. My hands were full enough with my father's reaction to the whole ordeal, I didn't need more tension from my already-tense relationship with my sister.

My father was incapable of containing his anger – an anger so deep that it prevented him from being helpful in any way, instead creating an additional layer of tension and angst to struggle through. He had cooked a stew of contempt in his stomach for Tom. He maybe hated the man more than I did, if that was possible. His wrath was crushingly all-encompassing and he expressed it through verbal outbursts and threats of violence. I worried that he would do more than just pop a set of Tom's tires. Could he snap and kill him? We were all grieving the loss and enduring the pain in our own ways, but his vicious version was hard for any of us to swallow. And seeing my face every day was just a reminder of the shit we were wading through. I didn't think it was possible for him to resent me even more than he already did, but apparently it was and he did. But I had learned the hard way where trying to make myself small for a man had gotten me. And I wasn't going to make that same mistake again.

23

WHO SAVED WHO?

I had never really learned how to be alone. I was born into the arms of my parents and my sister came along shortly after. I grew up surrounded by my immediate family and grandparents. I had an extension of aunts and uncles, myriad cousins, classmates, teammates, friends, boyfriends, college roommates, co-workers, my own baby and eventually a husband. I had never lived by myself or spent much time in true solitude and now, thirty-three years old, I was finding out that maybe I was no good at it. It felt foreign, uncomfortable and unrelenting.

The animal shelter in Augusta was opening shortly. I pulled my car into a prime parking spot facing the front so I could wait to see when they would unlock the door. When I had called the day before to inquire about their hours, the woman on the phone advised me to arrive early. 'First in line, first pick,' she said. As the minutes ticked by, more cars began to slide into the parking lot, filling up the vacant spots. I kept notice of the body movements of the other people in their cars, curious to see if anyone would emerge early from the warmth of their vehicle to form a queue on this cool spring morning. After the first person made a move, I quickly followed, just before a woman in purple scrubs appeared inside the glass door to unlock it, letting in the steady stream of hopeful adopters.

Inside, the shelter had an odour of animal faeces and cat urine so strong that I had to cup my nose and mouth to keep from gagging. Loud barks and shrill cries filled the registration area and bounced off the thick concrete walls. Behind the plate-glass window were rows of chain-link cages with dozens of dogs of mixed breeds and sizes, jumping wildly, pacing, wailing and wagging their tails, vying for any kind of attention. There were brown, mangy-looking mutts, little ones with white fur that had become yellowed with filth and a handful of pit-bull mixes. The room was chaotic with animals, all looking for someone to take them home and love them, someone to give them a second chance. I scanned the room a few times, passing over the wild- and angry-looking dogs and back again – and then, out of the corner of my eye, I saw her. She was a scruffy-looking girl, yellow with dark caramel-coloured ears and a nose to match, a tattered red collar around her neck. A Lab mix, but maybe with a bit of shepherd, which gave her a long snout; five, maybe six years old. She sat quietly with her paws slightly outstretched in front of her as the chaos of the pound encompassed her, her face so mopey that her embarrassment was palpable, almost human. I tapped lightly on the window to try to get her attention. She was unfazed and unengaged. She was scanning the room and her sad brown eyes caught mine for just a second. This isn't the way I saw my life going, they said. This isn't the way I saw my life going, either, I responded with mine.

'Excuse me, can you tell me about this one?' I asked the woman at the front desk.

'That's Penney. Brought in last week. People just dropped her.'

'Penney,' I said softly to myself as I turned back toward the glass wall, looking at the sad little yellow dog. Penney, I kept repeating in my head. She shared the name of the road where I grew up. Penney the pound dog, just looking for a different life – not too dissimilar from me. We were both dilapidated, broken inside, deflated and defeated, surrounded by chaos and craving a fresh start. A golden Penney, when I had none to my name. She met my eyes for another brief second and this time said: I'm stuck here. All I want to do is run.

Let's run.

'Let's get the hell out of here, girl,' I whispered to her through the glass. I had to move quickly to beat out the people who were scanning the room, looking for a good match too. 'Excuse me! I'd like to adopt the yellow dog over there. That one right there with the red collar,' I said as I pointed at Penney and pushed my way through the crowd.

It took just moments to fill out the generic form, but even that was a cruel reminder of the lonely abyss that had become my life:

QUESTION: *How many people are in your household?*
ANSWER: *One lonely-fucking-miserable-torn-apart woman.*

QUESTION: *Are there any children in your household?*
ANSWER: *No. My son, whom I love with all my heart,*
the brightest star in my sky, the sweetest soul I ever met,
to whom I've given all the love I know how to give,
has been taken from me.

I handed the application to the woman at the front desk, fearful she would ask me for clarification of any of my answers. She didn't and instead handed me a thin nylon lead. She then went behind the glass partition and returned with Penney. She helped me attach the lead.

'Do you want to take her for a walk around the parking lot before you commit to her?'

'No. We'll be just fine.' I hoped it would be true – that Penney and I would be just fine. The little yellow dog and I pushed through the front door and in that moment we both felt free. The air in that place smelled so bad you could almost taste the shit and I took a deep and thankful breath of the fresh air outside. Penney began to pull at the lead, clawing her way over the asphalt, grinding her nails down as she pulled me forward with all her might. She couldn't get to my car fast enough. I coaxed her into the backseat and we set off to Freedom.

When we arrived back home at the little farmhouse on Penney Road, I opened the back door of my car, releasing Penney into her new, free world. She took it all in but didn't move. She still smelled like the shelter, like shit and cat piss. Her coat was dull and scruffy, her eyes still droopy with sadness and shame. We needed to start anew. I led her to the end of the barn and tied her lead to an old rusty eye hook that my grandfather used to tie the horses to when they needed a new pair of horseshoes or a good brushing. I sprayed her down and lathered her up with Dawn dish liquid, then rinsed the suds away. I found an old horse brush and brushed her all over, pulling clumps upon clumps of old, dead fur from her body. She was cleaner, she was lighter, she was fresh, she was like new. I released her from the lead to let her do as she pleased. She immediately lay down, sprawling across the stone driveway, rolling and snorting and scratching her back, twisting her spine along the pea stones in sheer delight before she stood back up on all fours and shook it all off. There she stood, staring straight at me, her tongue hanging out of her toothy grin, her tail wagging happily, her ears perked. This was her second chance and she knew it. She shook off her old life and began to receive the new one right then and there. I admired her ability to move on so quickly. She let go of the pain and injustices dealt her, no grudges held here. She didn't have it in her to hold on to bitterness and anger. Her heart was open to love and trust again. I wanted to be her.

That first morning around three, I awoke to whimpering sounds. I guessed that Penney needed to go out for a pee. I stumbled through the dark, making my way to the screen door of the cabin with only a bit of moonlight to guide me. I unlatched the door to let her out and she ran out of sight into the dark. I waited for her. And waited. I called for her, whistled and clapped my hands. No sight. I didn't panic just yet, thinking she might just be sniffing around her new turf. I fumbled around the cabin in the dark, locating the chamber pot from under my bed and squatting over it to take a pee, hoping that by the time I was done, she would be, too. I threw another log onto the dwindling coals in the woodstove to waste just a moment more. I called again, clapped and whistled as loudly as I could. But she didn't return. She had bolted into the darkness. Fear started to come over me, realizing she might not come back to this unfamiliar place. Would she be able to find her way in the dark? Did she know this was her home now? Did she know she was safe here and would be loved? I called out for her from the porch of the cabin and listened closely, but not a sound returned. I stepped into the darkness, fumbling and feeling my way around the ground with my bare feet, calling for her over and over again. If she had run, she was gone. I began to wonder – if I couldn't even look after a dog for twenty-four hours, what business did I have being a mother to a human being? Maybe Tom was right – maybe I was incompetent, incapable and doomed. Maybe he was right to rip Jaim away from me. I made my way back to the cabin and returned to my bed, realizing there was nothing I could do until the sun came up. I somehow managed to doze off after beating myself up a bit more.

I awoke in the morning to the sun glaring in through the old windowpanes of the cabin, quickly remembering my sadness over losing the little yellow dog last night. The fire had gone out in the stove, but I didn't need it on this beautiful, balmy Maine morning. I pulled my legs from under the covers and stepped onto the warm, sun-kissed wooden floor. My mind returned to Penney: how could I have lost her? How far could she have gone? I hoped she was okay. I decided to busy myself with morning duties, which included emptying the contents of the chamber pot in the woods and cleaning out the porcelain bowl with a bit of pond water. I made my way toward the door, carefully balancing the half-full pot of piss in my hands and nearly dropped it when I saw her. Sitting on the front porch, with her back against the screen door, guarding her new home, was Penney, contentedly basking in the warm morning sun. She never left my side after that day. She needed me and somehow she knew that I needed her too. I may have saved her from that pound, but she was the one who saved me. Or maybe we saved each other. I may not have had a home or my son and my world had crumbled around me, but I had a pot to piss in and a devoted dog to feed me love in this complicated time. And I knew, in the bottom of my heart, that I was a good mother. I would get my boy back and we would see better days in Freedom; I was sure of it. Because today, for the first time in a very long time, I felt a twinkle of hope.

24

TO THE BAT CAVE

My days had become consumed with the tiresome grind of trying to free myself from Tom, who seemed hell-bent on keeping his squeeze on me for as long as possible. In divorcing Tom, I couldn't have imagined the bonfire that would be ignited. He was fighting to take everything. I had left him and he appeared to believe that the only fair punishment for doing so should be for me to lose everything and be banished to live out a sad and empty life. He fought me for everything from slip-covered couches to flesh and blood. With each battle, it felt as though he was digging me a grave. It was a deep and expansive emotional hole and when I was weak, it kept him in power. He pummelled me with a legal hurricane that I didn't have the money or emotional capability to survive. I could only imagine the hurtful things he said about me as a mother and as a woman. I could see it in the eyes of others, their heads filled with his stories. It seemed to me that he would stop at nothing until he had everything that mattered to me. Of course I knew that there was one way I could change the course of things: go back to him. If I went back, Tom promised to return everything he had taken. But I'd be living a lie, spending the rest of my life confined to the invisible box he wanted me to live in, dumbed down and wings clipped. I couldn't do it.

Tom was old enough to have lived almost a full lifetime more than I had. He had been through a marriage, witnessed the births of two daughters, built a house, built a business, endured a divorce, lost the house and fought custody battles. He had picked up a few tricks and knew how to navigate the court system. He made consultation appointments with every reputable lawyer within a fifty-mile radius, even though he had already hired a lawyer. This created a conflict of interest, clearing out any option that I might find decent representation to fight back. He had figured out the key words to use in court: 'She is emotional.' 'She is unstable.' 'She is unfit to be a mother.' There would be no quick and easy way to douse the towering flames with which he was fuelling this divorce. So I would have to endure, wait for the fire to die down, then pick up the pieces once the smouldering ashes had cooled. I'd have to dig deep to find the strength to rebuild my life, find a job and become financially independent so I could make a home that was a safe and stable space for Jaim to thrive. I had to prove to the lawyers and judges who were laying me bare on the examining table that I was, had been and would continue to be a good mother to my son.

While I was thankful for each day that I wasn't living under the same roof with Tom, I was mourning each and every moment that Jaim wasn't living under mine. I wrestled with the pain his absence brought me as I continued to slog through weekly legal meetings, court appearances, guardian-ad-litem interviews, therapy appointments and posse gatherings. The process was slow, invasive and degrading. I was living under a microscope in a petri dish of judgment. I was being assessed for every move I had made over the course of my short marriage and being scrutinized for every action I was taking now. What kind of a mother is she? Did she make good breakfasts, pack good lunches, get the boy to and from school every day and get him to bed at a reasonable hour? Did she tuck him in? Did she read him stories? Did she sing him songs? Did she work a lot? Did her demanding workload interfere with her ability to parent? If she worked long days, how could she be a good mother? All of eleven years old now, Jaim wasn't permitted to share his opinion. The courts didn't take into consideration the opinions of minors under the age of fourteen. As far as they were concerned, his voice meant nothing.

I had made his breakfasts and packed him thoughtful lunches with food he helped me pick out at the market. Warm egg sandwiches on good English muffins and fresh blueberries from the high bush in our garden, or a BLT on fresh sourdough bread with heirloom tomato and just a touch of mayo, the way he liked it (although he hated when the tomato made the bread soggy after sitting in his lunch box for a few hours). When the weather was good, we'd walk to school in the morning, grabbing a hot chocolate for the ten-minute journey, or ride bikes side by side. I tucked him in each night, with a kiss, a book and a backrub, then lulled him to sleep with his favourite Bette Midler song, 'Baby of Mine'. I ran a fan in his room at night to muffle the sounds of the inevitable fight Tom and I would find ourselves engaging in. I had worked long hours at the restaurant, sometimes eighteen hours a day, but I still made time for those morning walks to school and always made it up to his room for a goodnight kiss, even if he'd already drifted off to sleep. I wasn't perfect at this ever-challenging job of being a mother, but I always gave what I could when I had it. Did that make me less deserving of a child? *Was I a good mother?* The invasiveness of it all had me second-guessing everything about myself.

If you've been through a divorce, then you know that it just flat-out fucking sucks. There is no way to avoid the shame and pain that will splinter your life. For me divorce felt like a scalpel had been run down my chest, exposing my insides for public display so everyone and anyone could see the private tragedy that was ripping my family apart. Our small town gobbled up the morsels of gossip surrounding our divorce: *Depression, mental illness, addiction.* The whispers had people I hardly even knew shaking their heads, throwing sideways glances and indicting me on the street. It was hard not just to stay in bed and hide from the judgment. But

I also knew that if I wallowed, I would lose everything. If I stayed in bed, I would prove right all those who doubted me – that I was incapable of finding stability and strength. I had to get out of bed. So I fought like hell to rise.

For the longest time I had somehow convinced myself that the walls of that brick building were precious and that the restaurant I had built from scratch inside was defined by those walls. And when it was gone, I was sitting at the end of a dead-end road. At the end of that road there were only two choices: turn around and go back, or pave a new road. There was no way I was going back. To move forward I needed to forget about that building, move past the walls. I needed wheels.

The idea was hatched out of simplicity, with a side of survival. A small dream from years past that had never come to fruition, finding a new light. I had dreamed bigger than this tiny dream once, with eyes wide for that triangle made of bricks. I overcame the obstacles and caught that lofty dream – but maybe now, more than ever, I needed this small and simple less-than-lofty restart. The idea of turning an old trailer into a tasty little food truck all those years back returned to me. And for the first time I had a posse rooting me on, supporting an off-the-beaten-path idea that might have sounded a bit wild years ago. The search was on for a cheap old trailer to trick out and give a second chance. 'Wheels, kids. Wheels are what we need to get this gal really rolling,' Ivy said with a cool confidence as she sucked on her e-cig and pushed the classified ad she'd found my way.

The ad read:

FOR SALE: 1965 AIRSTREAM

LOCATION: BAT CAVE, NC

PRICE: BEST OFFER

Walls had never defined me, like I had once thought. It was what I brought, from my heart, hands and soul, to the space within that defined me. It was the personal touches like the handmade linen napkins, the vintage china I selected piece by piece, the big bouquets of seasonal flowers or the bud vases on the tables. It was the warm glow of candlelight and the hum of good music in the background. It was the dishes I was preparing each evening, with love and attention, dotted with edible flowers. It was what I brought to the table that defined me. I didn't need the walls that Tom had taken from me and letting go of that feeling and the need to fight him tooth and nail to try to get it all back gave me a remarkable sensation of relief. There was only one thing to do: 'To the Bat Cave!'

The old Airstream caravan had been sitting in a campsite for some time, left to become a home to the local rodents and snakes that had moved in and out of it over the years. Its once-shiny aluminium exterior had dulled into a milky matte finish and it was spotted with bits of sticky sap from the pine trees it had been living under. Inside, the original interior was dated, with dark veneer that was peeling in spots. The small galley kitchen had a shallow enamel sink, an inoperable apartment-size four-burner stove and a wooden plaque that read 'God Bless Our Camper'. There was a full-size pull-out bunk, plus a dismantled bathroom at the rear with a strangely large plastic bathtub. The smell of mothballs and mildew was overwhelming and had permeated the fabric of the cheap floral curtains. The windows were in need of repair and the few screens that were still in place were either tattered or dotted with holes. Parts of the brown-painted plywood floor had rotted or had been chewed by animals, evident from the droppings they had left behind. The water tanks were gone, the water heater bust, the electrical system patchy at best and the dinged-up bumper was spotted with rust. It was a real old mess and I wondered momentarily if I truly was crazy for taking this on. I wondered if Dave and Ivy were crazy, too, for cheering me on and delivering this old beast to my doorstep, believing I could pull off a small miracle with this dull wreck. The camper had clearly not been blessed by any God, reminding me that I was feeling pretty confident about my decision to quit believing in him all those years back when he had let my kitten die. This camper didn't need blessings, it needed a miracle in the form of another soul who knew what it felt like for imperfections to keep her from being loved – and a new set of tires to find her way back to Maine. The camper's unkempt state allowed for a good bit of bargaining, which meant I could get it for a steal. It would still take a lot of work to get it back into fighting shape and it would put me even deeper into debt, but it was the important first step of a bigger plan.

The old hunk of metal pulled up to my parents' farmhouse on a June afternoon. Dave and Ivy had volunteered to take the ride to hitch it up while I stayed at home, tethered to my legal battles and therapy sessions. A trip south to pick up a tattered old Airstream with the idea of turning it into some kind of mobile restaurant would only have sounded crazy to the courts and would have given Tom more ammo to make me look unstable. Dave and Ivy were game to do anything, but I knew that their generosity to travel such lengths would leave me feeling forever indebted to them. Sometimes I wondered why they were going to such distances for me, sticking by my side, through shit storm or adventure, ride or die. Was it out of guilt? Making up for the times they bent my ear, trying to talk me into going back to Tom while under his spell? Or was it because that's what good, honest, loyal friends do? Like family. Through thick and thin. Protect and fight for the ones you love. Like letting a dog loose on a rogue rooster. Our blood was thick like family.

The homecoming of this ratty camper was the most excitement any of us had had in a very long time. It was the first time in a long while that I saw a reason to celebrate, so I put together a little something to share with the weary travellers – a vintage-inspired menu worthy of the newest member of our posse. I made devilled eggs using fresh eggs from our coop and piped the creamy mixture of yolk and mayonnaise into the set whites with the pastry tip set my mother had given to me back when I was a girl. I sprinkled each one with a delicate dusting of paprika and flaky salt and arranged them on an antique egg platter. I made pigs in blankets, wrapping bits of hot dog with puff pastry and baking them in the oven until golden brown and puffy and served them hot with a ramekin of good mustard. I picked a few handfuls of lettuces from my mother's garden and tossed the fresh, tender greens with a homemade French dressing that was ketchup-orange and tacky in all the right ways. We sat in brightly coloured wicker pool chairs I'd unearthed from the barn and drank punch from little glass cups. Then we finished with small bowls of creamy tapioca, still slightly warm, with dollops of cream, slices of fresh nectarine and a scattering of blueberries. It felt so good to just feel normal. And I realized that this dulled little camper might just be the bright and shiny thing I needed.

After Dave and Ivy left, I didn't waste a moment before diving into work mode. I started by opening all the windows to let in the fresh air and swabbed each one down with some Windex. I wiped down the walls, counters and cupboards and shook out years of dust from the bed. Then I vacuumed up the droppings and the skeletal remains from the previous rodent tenants. I worked until the sun went down and it was too dark to see. I fell into bed, exhausted with the unique pleasure of hard physical work – something my body had missed.

In the morning light the insides of the Airstream didn't look much better than they had when it had rolled into the drive. I was discouraged – the hours of the previous day's scrubbing barely made a difference. It was still dark, dirty and in disrepair – and it still reeked. I stepped outside for a breath of air and headed to my father's toolshed in the barn. I fumbled around the disarray of tools and occasional empty beer bottles in search of a simple flat-head screwdriver. After a few minutes of digging, I finally found one. As I turned to leave, I noticed an old sledgehammer leaning against the wall. It stopped me for a moment. I could clean for days, weeks even, trying to bring this thing back to life, but the interior of this old Airstream would still be dark and depressing. I picked up the sledgehammer and walked back to the Airstream. As I stood inside, grasping the heavy tool in one fist, inhaling the unpleasant scents and looking over the sad interior, I knew I was making a choice for both of us. We were both ready to shake ourselves free of the choices others had made for us. We were done being confined by old stories. We could keep clinging to what had already transpired. Or we could let it all go.

I raised the sledgehammer over my right shoulder and took a giant swing, smashing the first thin veneer wall to pieces. With each swing, I recounted all the ways that Tom had hurt me.

For belittling me. For every time he put me down, made me feel foolish, emotional, young, dumb. For never letting me be myself.

Whack!

For intimidating me, bullying me and emotionally starving me. For making me believe I was only as good as he believed. For telling me he would ruin me if I left him. For never letting me grow out of fear that I would outshine him.

Whack!

For his drinking. For all the times he got so drunk that he blacked out. For when he shoved me, threw me, tore me down.

Whack!

For cheating.

Whack!

For lying.

Whack!

For taking my kid.

Whack!

Between each whack, I winced and wailed, letting out sharp cries and screeches. That same animal who had sat seething in her cage, craving release, was tearing her way out. I was letting go of all the shit I had been holding in the pit of my stomach. I was letting go of the voices – his and mine – that told me I wasn't good enough. I was letting go of the doubt, blame and shame. I was letting go.

When I was done, all that was left was an empty shell and a pile of debris on the ground. It was a small death that preceded a rebirth. Tom had taken the walls of my restaurant away from me, but he could never steal the burning love for cooking that ran through my veins. I would take this empty shell and I would rebuild the insides, trick it out and turn it into a mobile kitchen. I didn't need walls anymore, because I had wheels.

I was going to bring my supper club back. With the limitless possibilities a mobile kitchen could give me, I started dreaming about the dinners I could throw. I started putting together a contact list with emails and phone numbers of farmers and friends who had interesting places that would make for lively evenings, crossing my fingers I could secure use of the property. There could be pop-up dinners in open fields, with long tables set with linen runners and vintage plates tucked between the goldenrod. I could cook over an open fire, draping just-picked vegetables and pastured meats with smoke and char. I could tuck tables under the shade of an orchard, hang lights to twinkle above in the branches and make as many dishes as I could with the apples – savoury sorbets, soups, salads and tarts. I could host an evening in a local greenhouse with tables between the tomato vines, the grassy aroma filling our nostrils while we sliced into ripe, juicy heirlooms that had been doused with good olive oil and sprinkled with a pinch of salt. Or why not find someone with an old barn that could be transformed into a dining room and fill it with laughter, mingling the smells of fresh hay and good food? I saw visions of tables adorned with wildflowers, my guests feasting on all of the things I'd foraged and harvested that very day, from that very land. The thought of being behind the stove again comforted me. It reminded me of what I had to offer. It was like plugging into an energy source again and it gave me the momentum I needed to start to dig myself out.

25

BITTERSWEET BREAKUP
BROWNIES

Over the years, anxiety had become a part of my daily life. I had given it a cosy environment to thrive in between my demanding work life, broken marriage and the resulting depression. It started years ago, like a seed that had been planted deep inside. And over the years it grew, spreading its invasive roots throughout me. The drugs that had once helped me fend off the nervous twinges and suffocating attacks were no longer there to see me through an episode. I had quit the drugs, but the anxiety hadn't quit me. I could still feel its strong grip. It would start by squeezing my lungs and tightening my breath and then an inevitable layer of invisible bricks would begin to pile up on my chest. Next came feelings of fear and doom: my fingers would tingle, I'd get dizzy and my ears would ring. Now there were no little white, orange or blue pills to stop it, I had to figure out how to deal with it on my own. I missed the pills, but then again, I didn't miss the rage, mood swings, booze cravings and numbness. I didn't miss the way the side effects twisted me into an unrecognizable monster that had ultimately shattered my entire existence. I was going to have to learn to live with anxiety and I was going to have to learn how to do it prescription-free.

I tried yoga and breathing exercises. I tried acupuncture, aromatherapy and homeopathic sprays, mists and drops. Nothing took the edge off like the pills had. How quickly I had fallen into the delicious clutch of those drugs; how long it was taking me to remove the grasp of the great angst that had burrowed into a home inside me.

One day, recognizing my ongoing battle, my aunt gave me a small Ziploc bag of marijuana. She suggested that it might 'take the edge off' in a more organic and non-addictive way.

'Give it a shot; a little grass never hurt anybody. And it'll help you sleep like a baby.'

I was a strait-laced girl (at least until my love affair with prescription drugs began). And at thirty-three, I had never even smoked pot. The polar opposite to my sister, who started experimenting with drugs at fourteen. It was easy enough to get hold of in rural Maine; plenty of people were quietly growing it all over the place, but I just never had an interest, or maybe I had a greater interest in being nothing like my wild-child sister. The thoughtful donation was more intimidating than exciting. I was a pot virgin; I had no idea how to roll a joint or even how to hold the damn thing, much less inhale. If only my sister could see me now, fumbling around with this bag full of weed with no idea what to do with it. In my mind I could hear her laughing at me the way she had so many times before, the tone of her cackle laced with delight at my foolishness. I envisioned her in my mind, knowing just what to do with this stuff; rolling a big fat joint like a seasoned pro, lighting it up, taking a few big tokes and blowing smoke rings out of her mouth into my face, laughing all the way. She often seemed to find a strange joy in her occasional ability to make me feel feeble. I imagine it made her feel equal in some way, as the younger sister being wiser than her older sibling – comforting, even. Again I could almost hear her in my head, laughing. I could feel my face flush, my stomach uneasy. So I stuffed the small bag of weed into a Band-Aid box and hid it in my bedside table in the cabin.

The 150-year-old barn at my parents' farm had once been a dairy barn way back in the day. The old milk house was a square outcropping attached to the barn and had been converted into a summer kitchen. It was minimally furnished with a table and a few unsteady chairs that had been collected (often handed over for free) over time, not to be trusted to sit in for long stretches. There were a few aluminium pendant lamps hanging from the ceiling by extension cords, though – thanks to the squirrels that chewed through the wires – only a few actually worked. An old glass-front refrigerator and large two-bay stainless-steel sink had been salvaged from my restaurant when we were renovating and the custom pine counter with open shelving below had been made by my mother from some cheap wood that had been milled just up the road and lacquered with coats of polyurethane. There were mismatched sets of flea market dishes, platters, bowls and silverware that had been scavenged or given away, a vintage stand mixer, an old-fashioned egg beater, a crock filled with weathered wooden spoons and a few canisters filled with flour and sugar. My mother had softened the cold concrete floor with a coat of paint and an area rug that had been peed on at some point by one of the dogs – too nice to throw out, now suitable for barn use. She was always good at making something great out of so little. And last but not least, there was the four-burner GE electric range that had been in my apartment, the one I had started the supper club with a few years ago. Tom was happy to junk the old stove when we upgraded to a fancy induction range. I had been vocal about my sentimental love for the stove, but he didn't give a shit. But my mother was delighted to give the stove a new life in an old space.

The milk house summer kitchen was a happy place for me, a playroom of sorts. I could cook a simple meal for myself with fresh vegetables from the garden and eggs from the coop, or whip up a special treat for Penney on occasion, usually a sauté of some freezer-burned meat from our chest freezer with some cooked oats and carrots, topped with a dollop of yogurt. Uninterrupted and barefoot, with the summer breeze blowing through the open screens, I'd listen to old records that I had pulled from my parents' collection that was filled with albums that took them back to 'the good old days'. I began to discover that maybe being alone didn't have to feel so fearsome. I could be in that kitchen, with my good old stove, my good old dog at my feet, the crackle of Stevie Nicks in my ear and experiment with things like elderflower fritters, taking blossoms that I had foraged from the tree by the edge of the pond, dredging them in a batter of flour, icing sugar and soda water, frying them until the blossom turned golden brown, then sprinkling them with a bit more sugar before devouring the sweet, crispy treat. I found a scrap piece of marble that had been discarded by a neighbour – a bit imperfect with its cracks and stains, but perfect for turning out pastries and scones – and used it to hone a scone recipe, folding in candied ginger, brushing the buttery rounds with double cream, rolling them in simple white sugar, then baking them off into flaky pastries with crunchy sugared tops. I topped them with dollops of fresh cream and sweet strawberries that I picked at the pick-your-own-berry farm on nearby Raven Road.

Baking helped me relax. It gave me something to focus on while distracting me at the same time. I could use my hands, get lost for a moment and end up with something tangible and edible. One afternoon, I started to think about baking. And I started to think about relaxing. I started to think about baking *and* relaxing. I thought about the Ziploc baggie that was hiding in the Band-Aid box in my bedside table. I may not have known how to smoke, but I sure as hell knew how to bake.

In the summer kitchen I started collecting all the ingredients I would need: 225g butter; 250g dark chocolate chips, 200g white sugar; 200g dark brown sugar. I went into the chicken coop and gathered four freshly laid eggs. I measured out 250g plain flour and 25g Dutch-process cocoa. A couple teaspoons of vanilla and kosher salt – just a pinch or two. And the Ziploc bag of marijuana. I paused, staring at the ingredients, staring at the pot. I wondered if maybe Nina was the wise one all of those years, using a bit of organic weed to chase away all that was ailing her. I could almost hear her laugh.

'Well, here goes nothing,' I said out loud in Penney's direction, who was sprawled out on the kitchen floor, already in full relaxation mode.

In a small saucepan over low heat, I swirled the butter round and round, until it melted into a creamy yellow liquid, before removing the pan from the heat. I dumped the small green buds out onto the table and breathed in their pungent herbaceous fragrance before taking a vegetable knife to them, chiffonading them into a petite confetti. I added the chopped flowers – about a half cup or so – to the melted butter, gave it a stir and put the pan over very low heat, letting it steep and infuse. It was no different a technique than I had used a million times before at the Lost Kitchen, steeping creamy custard bases with chamomile tea, or sugary syrups with basil or rosemary for herbal sorbets, permeating a base with flavour.

In the top of a bain-marie I melted the chips of dark chocolate, then let it cool to room temperature. I saved a small handful of chips so I could dot them throughout the rich brownie batter so, in the oven, they would melt into the batter and make deliciously gooey chocolate ribbons.

I cracked the eggs into a small bowl, their yolks a rich orange hue – the sign of happy, healthy hens. I took the warm pan of butter from the stove and strained out the steeping bits through a fine-mesh sieve, pressing on them with the back of a wooden spoon to squeeze out every last drop of liquid. I whisked the fragrant butter into the eggs and added the vanilla, followed by a pinch of salt, before stirring in the cooled melted chocolate until the mixture was perfectly smooth. I took out a large mixing bowl and sifted together the flour and cocoa powder, then gently folded in the wet ingredients. I poured the batter into a parchment-paper-lined baking dish and, before I carefully placed it in the oven to bake, I ran my finger through the velvety batter and took a taste. It was rich and chocolaty, buttery and delicious, with hints of vanilla, salt and the green pine notes of the marijuana. I dipped my finger back in again for a second taste. *Not bad.* Maybe next time a pinch more salt, but not bad for a first try. I smoothed out the batter, licked the spatula clean and slid the baking dish into the oven. I set a timer for twenty-five minutes and began to clean up. The sides of the mixing bowl were lined with the remains of the batter. I used the rubber spatula like a squeegee to lick every last bit of batter from the bowl, just like I used to do with my mom when I was a kid. And like a kid, I watched the brownies baking in the oven, impatiently waiting for them to be ready. The edges began to puff, the surface began to crack and the timer went off. I pulled the pan from the oven and gave it good whack on the table, making the brownies more even and concentrated in their gooeyness.

The brownies needed to cool before being cut into, which was fine because I was suddenly starting to crave vanilla ice cream. Perfect, I thought. I'll make a run to Knox Ridge and grab a cone at my dad's old diner while I wait. I hopped in my car and took the five-minute drive to the restaurant where I had spent so many hours as a kid, as a teen and as a pregnant single young mom, slinging burgers and twisting cones. My father had sold the diner a few years back, but it remained virtually unchanged. I stepped up onto the wooden platform of the dairy bar and rang the bell that was located just next to the service window. The familiar buzz, unchanged, echoed from within. I ordered my small vanilla cone and paid with a handful of change. When the girl behind the counter handed it to me, I couldn't help admiring the perfect twists, just the way my dad had seared into me long ago.

'One, two, three twists – nice!' escaped my mouth. 'Hey, excuse me,' I continued. 'I think I'm craving some rainbow sprinkles. Would you mind throwing some on this cone?' The cone reappeared, covered in an explosion of colour. Red! Pink! Green! Yellow! Even blue and orange! It was so vibrant, so crazy beautiful.

'Wow!' I blurted out. 'So cool.'

I climbed back into my car, feeling strangely electrified about this kaleidoscopic cone in my hand. I couldn't wait to just put my mouth all over it. I made my way around the cone with my tongue. The ice cream was soft and cold and so creamy, so ridiculously, unbelievably, mind-blowingly creamy. It was the best fucking ice-cream cone I had ever eaten in my entire life. The sensation in my mouth was so pleasurable – sensual, even – and I couldn't help moaning with delight over how outrageously delicious it felt on my lips. *Wow*! I thought. *Fucking-so-good-wow*!

I made the slow and winding drive back toward Penney Road and I couldn't help noticing how good the rushing air from the open window felt on my skin, how clear and crisp the music wafting from my speakers sounded. The wind was good, the song was good and that cone – damn that cone! As I descended the final small hill before I'd take a right onto the familiar dirt road, it felt like I was on a carnival ride.

'*Wheeee!*' I shouted.

I realized then that there was no rush to get back to see if the brownies had cooled. Because I was already fucking stoned. High for the first time in my life at thirty-three. From brownie batter. And in a mile, I'd be back at my parents' house high, high, high. I started to feel paranoid and a bit freaked-out. Would they be pissed? *Could* they be pissed? Was I gonna get grounded?

The mile seemed to drag on for hours as my reality had become strangely skewed and slow moving. I managed to park my car. I managed to get out of my car. But I wasn't sure how much more I could manage because my deliciously luscious high had begun to turn. My hands and toes began to feel tingly and numb and my motor skills were off. I felt outside my own body, outside reality. I just needed to lie down. The sun had set, I was paranoid I couldn't hike my way down the hill to the cabin in the darkness in my stoned state. I lowered my sunglasses as I crossed my parents' driveway, thinking the shades would conceal my glassy half-mast eyes and I could just sneak onto their couch without them seeing me. Because I was wearing sunglasses, right? I did make it to the couch, but not unnoticed by my mother, who was in the kitchen. She came to the living room to check on me with the intuition that clearly something was up. My altered state got her worried. She was as paranoid as I was, but paranoid that I had taken something – a bottle of pills, maybe – trying to end my life again. I reassured her that I wasn't trying to kill myself and that it was just a case of wickedly spiced brownie batter that had a hold on me.

'Mom, I'm just stoned,' I told her. 'I don't want to be anymore. How do I shut it off?'

'You don't. You wait,' she said disapprovingly, before turning and marching back into the kitchen to ignore me for the next hour or two.

I stayed on the couch waiting for the crushing high to wear off. When I closed my eyes, it almost felt worse. I was nauseated and out of touch with reality. I even caught myself at one point sitting up, examining my hands, questioning, Did I black out and kill Tom? I was assured later after recounting my experience to Ivy that killing someone while high on marijuana was highly unlikely. 'It's a peaceful drug,' she promised.

The high did eventually wear off, a few hours later. Some of the drug's effects must have lingered inside of me, though, because when

I came to, I had a raging craving for something sweet. I found my mother in the kitchen eating dinner in solitude at the counter. She didn't have to say anything for me to know that she wasn't pleased with me. Her passive disapproval was not too dissimilar to the day I got kicked out of Sunday school as a kid. Like a kid, I rummaged through the kitchen cabinets and found a bag of marshmallows, a box of Nabisco graham crackers and a bar of milk chocolate. I took a skewer and pierced a marshmallow with its tip, turned the gas on the range to low and roasted it, turning it slowly. I could feel my mother's quiet and frustrated gaze behind me just as I heard my father come through the front door. It was past nine o'clock now and my dad was definitely buzzed from God knows how many beers, but tonight he was stoned *too*, his eyes bloodshot, his stagger slow and calm – happy, unlike that of a vodka-filled man. He flicked on the radio and joined me at the stove, placing a saucepan on the burner next to the one where I was spit-turning the marshmallow. He added a few tablespoons of olive oil to the pan, then added a layer of popcorn kernels. He covered the pan and started to shake it in a slow circular motion around the flame, whistling little high-pitched tunes of merriment along with the radio. It reminded me of that day at the diner when I was a kid, seeing him joyfully whistle away, on the line next to his father as they flipped pancakes over the griddle. Now here we were, father and daughter, popping popcorn and making stovetop s'mores, a bit stoned, but at peace with each other for the first time in a very long time. I joined him, whistling in harmony. We weren't the best of friends and maybe we never would be. We didn't see eye to eye, but maybe, just maybe, this seemingly inimitable moment could help us find a way as father and daughter.

The next morning I awoke to discover the mess I had neglected to clean up in the summer kitchen. I stuffed the untouched brownies into the trash, vowing to never do that again. I hoped my dad and I would see more of each other as we had the night before, but maybe through a bit less of a haze.

26

POTHOLES AND PAVEMENT

My dad's Ford truck was a beast. It was big, clunky and the suspension so stiff and heavy that it would jostle me around the cab like a rag doll when I passed over the many potholes of Penney Road. It took effort to climb up into the cab and I'd have to sit on the very edge of the bench seat to even come close to reaching the pedals. It was a struggle to drive and I hated the way it made me feel weak and small. At the mercy of something bigger and stronger than me.

I had never hitched up, trailered or towed anything before and a twenty-four-foot Airstream was not going to be the easiest place to start. My dad had mad trailering skills. He had years of practice under his belt and plenty of time to teach and share his knowledge with me. However, when I leaned on him for guidance, I realized that what he didn't have was any interest in doing so. 'Figure it out,' he told me, flat and firm. The response was a familiar one: *Figure it out* was his generic reply to blow me off. His interest and patience levels were low when it came to teaching, explaining or spending time with me.

Things had gone down similarly when I was learning to drive my first car, a 1984 VW Rabbit convertible. I was sixteen years old and had no idea how to drive a manual five-speed when my father delivered the old thing home to me one afternoon.

'Can you show me?' I asked.

'Figure it out,' he told me before he hopped into his truck. 'Take it for a drive. What's the worst thing that can happen? You'll burn the clutch out, then you'll just have to buy yourself a new one,' he told me nonchalantly before speeding off to the general store for a case of Budweiser, leaving a trail of dust in his wake. I couldn't afford a new clutch. But I also couldn't afford to wait for him to miraculously find the interest in teaching me. My mother's fragile hands and worrisome mind were consumed with the teenage tumbledown of my sister, Nina. Keeping her in line was a full-time job for my mom and one my father wasn't equipped to help with. My father saw emotions as a sign of weakness and weakness was not masculine. He had been raised to ignore emotion and bury it deep, because that's what a man does. So when the day came that his younger daughter became an emotional wreck, he did what he was taught: he ignored it, buried it deep. The responsibility fell heavy on my mother's shoulders instead. I kept my asks of my mother to a minimum, sympathizing with her struggles to keep my sister on the rails. I could feel that the wheels of this car might offer me a bit of freedom to escape the cloudiness of our home for brief, needed moments. But I'd have to learn how to make the car go on my own. So the only thing to do was to just start trying and hope I learned quickly. Maybe the wheels were just enabling me to ignore and bury my emotions and anxiety too. We were all coping in our own quiet ways.

It took me twenty minutes before I was finally able to get the car out of the yard, though it felt like hours. I worked tirelessly to find the release spot on the clutch in first gear as the car would lunge and sputter and come to a violent stop. Then I'd have to start all over again. When I finally managed to make a successful start and accelerate the car out of the driveway, I was relieved to discover how much easier it got once I got rolling. From first gear to second, then second to third with a bit of a grind, I flew over the potholes and threw the car into fourth gear, afraid to slow down and afraid to stall out. I cruised along the entire mile-long stretch of Penney Road until I saw the stop sign. I began to anticipate the stop and stall-out that would inevitably happen in a few hundred yards. The wafting cloud of burned-clutch smell caught up with me as I came to a full and complete stop. I checked my rearview mirror for the rare chance of a car behind me before I attempted a few more failed starts from first gear. My heart nervously sputtering, the burning-clutch smell growing stronger. I finally got the car going again and sped along, aiming to just keep the thing moving. For the next few hours I just drove. I drove and I drove and I drove, avoiding any main roads and sticking to the series of dirt roads that surrounded our house. I looped around quiet wooded bends, past bubbling brooks, up and over hills, past open fields and old forgotten cemeteries. I messed up so many times. I ground down gears and I stalled over and over and over again, knowing that every time I was increasing the risk that I'd have to work all summer long to pay off the parts that would need replacing. I left ripped-up tire marks and long tail-like skids in the dirt along the way, but there wasn't a soul around to see it all go down. I started to feel free, confident, even a bit masculine with my little car. The burning smell began to fade and I got better turn by turn as I dropped the car into second gear then accelerated again and shifted up. I took my time at the occasional stop sign, working on smoothing the transition between clutch and gears, getting silkier by the mile. And when I was good and ready, I'd venture out onto the main roads, knowing that there would be no stopping me once I hit pavement.

Here we were, years later and I still didn't have time to wait for my father's tutelage or energy to waste seeking his attention. And now I was the daughter in the tumbledown turmoil, consuming my mother's hands and mind. And even if she knew how to trailer and tow, which she didn't, I sure as hell wasn't going to ask her. I was hell-bent on learning how to trailer this Airstream and getting out of this mess of my own making. I spent a few afternoons fiddling with the rig and all the metal bits that made up the hitch, trying to decipher which parts did what and how. Whenever I was stumped, I called Dave, who had trailered the old thing up from the Carolinas and had gotten a feel for how to manage the rig and he would walk me through it with patience and kindness, ensuring I was hooking it up properly. I practised backing up the truck, making my best attempt to get the ball as close to the socket in as few tries as possible. I'd inch the truck back in reverse, relying on intuition. After each move I'd put the truck in park and jump out to see what my manoeuvre had produced. I'd take note, climb back into the cab and reverse again, readjusting or inching closer before checking again and again and again and again. It was slow going, but eventually I could rule that hitch, hovering the socket over the ball in just a few moves. From there I would twist the heavy metal lever that lowered the trailer down onto the ball before locking the socket in place and attaching the electrical cord to illuminate the Airstream tail-lights. The sense of strength I felt when the entire weight of the trailer was in my hands – if that wasn't what having balls felt like, I couldn't imagine what else did.

The next great feat would be to learn how to tow and trailer the aluminium beast. I'd have to figure out how to handle it on the road, understand its braking, feel its acceleration points, discover how to make clean turns and most challenging of all, figure out how to back it up. Just like with my VW Rabbit, it came with practice, patience and trust in myself. No one was around to see all my failed efforts and fuckups; it was just me and my ripped-up tire marks and skids. In good time I was able to leave the safe back roads of Freedom, pull the old aluminium rig onto the paved roads and see if I could salvage what, if anything, was left of my life in the kitchen. I would set out on the road with my kitchen on wheels and take to fields and farms, greenhouses and barns, orchards under the stars and anywhere else anyone would adventure to join me. I had tables and chairs, some mismatched china and silver, an old propane stove, a vintage refrigerator and a couple of Weber grills too. I was only missing one thing. It was going to take a journey to regain custody of Jaim, to prove to the courts that I was a strong, true and able mother. Journeys take time and the first few miles of that journey were in my rearview mirror now, which at the very least was a steady start.

I set off early that Wednesday morning with Penney by my side in the cab of the beastly Ford, Airstream in tow over the bumpy dirt road. I was cautious not to go too fast, fearing that the tables I had built and piled in the bed of the truck would be thrown out, or that the old refrigerator that weighed a zillion tons would break free from the bolts that were fixing it to the inside wall of the trailer. I was headed for pavement for the first time, nervous and eager. I flicked my blinker switch to the right as we rolled up to the flashing stop light on the ridge. I gave a little wave as I passed the tractor shop, the convenience store and of course the diner. We headed east toward the coast, making our way down the hill past Ingraham's dairy farm, past all the wooded lanes and sharp narrow corners around Sanborn Pond. I could feel us getting closer to Belfast long before the cool salt air blew in from the ocean because my breath started to shorten and my stomach started to churn. Like Pavlov's dog, I felt an automatic response to approaching the town that was the epicentre of my pain. The restaurant was still there, but Tom had replaced it with some vegan so-cool-Southern California bullshit that served things like quinoa bowls, avocado toasts and 'massaged kale' (no offence to quinoa, avocado or kale). And my kid, the brightest star in my sky – my flesh, my blood, my everything – was living upstairs with the monster of a man who was keeping him from me. I wanted to shake, scream, cry – but I didn't. I buried it deep in my gut and just kept driving.

I turned onto Route 1 North. It took all the way to the bridge in Bucksport, twenty miles later, before my stomach and breath began to soften. A few miles further I couldn't help myself as I veered into the Bucksport McDonald's parking lot. I wasn't skilled enough to pull up to the drive-thru with this rig. Instead I parked along the outskirts of the lot in the easiest, most manoeuvrable spot, one where I wouldn't have to reverse. I counted out four dollars in change and ran inside to place my order – a Happy Meal with chicken nuggets, sweet-and-sour sauce and a chocolate milk. It was cheaper than the 'adult' meal and chocolate shake that I was really craving. Jaim loved chicken nuggets. Sweet-and-sour sauce and chocolate milk, too. I couldn't help thinking how much he would get a kick out of towing this aluminium spaceship over the roads. With Penney by his side, a box of chicken nuggets in his lap. A sticker the shape of Saturn was still on the passenger-side truck window, where Jaim had stuck it years ago. It made me smile sometimes and other times cry. No matter how deep I tried to bury it, my heart ached endlessly over how much I missed him. He had been with Tom full-time for months now, with the exception of a few court-allowed visits with supervised conditions. The brief time with him felt more like a punch in the gut than the 'kind' gesture Tom portrayed it to be: 'You're lucky I've let you see him at all.' And when our short visits would come to an end, Jaim would inevitably cling to me, melting into my body, which would in turn appear to upset Tom. I could hear Jaim's pleas echoing in my head alongside the everlasting vision of Tom prying him from my body. It was hard to feel anything but infinitely incomplete. I ate the nuggets in the truck, feeding Penney every other bite, my thoughts stuck on my missing kid, loathing the man who had ripped him away from me and frustrated with myself for my part in getting us here.

I took a right off Route 1, not too far beyond the McDonald's and headed toward Blue Hill. Just past the blueberry barrens, I began to make more precise turns as the roads began to narrow. A right-hand turn by the convenience store with the greenhouse on the corner, then past the Bagaduce Lunch and over the tidal river. Another right and then a quick left by the big barn with the plastic goose lamp in the second-story window and we were nearly there. The yellow lines disappeared from the road as we entered Brooksville and weaved our way around the sharp and narrow corners. The road ended when we T-boned with the Coastal Road and there it was, straight ahead: David's Folly Farm. It was a big white farmhouse with a huge three-story red barn – the place where I would host my very first dinner on wheels. I had passed their rustic and beautiful farm before, slowing my car to eye the big barn from the road before pulling into the neighbouring small bakery for a hot crusty loaf of wood-fired bread. The bread was worth driving hours for and the potential for this farm was obvious – a prime spot to host a big pop-up dinner. Like the underground suppers I had hosted in my apartment – but with all this space, even bigger! And as with the old supper-club dinners I had hosted dozens of times before, pay-as-you-please, bring your own bottle of wine. Guests could leave a suggested donation for the meal, affording me the cash to buy the ingredients and pay the friends I would need to pitch in to pull it all off. With the excitement of this grand dinner growing more real, I was thrilled to land in their yard and begin.

I pulled the truck and trailer into the dirt drive and bounced slowly over the first potholes I had seen on this journey since Freedom. The family who lived here were practically strangers, but I felt surprisingly at home already. I had met the Altmans only once before through a neighbourly friend-of-a-friend introduction and I wasted no time pitching them my wild idea of a big glorious dinner in their beautiful old barn. I could see the excitement in their eyes as they nodded their heads up and down in agreement, giving the green light for me to cook my little heart out on their farm. They were eager, excited and willing and I was over the moon for the chance to bring this dinner vision to life.

The lawn in front of the house was happily scattered with children's toys: buckets and spades, bats and balls, overturned tricycles and a swing hanging from an old maple tree. I carefully swung my caravan around and began to back it slowly into place, taking my time, cutting the wheel back and forth in a novice effort to nestle the Airstream nice and close to the large barn door. Only then did I realize how much the manoeuvring of the trailer in reverse felt like the push and pull of a boat tiller, turning the wheel in the opposite direction I wanted the trailer to go. Tillers made me think about Tom and thinking about Tom made my blood boil and made my heart feel like a scorched lump in my chest. But this time I was snapped back into a happy place when I saw a little boy, all of two years old, come whipping around the corner on a trike, bare-bottomed, head full of curly blond locks, with bright blue eyes and a big smile. He was followed by his four-year-old sister in a sundress, who was skipping barefoot with wild glee. A short parade of tabby barn cats followed close behind her. The kids were shrieking with excited delight as they greeted my caravan, as though it were a grand parade. Their mother, Emma, appeared in the doorway of the barn. She was a tall, rugged beauty, with a short brown bob and warm glow of softness. She smiled brightly and waved her arms with enthusiasm. Her husband, John, followed slowly behind the kids and kittens on his orange Kubota tractor and I could see immediately where the little one got his curls. I put the truck in park and hopped out. Emma approached and grabbed me as if we were old friends, giving me a hug so long and strong that I thought it would last forever or maybe pop a small rib out of place. No one had ever hugged me this hard, this long, and no one had been this happy to see me in as long as I could remember. Their kindness took me by surprise until I realized they had no idea what I was going through. They had no idea about the train-wreck-like state of my life. How refreshing it was not to feel judged, not to feel embarrassed or ashamed. Their ignorance of my messed-up world was a gift and for a moment I forgot about all the lawyers, the guardian-ad-litem and all the contention that was consuming my life. For the first time in a very long time I started to focus on the goodness that was in front of me and for a moment I thought I knew what normal could feel like again.

The Altmans took me in that night as if I were a long-lost sister, even though I was a near-stranger who had turned up at their door. They put me up in a small cabin on the edge of their vegetable garden, where they would occasionally house farm apprentices. They fed me a dinner of fried seafood from the Bagaduce Lunch with French fries and coleslaw. With fresh sheets – and miles between me and Freedom – it was a momentary feeling of heaven. Snuggled under the down duvet, surrounded by the hum of crickets and the murmur of goats settling in for the night, with Penney on the floor by my side, I fell asleep.

I awoke in the morning to the immediate reality and pressure of the task ahead – I had two days to prepare for the sixty guests who were coming to my first dinner since losing my restaurant in the not-too-far-away town of Belfast. But as much as I felt the need to panic, I was hungry to get back to doing what I loved. I looked forward to a day when I could pour my emotion into cooking and not into my private life. Emma came to pick me up at the cabin so we could make our way to the lower fields, where the Altmans' hens were frolicking in the pasture. We were followed by the kids, the kittens and Penney, too. John motored behind in his four-wheeler, bringing up the rear. Today we would be slaughtering thirty-two chickens to be served at the weekend's dinner. I straddled the wire fence that contained the flock and started herding and catching the hens as fast as I could. Catching the hens conjured up memories of my sister and me in our parents' henhouse. We spent hours playing in the barn and on hot days, looking for ways to stay cool, we would harass the hens for our own amusement. Because we discovered that if we grabbed them by the tail feathers, they would flap their wings wildly, giving us a fan of cool air on our faces. I continued to round up the hens with Emma, grabbing them one by one, holding their wings firmly and placing each one gently into the crates John had brought down on the back of the ATV. Once each crate was full, we caravanned back up the hill to a small aluminium trailer that the Altmans had transformed into a slaughterhouse. Inside was a simple setup with three metal kill cones, a vat of scalding hot water and a large plastic drum for defeathering. We decided John and Emma would kill their birds themselves and I, along with a neighbour from across the street, would gut and process them. The kids and kittens were hovering around our feet with excitement over all the commotion.

John placed the first chicken beak down into the cone, pulling the bird's neck through the bottom hole before grabbing its head and severing its carotid artery, jugular and windpipe with a quick swipe of his sharp knife. The warm blood drained into a bucket below. He took another chicken and did the same and then another. He let the three chickens rest for a few minutes, waiting for the steady trickle of dark blood to slowly come to a stop. He removed one hen from its cone, holding her by her feet and dipped the lifeless bird into the hot water, dunking and stirring for a few moments, which would make the feathers easier to remove. He pulled the wet limp bird from the water bath, steam rising from its body, and began to pull the feathers off by the handful until it was bare and fleshy. Then he took a pair of shears and clipped off the head and feet, the bright red comb and deep yellow claws falling to the floor of the trailer, forming a pile as he moved on to more birds. The kittens were starting to get especially excited, the kids too.

'What are we making, Dada?' one of the kids piped up.

'We're making chicken,' John casually responded as he continued, slitting the throat of another bird without pause.

'*Mmm!* I love chicken!' The little girl squealed with delight, counting all the ways she loved her chicken prepared and how much she'd look forward to the meal we'd make together with the bird that was dangling from John's hands.

I couldn't help pausing so I could hold on to this moment. Even with blood everywhere, heads and feet piled up on the ground, her pure understanding of death was shockingly beautiful. She was being raised with the knowledge of where her food came from. She would never mistake a tasteless, antibiotic-filled bird that had been sitting for weeks wrapped in plastic on a grocery-store shelf for one that had lived its life free in the field eating grubs and basking in the sunshine. She wouldn't flinch at the draining of its warm blood, the plunging of its lifeless body into hot water, the clumps of feathers being pulled from its fleshy skin or the extraction of its complex innards. Because that was how you make chicken. She would learn to cook it as her mother did – brined, roasted, fried or sautéed in butter. I wished for Jaim to be here now, to see and understand this. I could only imagine how Tom would spin it to the lawyers – the blood, the heads and feet piled up on the ground. What kind of a mother would do such a thing?! they would protest. And I'd respond, 'The good kind.'

Emma handed me a moist, fresh chicken and I scurried into the barn kitchen to take my part on our production line. We had set up a stainless-steel table with plastic cutting boards, a few sharp knives and a big plastic tub filled with ice water. I laid out the first chicken on my board and began to work my knife around the back end of the bird, making a V-shaped slit around its vent, careful not to puncture the intestines. The guts were still warm as I felt my way around inside the bird, locating the organs, then cupping my hand and moving it in a circular motion to help free the connective tissues from the cavity wall, just like my duck-farmer friend, Gina, had taught me a few years back. One crisp fall afternoon, Gina and I had single-handedly killed and gutted sixty-eight ducks, taking a few pauses to sip cold swigs of sparkling cider when we needed a break from the strong smell of the warm guts, or if I needed to pause to refine the technique. It was the first time I had ever killed a living thing with my own bare hands, feeling the warm blood trickle down my arms, watching the life fade away from the creatures' eyes. I hadn't forgotten that day and the feelings of simultaneous sadness and power, nor had I forgotten my way around a bird since. With my fingertips I dug into the rib cage, locating each lung and freeing it before grasping the top of the windpipe and tugging gently, with a bit of force, as I felt the pop and release. I pulled the innards from the bird and laid them out on the plastic board, spraying them gently with fresh water, then meticulously carving away the good bits to keep: the liver, for a silky smooth mousse to be served with slices of grilled bread. The gizzard for a rich and gelatinous stock. The heart to marinate and skewer with rosemary sprigs, then grill over a hot bed of coals – though the truth was, it would never make it past a raw snack for Penney.

I sprayed out the empty cavity and plopped the clean hen in the tub of ice water to chill while I kept working on the steady line of freshly plucked chickens that began to pile up. We killed, cleaned and bagged up thirty-two chickens that afternoon and the following day I would cut them up and add the breasts, legs, thighs and wings to a flavourful brine of salt, sugar, peppercorns, juniper berries and a few bay leaves, infusing them with flavour from the inside out. After a full night's soak, I'd gently poach the meat, then roll it in buttermilk, flour and ground cornflakes before frying it in a deep vat of hot vegetable oil. I'd serve the delicious brown pieces crispy and hot with a good sprinkle of Maldon salt to all sixty people on Friday. It was going to be the freshest and most beautiful chicken I had ever put my heart into. And if the best ingredient was love, then this was going to be one hell of a dinner.

My mother made the winding drive from Freedom to the farm and joined me in the cabin the eve before the big dinner. She was ever ready to pitch in any way she could, ensuring this thing would be a success. She was able and willing to do anything from setting tables to chopping herbs and slicing tomatoes. I needed this success and she did too. There was a lot riding on this dinner. It was more than a meal. It was a symbol and would be the beginning of proving that I was able, that I could keep cooking and find a way to make a living, make a life – proof that I was okay. This proof would only get me closer to my son and only get her closer to her grandson. There was little sleep to be had the night before the dinner. The anticipation keeping me tossing and turning. I awoke early that morning just as the sun began to peek through the trees. My mother was already up and sweeping the barn and putting the finishing touches on some hessian runners for the tables. My mind was swirling with the long checklist of things I had to accomplish before the carloads of guests would descend upon the farm at 6:00 P.M. I got dressed and pulled on my wellies, then left the cabin with an empty wicker basket to forage for some summer goodies for our feast. But first I stopped outside the cabin door to pick a few handfuls of fresh raspberries from the wild bramble for breakfast. Ripened by the warm summer sun, the flavour was sweet and bright in my mouth, awakening my taste buds for the day. That kind of pure raspberry flavour was rare and special and I savoured it for the split second it rested on my tongue.

I followed the tractor-flattened path through the vast back fields of the farm. Penney scampered ahead, sniffing and wagging her tail, turning back periodically to make sure I was still with her, still okay. I was okay. I stopped along the way to snip tiny white wild strawberry blossoms and munch on patches of ripe wild blue-berries. The air smelled of anise and warm hay, reminiscent of the way our back field smelled when I was a little girl. It brought me back to that place, where my sister and I ran barefoot through the fields of goldenrod. Where we spent countless afternoons playing in the hayloft with our cats, following the sounds of tiny mews to search out clutches of baby kittens hidden between the bales of hay in their warm nests. Where we sold eggs and vegetables from my mother's garden by the roadside along with preserving jars filled with big bouquets of white-and-pink pastel cosmos. Where we were innocent, happy and free. I pulled off my rubber boots, craving the feel of the earth under my feet. I had missed the warm crinkle of the dry summer grass between my toes. I paused to pick more wildflowers and I thought about all of the times I had vis-ited my mother's garden with an empty basket, returning to the kitchen with mounds of nasturtium, chives and oregano blossoms, all of which we'd sprinkle over whatever was coming out of the oven. I had let go of that girl when I met Tom because that wasn't the girl he seemed to want. He didn't want wild. He didn't want a dreamer. So I let go of her out of fear he wouldn't want me, out of fear he would discard me, as my father had. I had lost her, that girl who didn't care about chicken shit on her feet or mud on her clothes. I had been living some safe and sad version of someone else for far too long, trying to appease others.

Leaving my boots behind, I continued along the trail barefoot until I had walked so far that eventually the farm disappeared from view. The field was so peaceful that the only movement besides Penney's and mine was the light breeze that wafted over the tall grasses, swaying them back and forth, back and forth. I turned in slow circles, taking in the beautiful field. I inhaled the smell of the air. With each step I felt as though I were extending a hand toward that little girl I had left behind. I looked into her eyes and told her what no one else had – that she was perfect, that she was safe, that she was going to be okay. She put her hand in mine and simply said, '*I forgive you*'.

I walked a bit further along the path and came around the corner to discover the saltwater cove that hid at the back of the property. I took in the magical wonder of this beautiful, private spot nestled against pondlike, bluish-green water, surrounded by pine trees and a sandy beach. I made my way to the edge of the water as the tide was heading out and took a perch on a piece of driftwood. I pushed the coarse sand and pebbles around with my bare toes, enjoying their coolness. Penney had waded into the water and just stood there, contently cooling off her warm belly, wagging her tail all the while. I stood and stripped down to my underwear, then waded into the frigid salt water, crossing my arms and clutching my breasts, stopping when the water reached my navel, taking a deep breath. From here on out, I would open my eyes and ears and, most of all, my heart. I'd make a promise to live my life with authenticity and truth. Tonight's dinner would symbolize the eve of my rebirth.

DINNER at DAVID'S FOLLY FARM
BROOKSVILLE, MAINE

MENU
Little Island Oysters with Cucumber Mignonette
Fried Folly Farm Chicken
Heirloom Tomato & Basil Salad
New Potatoes with Mustard & Marjoram Vinaigrette
Buttermilk Biscuits with Jersey Butter & Honey
Maple Custard with Blue Hill Blueberries

Tonight we would celebrate honesty and simplicity. We would dine on salvaged barn board tables that I had built with my own two hands – I still had the splinters to prove it (plus a small scar on my upper right arm where the table saw kicked a piece of wood back at me). We would serve from vintage mismatched plates and silver that I had collected at tag sales over the summer, with napkins that my mother and I had sewn into neat little squares from scraps of fabric, using my grandmother's sewing machine. There were vases filled with wildflowers from the back field that I'd plucked that morning. We would feast on oysters – pulled fresh from the Bagaduce River just down the road – served with finely chopped cucumbers, shallots and fresh dill from the garden. There was the fried chicken, raised and slaughtered right here on the farm and an heirloom tomato salad with tomatoes picked just hours earlier from the hothouse, plus an assortment of basils from the garden, a drizzle of good olive oil and a sprinkle of flaky salt. We'd have tender new potatoes, freshly dug and dressed with a mustardy vinaigrette and sprinkled with fragrant marjoram. And big flaky buttermilk biscuits served with cultured local butter from the farmer's market and honey that was bottled across the street by the neighbour. We'd finish with sweet maple custards made from rich farm eggs and cream and garnished with local blueberries, dollops of whipped cream and the tiny strawberry blossoms I had collected that morning. Tonight, along with sixty guests, including a handful of faithful friends and my dear mother to help me set tables, slice tomatoes and pull the whole thing off, I secretly celebrated a rebirth. The old barn came alive that night with the sounds of laughter and the clinking of glasses. The candlelight flickered from the summer breeze that found its way through the airy space and from the bright conversation that bounced around the tables. I watched my dinner guests savouring dish after dish, devouring the chicken down to the bone, licking their fingers and pouring more wine before polishing off their desserts. The utter joy in the room was palpable. I had brought joy to this space and made a warm memory for my guests. As I looked across the room, my heart filled with pride, I caught a glimpse of John and Emma at the other end of the barn, with drinks in their hands, gazing across the room with pride in their eyes, because their barn, the place they called home, was bringing so many people so much joy in this moment. It was the first success I had felt in a very long time and proof I was surviving a storm that had tried so hard to drown me. And all I could think was: Look out. I was back and I was going to be better than ever.

PART FIVE

FREEDOM

27

LEAVES OF THREE

I was carrying on, moving forward, ploughing through the storm that my contentious divorce was pouring down on me and getting through it one off-the-beaten-path supper at a time. I was regaining my strength, rebuilding my life slowly and trying to prove to the courts that I was a worthy-enough woman to regain custody of my son, who was now twelve. Even though I was no longer using prescription drugs, I was stuck now, forever, with the stigma they had left behind. That one weak and unintentional moment in my life had stripped me of the one thing I felt I was put on this earth to do – be a mother. Between prepping for the dinners, cooking, packing up the Airstream and doing it all over again, my mind couldn't escape the inevitable question: Had I lost him forever? The thought of the answer being yes was heavy and horrifying enough and the gaping hole in my heart big enough, that I had no choice but to keep fighting to get him back. Stopping, at this point, would be crippling.

The summer rumbled on, as did I, hosting elaborate dinner after dinner in barns, on farms, under the shade of apple orchards and in wide-open fields. The wheels on that trailer kept me rolling forward. When I wasn't cooking, there were therapy sessions, legal appointments and court appearances. I was proving that I had kicked the drugs, that I was capable of working and that I was paving the way for a new and healthier life. And eventually it was enough for the court to rule against Tom and award me two days a week with Jaim, unsupervised, while our messy divorce lumbered on.

Jaim, too, had been deprived; I could feel it in our embraces. He hugged me harder, held my hand longer and stayed close by my side. It had damaged him and he had been robbed of moments together that we could never again recapture. I couldn't help growing a bitter resentment for Tom and all the things he had taken. I knew the depth of the scars in my heart from it all and feared how deep they were in Jaim's, hoping this wicked breakup hadn't completely ruined his sweet, kind soul. He didn't deserve it, any of it and here he was, a casualty of battle. There was goodness still to be found, though; we had the future to look forward to and a different outlook that reminded us both to love each other fiercely when we had the chance. Our precious moments together were no longer taken for granted. We would go swimming in the ocean, treat ourselves to ice-cream cones and look for the best spots for fry baskets. We'd go for walks down the dirt road with Penney or take day trips on the ferry to Vinalhaven just for the ride across the water. We'd walk the granite breakwater in Rockland or go to Owls Head to visit the transportation museum, but mostly to get a seven-napkin burger at the old general store.

But our well-spent time together would inevitably come to an end and both Jaim and I grappled with the excruciating transition and the departure. Jaim would clutch me, holding me like it was for dear life with embraces that would never end if he had the choice. I had to pretend to be upbeat about his going back to be with Tom; I had to conceal my tears and not break down, even when he cried. There were times when I couldn't control my tears during our handoffs, his hugs growing tighter. Tom would glare at me with his hateful slanted eyes, telling me I was too emotional – unstable, even. I couldn't help feeling that he vindictively revelled in my emotional moments, because his views of emotions were not dissimilar to my father's: emotion equated with weakness. He could run back to his lawyer and tell him that I cried, using my tears against me in court as evidence of instability, increasing the likelihood that he would retain custody. There were times when Tom would physically pry Jaim away, breaking the embrace he was desperately trying to maintain with his mother. In public parking lots, at petrol stations or wherever the highly visible meeting spot for transitioning was for the week. It all felt so wildly wrong and I feared the detriment it was causing Jaim and his psyche, worried the effects would last a lifetime. I watched him use Minecraft as an escape. The virtual world became a place where he could get lost for a bit, forget about his real world and build a new one from scratch and be lulled by simple chorded melodies. But he could dig only so deep and build only so high and eventually the game would end and he would be back to the reality of the fractured world we had created for him. *We* did this to him. It was *our* fault. My own feelings of helplessness were followed by self-blame and loathing I fought to fend off, out of fear of spiralling down again and losing him again. I used my weekly therapy sessions to sound off on all the pain I would feel when Tom would take Jaim back. I was learning that I'd have to change the way I internalized his departure to keep myself from going mad again.

When Jaim wasn't with me, I had to spend my time wisely, plotting my next work moves. I couldn't be transient forever. I'd have to put down some roots and build a life, for Jaim and me, from the ground up. Somewhere where Jaim and I could feel accepted, be ourselves, be understood and be okay. We needed a house to call home. We didn't need much to be happy, something simple would do. When I closed my eyes I could see it: an old clapboard farmhouse with peeling paint and a screen door that would creak when it opened in the summertime. I could see the wide pumpkin-pine floors that I could refinish with a good sanding and a fresh coat of glossy urethane to make them look like new, but they would still groan and grate to remind us they were more than a hundred years old. Maybe we'd even get some chickens and let them run around the yard, wild and free as they pleased, filling their bellies with grubs and worms from the grass. Yes, I could see it, I could feel it and I knew in my heart that we'd get there someday.

At the wheel of my dad's clunky truck, Airstream in tow, Jaim and I, with Penney between us, set off. Four Season Farm in Harborside was home to master gardeners Eliot Coleman and Barbara Damrosch. I was tickled that they agreed to my inquiry to use their farm and to host a few pop-up dinners there on an August weekend and even more so to have Jaim along for the ride. We made our way over a pine-lined road, passing fields of swaying goldenrod, rounding rocky coves and rolling through blueberry barrens before coming to the little dirt drive that took us to the famous farm. I parked our rig beside a sprawling field of Tuscan kale, unhitched and hunkered down for the evening, anticipating a long day to come the next morning. Tucked into our aluminium camper, we were cosy in our sleeping bags and slept like babies with the comfort of being together on this adventure.

I awoke the next morning to begin preparing for the evening's feast, excited to take in the land around us. We had to pick up freshly roasted coffee from the girls at 44 North in Deer Isle (Jaim even got to help roast it) and big bags of oysters to fetch from the Bagaduce River. On our way back to the farm, I slowed as we approached the beautiful horseshoe-shaped cove we had passed the day before. I could see hot-pink sea roses lining the shore and got to thinking that we could scavenge for wild goodies to embellish the dishes I had been creating in my mind. I parked and Jaim reached for my hand as we made our way toward the beach. Penney scampered along in front of us, splashing in the frigid waters with joy. We dug around the mud, wondering if we might be lucky enough to find a clam (we weren't), then skipped flat beach stones over the calm morning water. The waves from Eggemoggin Reach were rolling ever so softly in to the sand-and-stone beach and we could see a small sailboat drifting through the light fog, bouncing along the crests of salty water. It was a slice of Maine perfection straight out of a postcard or the Robert McCloskey book *One Morning in Maine*, which I had often read to Jaim before bed. It was the stuff dreams were made of and I took a deep breath to inhale that moment, tattooing it in my memory, never wanting to forget the freedom and contentment I felt as I watched Jaim digging happily in the sand and Penney splish-splashing in the waves. We were all okay, practically normal, crisisless, even joyful, as if the haze of hell that had been hovering over us had lifted like a quick fog. Our battle was far from over, but the short adventure we were on together let us momentarily feel it was. I was blissed out on the moment as I gathered wild mustard beans for salads from the high-tide mark, sea heather for a cocktail, perhaps and some wild rose hips for a savoury jam that I would pair with pork chops. I placed my treasures into my basket and spotted some wild purple thistle by the roadside that would look perfect arranged in a giant vase. Then, out of the corner of my eye, I spotted a spray of tall twigs with lime-green baubles – they were foreign to me and beautifully unique – the perfect complement to my thistle arrangement. I parted the hedge of weeds, pushed my way through the bramble and with my pruning shears in my back pocket, harvested a half-dozen stalks of the green gold. I slung the tall stalks over my shoulder, took another deep breath and lovingly cradled the stalks with their shiny leaves against my neck as I took in the warm scene of Jaim and Penney playing fetch at the water's edge. *Heaven.*

Back at the farm I began to play with my newfound goods, stuffing a giant clear vase with the thistle and mystery stalks I had collected. I played with the arrangement for a good ten minutes, pruning it carefully, while Jaim sat reading a book beside me. I wanted it to be perfect, like the day we had had together. As I finished arranging, rain began to fall. At first I didn't think anything of it – I had planned dinner in one of the greenhouses that housed the tomato crops on the property, envisioning the tables mingling romantically between the tomato plants, surrounded by the fresh and herbaceous smell of the vines. But, amplified through the structure, the rain hitting the clear plastic siding sounded more like a shooting range than a peaceful spatter. It continued to pour throughout the day and the more it rained, the muddier the path between the kitchen and the greenhouse became. My mother, who had come up to lend a hand, was sopping wet from running between the two. Jaim was no longer feeling so patient with my preoccupation with preparing for the dinner and I was increasingly feeling the stress of pulling it off. Our picture-perfect day had turned into a wet, muddy, loud mess.

I took one look at Jaim and my mom – grumpy, sopping – and knew the right thing to do was to send them home, back to Freedom. It pained me to part with Jaim, knowing that we had had so little time together, but a night like this called for a hot bath, a good movie and some popcorn for the kid. I hugged Jaim goodbye and just in time, my support staff arrived, a hardworking mix of friends lending their able hands. They helped me finish up my kitchen prep and set the tables and tend to last-minute details. As guests arrived, they mingled happily, seemingly unfazed by the sprinkling of rain that sounded like a thunderous downpour from within the greenhouse. They nibbled on bites of local cheese and bread, sipped on gin-and-tonics with farm-fresh cucumber and foraged sea rose petals and ogled my over-the-top floral display.

'That's quite an arrangement!' my friend Anne exclaimed as she was passing small canapés for guests on a silver tray. 'Is it a joke?'

'What do you mean, a joke?'

'Erin, it's fucking poison ivy!'

What? *No!* It couldn't be. This wasn't the 'leaves of three, let it be' shiny forest-floor covering I had grown up with, that my grandmother and mother taught me to avoid like the plague. This wasn't the evil plant that caused a bubbling red rash on my legs and ankles when I ran barefoot through the woods as a little girl, or all up my legs and ass the time I fell in the field in my sundress. This couldn't be the same thing! *Could it?*

'It grows different up here,' Anne explained. She told me a story about a camping trip she took with her family on the rugged coast somewhere in Penobscot County. After the tents had been pitched and the fireplace set, it was time to sit around the campfire and relax for the night. Anne set off to the edge of the woods to find herself the best stick so she could whittle it down into the most perfect marshmallow roasting stick of the summer. She was determined to make it a good one. She found the perfect stick, just-right thin and trimmed the end to a fine point with a jack knife. She placed a fluffy white marshmallow on the freshly whittled tip and placed it over the campfire in the perfect spot with the hottest coals. Anne turned the stick slowly, pretending it was on an automated spit, working with the coals of the wood fire to toast the sugary delight to the perfect golden brown, crunchy on the outside, soft and sweet and melty on the inside. She stuffed the puffed, gooey treat between a few graham crackers and a square of milk chocolate, proclaiming quietly in her mind that this might just be the finest one she had made this season. She savoured each delicious bite, taking in the flavourful aromas of the woodsmoke as she swallowed. And in the morning, she awoke to find her face and throat completely swollen and red because she had, indeed, whittled a marshmallow stick out of poison ivy wood.

It was fucking poison ivy and I had made a great big, gigantic, beautiful bouquet of it. I had lugged the stuff to the car tucked under my neck. I had pruned it with my bare hands. I was covered with the poisonous oils and by morning I would surely be covered in red rashes. The thought of it immediately made me start to itch all over. But the damage was done and all I could do was continue on with dinner, calmly discourage guests from approaching the lush arrangement and sleep the day off in the Airstream, alone. My cravings to settle down, find a real home to call my own and a kitchen to practise my craft grew stronger as the itches on my neck and arms did too. The poison ivy was reminding me that my struggles were not over, that there was still such a long way to go.

But despite the big step backward that evening, I had made it further than I ever imagined. I made a list in my head of all that I'd accomplished as the rain drummed all night on my aluminium shell to keep my mind off my itching skin:

This summer I:

Learned how to build a good fire, with good draw, to keep warm on cold Maine mornings.

Used a table saw for the first time and built eight tables from reclaimed boards. Have the splinters to prove it and luckily all my fingers too.

Gutted a 1965 Airstream with my bare hands and turned it into a mobile kitchen.

Learned how to drive and tow a twenty-four-foot trailer with a big-ass truck.

Cooked my heart out in a barn, in an apple orchard and in a greenhouse in the pouring rain. Made some people smile, brought some people joy.

Kicked my prescription-drug addiction. Swore to never touch another Xanax or Klonopin, upper or downer again. (Got high on pot brownies for the first time ever – won't do that again.)

Adopted a dog. Still questioning who saved whom.

Walked barefoot through a field, swam in the ocean, found myself.

Got my son back.

28

TAKE ME BACK

Second chances in a small town seemed to be few and far between. Heck, even first chances were something of an anomaly. But Freedom had taken me back, over and over again. It had let me grow up, barefoot and free as a little girl, then given me the space to learn and work and discover. It had given me a place to come home to and give birth to my son, allowing us the safety and simplicity we needed in a complex time. And then once more, it gave me the space to restore and rebuild myself from the inside out. Freedom was my home and it was always there for me when I was in need. I could see it now – my heart had been here all along and there was a good life to be had in this tiny town in the middle of nowhere. Freedom had been giving me hundreds of chances – it was I who had yet to give it one.

I wasn't the only broken and lonely soul in Freedom: there was the old mill. The one my sister and I would parade past every Fourth of July in our retired dance recital costumes from the year before. The sad and neglected structure listed dangerously to one side, its rusted metal roof warped from the many years it had been forgotten. It appeared as if it could collapse with a single gust of wind or wash away into Sandy Stream, which flowed beside it. Until it got its second chance.

The cavernous mess of a building had been long forgotten and was in such disrepair that anyone would cringe at the thought of bringing it back to life. A project to restore the mill would be daunting, take at least a few years' time and – well – some might say was just plain crazy even to entertain. The crumbling heap of old wood wasn't for the faint of heart or for those looking to make a quick and easy investment. It could only be for someone who saw something that nobody else did, someone whose heart was bigger than their logic. It was for someone who believed in leaving things in the world a bit better than they found them, someone who believed in second chances. That someone was Tony Grassi.

The quiet rumours had been spreading around town about the old mill's restoration, the same way they had about me. I first caught a whiff of the giant undertaking while I still had the restaurant in Belfast. My friend and farmer, Polly, had come by that morning to drop off goods from her farm and casually mentioned the mill and her in-laws' plans to breathe new life into it. Villageside Farm, which she ran with her husband, Prentice, sat on the land behind Sandy Pond, which abutted the plot where the old mill sat crumbling. As she handed me bags full of baby lettuce heads and microgreens that I stuffed into the refrigerator, she said: 'If you know of anyone who might be interested, they'd be looking for a tenant.' It was welcome news that the old building at the centre of my hometown was finally getting some long-overdue love. I had always been intrigued by the place, eerie as it was, perched at the top of Mill Street on its massive granite-block foundation. I had been forbidden to get close to it when I was a girl, since it looked like it could topple over at any time. But it was always the tiniest bit romantic to me, the way it sat next to the cascading water of Freedom Falls. Polly continued, telling me about the restoration and how it would take a team of historians, architects and contractors led by her in-laws, who wanted to create a space for people to gather. I was flattered that she would think of me as a potential candidate – a second restaurant, perhaps.

It sounded like a dream. But I told her that I was all set, satisfied with the restaurant I had just built from nothing – and I wasn't exactly lying. But I also didn't mention the fact that my marriage was crumbling. That I was working eighteen hours a day, pumping myself full of prescription drugs and alcohol just to keep going. I was barely staying afloat; opening a second restaurant was out of the question.

But a year had passed now. Life had changed dramatically. My restaurant was gone and so was my marriage. I was back living on Penney Road, penniless. I had lost everything, but that also meant I had nothing to lose.

A lot had changed in a year for the mill, too. It had been through its own rehab; stripped down to its bare beams, its dead shingles removed, the rot exposed and taken out. It had taken a village of timber framers, stonemasons, engineers and carpenters to get it back in line with the shape it had once been. And when its timbers were finally back in alignment, it was as if it sighed with relief. At heart the structure had been strong enough to keep it standing, bolstered by the power of its granite foundation. Tony had seen that strength and possibility, seen the way it could breathe new life into the sleepy little town and support the agriculture that rooted people there. His wife, Sally, stood behind him, never questioning her husband's crazy notion.

The mill sat quiet and peaceful that late summer evening. The construction crew had gone home for the night. The stream filled the air with a quiet white noise and all around me were the scents of cedar and pine wafting from the fresh shingle exterior. There was still work to do on the building, but the majority of it had been done. The front doors were unlocked and slightly ajar; there was nothing inside except sawdust that floated across the floor with the breeze as I came in. And as I made my way into the interior of the place I had long been forbidden to go, a warm feeling came over me. Gone were the jagged panes of broken windows, the gashes of spray paint and the scents of urine and warm beer. Instead the six windows that lined the empty room let in soft light through their new panes. The walls and floors, made of reclaimed barn board, filled the space with their freshly hewn smell. It had been reborn. And I knew in this moment that I had found it: a new home for the Lost Kitchen.

I could see the tables scattered around the room, one by each of the windows so you could feel the breeze roll on a warm summer's night and watch the warm candlelight flicker against orange dusk. I could see the kitchen, set in the centre of the room where I could cook as though entertaining guests in my very own home. There would be a counter with a few stools for friends to sit and watch me tend the stove. I could float from table to table serving small bites that came fresh from the oven. Soft music would meld with the sound of the stream outside and bounce around the old pulleys in the ceiling that were still intact from the sawmill days. And flowers, of course. So many flowers! There would be bud vases on the tables and big foraged arrangements wherever I could fit them on the counter. I would display a collection of cookbooks and dot the room with tiny lamps when the moonlight wasn't enough. I envisioned where a big cast-iron enamelled farm sink could go, with a vintage refrigerator alongside. It would look as though they had always been there, had never spent a moment discarded or forgotten. I was dreaming with all my heart now, for the first time, as if Freedom was where I belonged.

The idea was crazy – a restaurant in the middle of nowhere, in a town of fewer than eight hundred people. Would people drive to Freedom for something as simple as a supper? I didn't know and if I stopped long enough to think about it, I feared I'd start doubting myself. Just keep going, girl, I told myself. Put your head down and your heart into it; you'll know what to do – you'll feel it in your bones. It was the nicest thing I had said to myself and truly believed in a long time.

It would take more than convincing myself, though. I knew that the odds were not in my favour and that the rumours were still flying around me like a swarm of torturous blackflies: I heard she's completely nuts! I heard she abandoned her restaurant and kid! I heard she clawed his eyes out! I heard she slit her own throat! One afternoon we sat in a set of folding chairs in the corner of the nearly finished mill – Tony, Sally and me, with Dave and Ivy by my side to lend me their support and to show Tony and Sally that I couldn't be the girl the rumours had described. Surely if I was flanked by my competent and level-headed friends I could be taken seriously, no matter how nutty the idea I was about to present to them. So I began, painting the picture for them that I saw in my mind. There were moments when I heard my own words and wondered if I really was crazy. But my pounding heart kept me pushing this big, bold idea around the room. I finished. I paused. I smiled a bit nervously. They nodded, smiled and asked to take a think on it. We would reconvene in a week's time and they would give me their decision then. I couldn't tell what they were thinking. They were both so polite, patiently listening to my dreamy rant. If it was meant to be then it would be and if it wasn't, it wouldn't. Either way I was counting each breath, waiting for the week to go by.

Logic is the death of dreams. And it turned out that Tony and Sally favoured dreams . . . and second chances. We shook hands in agreement, them taking a chance on a girl fresh out of rehab in the thick of custody hearings with not a penny to her name and me with an opportunity in a place that defied everything I knew to be true. We shoved all logic aside and we bet on visions and second chances, giving the Lost Kitchen, the old mill and me with it, a new life in Freedom.

29

STARTING FROM SCRATCH

Starting over from the beginning and building a restaurant from the ground up – in the middle of nowhere, no less – was a daunting task to consider. I was a woman in a male-dominated industry with no culinary degree and a tattered past that I was still fighting to recover from. Even after a year's time, my divorce was still painfully carrying on with no clear end in sight, adding a messy twist to the already-challenging task. But I had done it once before and that made this time around feel a little more focused. Even so, there was an entire kitchen to build, tables to make, chairs to pick out and paint, licences and permits to put in place, equipment to secure – not to mention the worry of how I was going to pay for it all. There was staffing to manage, menus to plan and lists of things I'd need but really couldn't afford. I'd need to build a walk-in refrigerator, buy an expensive commercial dishwasher, a three-bay sink, a sturdy stove and a hood with good ventilation and a fire-suppression kit that was mandatory – and pricey. Not to mention all the other small gadgets that would amount to a rather large list. I had lost every pot, pan, whisk and spoon the day Tom changed the locks. I might not have had the kind of money you'd need to open a restaurant, but I wasn't about to let that reality crush my dreams now. I was a born-and-bred Mainer, which meant I had scrappy Yankee frugality pulsing through my veins. I found ways to do things on the cheap and raised money to buy the things I couldn't skimp on. I begged and borrowed bits of money from friends and family who saw a glimmer of promise in me, pledging payback with good meals in exchange. I took donated pots and pans and old stand mixers that people didn't want or need anymore. My father even donated a dinged and dented food processor that needed to be pressed just so in order to turn on – and was so dangerous that I had to remind myself to make sure my hands were clear of the blade when I used it. I went to every flea market and antique store in a fifty-mile radius and collected old platters and plates, cups and saucers, a sturdy juicer and a set of copper colanders, secretly hoping that Tom had pawned my grandmother's dishes to make a few bucks and that I'd find them. I didn't, but I did find vintage silverware for a buck apiece that would shine up just fine with a little elbow grease. I found a big old porcelain farmhouse double sink with pedestal legs for sale in a classified ad and an old Frigidaire icebox from the fifties that still ran like a charm. I found that with a few crisp dollar bills in your hand you could easily bargain with the seller and beat the price down. I found an old Hoosier baking cabinet that was tired and in need of repair, which made it a prime candidate for negotiating a better price. I'd strip it, sand it and give it a fresh coat of charcoal paint along with a set of porcelain draw pulls to match its enamel top. I could already see the shiny glassware that would line its shelves.

There was a rumour floating around the dirt roads of Freedom that my high school maths teacher, who lived a mere three miles away, was in the process of tearing down his barn. I took the short ride down the street to find out and I could see it was true when I pulled into the front yard. Instead of pouring loads of money into saving the old structure, he was letting it go. The death of this barn meant its boards were being removed piece by piece in order to be repurposed. The thick floorboards stretched some fourteen feet and would be perfect for a long table that would sit at the centre of the dining room. If you looked close enough, you could make out hoofprints in the wood. I could see people mingling by candlelight at this rustic table while they laughed, sipped on wine and feasted on course after course – at this table strangers would become friends.

The thinner, weathered wall boards could be transformed into an island for the homelike kitchen I was envisioning, topped with a poured-concrete countertop to make a functional yet cosy space to assemble dishes and serve them to guests mere feet away. When you throw a good party, it's inevitable that everyone ends up hanging in the kitchen. The kitchen is the beating heart in any home. That's what I wanted my kitchen to feel like. Just like home. I wanted my stove smack dab in the middle of the room for all to see and feel. I wanted to mix and mingle with guests between plating courses and serving soups and salads. I wanted them to hear the sizzles, catch glimpses of flames from the stovetop and smell the aromas of the ingredients I was preparing wafting through the air. I wanted to see the joy on their faces as they tasted each bite, because witnessing that joy filled my heart and all the empty holes it had in it. I wanted to be able to feel the energy of the room and gauge the subtle changes that would make the evening feel perfect, like turning up the music a bit when appropriate, dimming the lights as the sun set, or flicking on a fan or two on a warm evening. I wanted to do more than cook: I wanted to serve; I wanted to entertain and host; I wanted to take in strangers and feed them my love on a plate. As a woman, I felt a most innate joy in caring for people. Something that felt so natural to me, something that I craved to do.

I had built a restaurant from scratch before, but this time it felt like there was more to prove. There were people who had loved the good bit of gossip I had given them to chew on and enjoyed watching my tumbledown – wouldn't they just love a little more?

Tom appeared to be all too eager to dig an even deeper hole for me. He seemed to be making efforts to amplify my faults around town, hoping it would reach the ears of anyone he thought might support or believe in my efforts to start all over again. But if I could pull off something so nearly impossible, build a real business and make a good life right here in Freedom, there was no judge or court or asshole soon-to-be-ex who could testify that I wasn't capable enough to be responsible for my own flesh-and-blood son. My entire life was on the line, whether I liked it or not. So I would fight, I would rise, I would show him, I would show the world, but most of all, I would show myself what I was made of and I would show Tom that without him my life was happier, healthier, stronger and better than ever.

I wasn't a chef; I was a good, simple cook. I could sear up a good piece of fish with potatoes like my grandfather; I could make an old-fashioned butter cake with rhubarb and a thick custard sauce that reminded me of my grandmother. My knife skills were sub-par at best and I had no idea what the eff *mise-en-place* or *garde-manger* was. I knew butter, I knew salt and I knew how to dress a salad with the just-so amount of vinaigrette and whip cream to a faultless glossy peak to stand soft and proud atop a creamy pudding or pie. I made food that reminded me of my mother, food that reminded me of my father, food that made me feel close to my grandparents, even though they had both been gone for a few years now. I could still feel her hug, I could still hear his whistle and the spicy taste of nasturtiums, beetroot greens with a splash of vinegar, mashed potatoes with butter and salt and pepper, fresh ripe strawberries dusted with a spoonful of sugar and drizzled with a bit of fresh thick cream – with one taste I could feel them still. Their memories lived on with every bite. I could remember the songs he would sing, her laugh and infectious smile, the crow's-feet wrinkles in the corners their eyes. Their warmth, their love, the feelings and the memories they gave me with those soft and comforting dishes. It was the power of good, simple food. It was the food I wanted to cook and the way I wanted to make people feel: nostalgic and loved. Nothing sous-vided, nothing frothed or foamed or forced or trying to be the best award-winning anything. It wasn't cutting-edge, it wasn't sprinkled with gold flecks or garnished using tweezers. It was food that, with one bite, swaddled you, reminding you of your childhood, of someone you loved and of the one, the few, or the many sweet moments they gave you. It was as humble as new potatoes, fresh from the ground on a hot early-July day, creamy and sweet, their skins so soft and tender that all you wanted was a pinch of good crusty salt and a pat of butter to melt over the top of them, maybe a sprinkle of fresh dill if you were feeling fancy. It was tomatoes, ripe, tender and sweet as the fruit they were, fresh off the vine, still warm from the summer morning sun, needing only a drizzle of olive oil, a pinch of salt and a few shreds of fresh basil. It was a good shard of cheese atop a slice of crusty just-baked bread, with a dollop of creamy honey or a slather of sweet berry jam. Because long after a plate had been licked clean, it was the way you felt while you were eating it that carried on for days, months, years. For me food wasn't a competition about who could make the best dish. Its greatest power was to take taste and turn it into a long-lasting memory. As a girl, I had learned from my father that good food could be a vessel, a way to show love, even when you might not have the words to say so. I could feel in my soul that this was exactly what I was meant to do now, but the question remained: If I built it, would they come?

We opened on the Fourth of July. It felt fitting: Independence Day in Freedom. Twenty-five years before I was parading past this very spot on this very day with my sister in the annual Freedom Field

Day parade wearing a cancan costume, staring up at the crumbling heap of a mill as we passed by. Never in my wildest dreams could I have imagined I'd be standing within the old place, reborn now, housing this wild idea of a restaurant with me at the helm, about to embark on a voyage into the unknown. I had no idea if it would sink or float, so all I could do was cook my heart out and see what would come of it. I would put every ounce of my love on each and every plate and garnish it with a tender sprinkling of edible blossoms. It was simple, honest, feminine and so very me. The room was full that night, flooded with familiar faces from the first restaurant and my supper club; people who were eager to get another taste of my cooking and were willing to drive to the middle of nowhere to get it – for some, a hundred miles. It was just as I had pictured it, but even more beautiful in real life: joyful chatter mingled with the sound of the waterfall outside and the light breeze blew through the open windows and kept the candlesticks fluttering. The air smelled like the ripe strawberries I had just picked that morning, before the July sun became too much to bear, now sitting in a big antique bowl on the side counter. Their telltale pink juices still stained my hands. And as I stood before the crowd of happy diners and raised my glass, clinking it with an old butter knife to get their attention before the start of the soup course, my heart pounded with a mix of nervousness and immense pride as I took in the smiling gazes of the crowd. I told my guests the story of the menu I had made for them that night, admitting to them my fear of soups, but that this one had come out damn good. Soups were complex to me, with their layers of ingredients, from the stock that took hours to build, to the intricate ingredients that had to be picked with care in order to create deep, nuanced flavour. (I omitted the fact that I believed the process always knocked me a little off-keel because I never believed I was good enough to accomplish it.) I told them about the organic chicken that had been raised by one of their servers this evening, Victoria, at her farm just a few miles away. That it had been brined overnight with bay leaves and juniper berries. We would finish with strawberry shortcake, the destination for those fragrant berries. I raised my glass high, suggesting a toast. The room followed, lifting their glasses of wine toward the ceiling, up toward the old weathered timbers and pulleys. We toasted to finding ourselves tonight in Freedom, the middle of nowhere, a place that was becoming more and more the centre of my universe.

30

WOMEN OF WALDO

I was quickly learning that just because I had opened a restaurant once before did not mean that it would be easier this time. There were systems to iron out, kinks to fix and help to groom. There were dishwashers who would call in sick, as well as equipment that would break down and produce that wouldn't show up on time. It was a moving vessel, like a sailing boat, where I had to stay agile, dealing with the wind and adjusting accordingly, trimming the sails until it was running tight and tidy. There would be days of smooth seas and days where the churning water threatened to engulf me for good. There were so many details, from the love and attention it took to produce each dish on the ever-changing menu to the days' worth of prep that went along with it. The candles had to be kept burning through the night, the music flowing to suit the room, the flowers fresh and vibrant, the toilet paper in the bathroom needed to start each evening with a perfectly folded point. Details, details, endless details. Wednesday through Saturday at five o'clock the front door would open and the show was on, the curtain was up, whether we were ready or not. My heart would start pounding at four, knowing the flood of guests would be lining up within the hour. Because we had built it and they were indeed coming – by the carload. Every night, booking out the tiny eight-table dining room. What so many had said was impossible was not only alive, it was thriving.

Almost overnight I was back in it, working sixteen- to eighteen-hour days again, sleeping little, eating even less. And on top of it all there was critique to put up with – people who would come to dinner and return home, sit at their computers and tell the world what they really thought of me through an online review. I'd pore over the comments, sometimes shedding a tear or two (or more, sometimes lying in bed, hating myself for all of my imperfections). I had put myself on a public platform by being in that open kitchen. And food was emotional, after all, so it seemed only natural that there would be feelings and thoughts to go along with it for all involved. Feeding people felt so personal and intimate and when I felt that I had faulted in some way, let someone down who had come through my door for a meal, it would ding my heart in a most personal, intimate way that felt so public and painful when I would read it online. I couldn't help but even feel shame on occasion. If I didn't want to be swallowed alive, I'd have to learn to not let it gouge me too deep. I'd have to restrain myself from responding through a public forum because I knew feeding haters would only give them power. I'd struggle to stay silent on the outside, but on the inside my mind would churn with thoughts and feelings. I'd have to learn from the inevitable negative comments, the shots at me, use them as a tool to look at myself real deep and ask myself, Is there something I can learn from what they are saying? Can I use it to make me stronger, better? And if there was a shred of truth or lesson to be learned from it, I'd take it, run with it and use it to improve whatever it was that I had effed up. But if someone was ripping on me for no good reason? Don't feed the haters, they bite. Shake it off, eff 'em and keep going, girl.

How would this time be different from the last? What would stop me from washing down anti-anxiety drugs with a swig of booze to allay the anxiety of all the same stressors that were coming back all over again? Not this time. This time was different. I was different and my toxic ex was out of the picture. I was cognisant of the importance of managing balance in life now, focused on rebuilding a better, happier and healthier life. And this time around, I had a village of support by my side to see me through it.

It was organic, the way that this village of women came to join me. We weren't sisters. We didn't share blood, but we each had our reasons and our own path that led us to this wild idea of a restaurant in the middle of nowhere. It was as if we were led to one another in an accidental way that was by no means an accident at all. We came together as old friends, some of us strangers, some friends of friends and neighbours living in the same rural Waldo County. Some who knew me and believed in me before and still believed in me now. Some who were just getting to know me but harboured no judgment over the gossip of my past. What we had in common was that we were all making and building a life here in this rural place that sometimes felt like the middle of nowhere and knowing that we weren't alone lent some sort of comforting strength. We were mothers, sisters, wives, farmers, makers and teachers. Each of us looking for just a little something to be a part of, to build and to be passionate about, to share and celebrate. And while none of us had been professional servers or sommeliers or had culinary degrees, we each brought a different strength to the table. Living in Maine can feel isolating and challenging, punctuated by hard work and hard seasons. It can eat you up and grind you down if you let it. We needed a village to lean on – craved it, even – whether we realized it or not. An epicentre at which to root ourselves, professionally and personally. As we quickly realized after opening the Lost Kitchen, this wasn't just a place to work; it was a good life. We found a sisterhood in what we had built, one that was emboldening us to burn brighter.

There was Anne, who would bring buckets of bolted brassicas and coriander to accent the evenings' dishes and keep the crew in stitches with her quick and witty jokes, reminding us never to take it all so seriously, occasionally reminding me about my poison ivy arrangement mishap. And Ginger, who would show up after a long day of working on her farm with a calming energy that always made the busy evening on the line feel a little more relaxed. She could plate salads so light and elegant that they looked like the leaves fell from clouds.

Gina slaughtered ducks by day on her poultry farm and helped fry the legs into a crispy confit at night. She was dedicated and driven and beneath all the toughness and tattoos was a heart so deep and warm I felt protected when she was around. The Flynn sisters would float about the dining room with their downright beauty and grace. Born-and-bred Mainers, they were pros waiting tables. Hell, they'd been doing it since they were young girls, just like me, which is how we met all those years ago. And there was Ashley, who had been helping me out since the quiet supper-club days. We were busier now, but still the same great friends. She'd spend her days growing fresh flowers on her farm and by night she worked the dining room as a server, setting dishes next to bud vases filled with the flowers she had herself grown from seed. It made us both so fucking proud.

There was Krista, who showed up looking to wait tables, but her knowledge of produce and her willingness to learn any task screamed that this girl belonged in the kitchen. Her farm would provide us with an endless garden of edible flowers. Each day she arrived at the restaurant for her evening shift with a wooden crate filled with jars upon jars of beautiful blossoms that we would dot on the dishes we were composing together. And then there was Heather, who walked through our doors with a huge fear: food.

It had literally become her enemy. When she touched gluten, her skin would break out in a fit of rashes. When she ate dairy, her stomach would twist in pain. She was on a mission to face her fears head-on by working in a kitchen, handling food every day. She had never shucked an oyster before, but became a pro and could shuck any dude behind a raw bar under his station. Food didn't scare her anymore.

Nancy arrived one morning with a basket full of big high-bush blueberries and plump gooseberries from her garden for sale. Her timing was impeccable: the fruit would be perfect for the evening's dessert and I was desperately seeking some extra help with a handful of daily random tasks. Without hesitation she jumped in, full-hearted, helping out in any way our little kitchen needed; from pressing linens and aprons to chopping herbs and prepping cookie dough, even greeting guests as they arrived for dinner with a kind smile and the evening's menu. And then there was sweet Katharine. By day she would prep with me in the kitchen, with her even-keeled spirit. By night she, too, would greet guests as they arrived, guiding them down to the wine cellar to grab a bottle or two to pair with the evening's menu.

Helen grew the most beautiful heirloom tomatoes you could imagine. Pinks, yellows, greens and a red variety so deep and rich it almost looked like chocolate. Each morning she'd bring bountiful boxes of the seasonal fruit into the kitchen for her prep shift, to be served that evening. She'd save me sometimes by tucking a baked good or a warm egg sandwich at my station to keep me fuelled for the long day ahead. A compassionate listener, she sometimes made early morning prep feel like free therapy to us both: chopping, listening, offering each other sage advice and occasionally having a good cry when needed at the shallot station.

Victoria raised organic chickens, tomatoes, peppers and every variety of basil that existed under the sun. She was a spreader of love, always checking in, making sure all was well. She'd keep us hydrated; our water bottles full – and our wineglasses when we needed it. Her nickname became Vicki Vino for the nighttime crew. Then there was Lauren, who started on prep at my first restaurant, then moved on to hostessing before she found her happy place working the wine cellar and helping serve dishes around the dining room. She'd salivate on both tenderloin and lamb-chop night, hoping for a scrap of nice rare meat at the end of her shift – which I'd always make good on in exchange for a bit of her dry humour, which would keep us giggling through the night. We were also entertained by Maia, who would fill us full of gossip and stories while polishing glassware before service. She had never waited tables before, but what did that matter? She'd learn, as we all were learning, how to walk softly in the dining room, set silverware down just so and to serve from the left, clear from the right. On warm August days she would bring us giant boxes stuffed with ripe wild blueberries from the barrens she farmed in the neighbouring town of Montville. Her heart was so deep and endlessly kind and her spirit so warm it could be felt around the room as she conversed at length with guests about where they came from and what they had in common, making them feel at home, like they were in somebody's home, having dinner and making a new friend.

Alex had the most fine-dining skills of any of us. She'd picked up her technique at other restaurants along the coast, but it was her natural, innate grace that made her shine in the dining room. She'd teach us all the fancy serving tricks she had. With an unflappable softness, she'd glide around the restaurant like a ballet dancer with her quiet steps and warm smile, gently placing fresh silverware or exchanging carafes of water without so much as disturbing the flicker of the candle on the table. Then there was Carey, who brought the most fine-kitchen skills. She had worked in some notable kitchens and came to us with more knife skills than the rest of us combined. She'd teach us fancy bits of chef lingo and formal kitchen protocol.

Aunt Rhoda, my dad's sister, managed the office, paying bills and taking care of payroll, license renewals and insurance. With my friend Dave by her side lending constant help with everything from formulating spreadsheets to accounting to tax advice. He had worked for IBM and was a computer wizard, putting systems into play that made the back office hum and answering every technical question we ever had without a moment's notice.

And behind each of these great women we had our one man, T.J. The drummer to our band, the keeper of the beat. T.J came to our rescue as our fearless dishwasher. He lived across the street from the mill with his schoolteacher wife and their two daughters. He was surrounded by women by day and it was certainly no different by night. As a result he was a hell of a good sport and being outnumbered didn't bother him one bit.

And then there was Nina, who had come to help me handle the reservations and phone lines, engaging with guests with her authentically bubbly people skills. She and I were sisters bound by blood, but there had been a long history of little warmth between us. Had we been given the choice, neither of us would have chosen the other. The truth was that we were night-and-day different, starting from the day we were born. My mother described me as a miserable baby. I was fussy, colicky and needy. I nursed a lot and slept little (my mother sleeping even less). I needed constant contact, whether it was being held, rocked, bounced up and down, or read to. Realizing that it didn't matter what she read to me, she read recipes from cookbooks while she bounced me on her hip in the kitchen. Then it only made sense that when I was a toddler she couldn't keep me out of the refrigerator, finally having to resort to duct-taping it closed.

Nina was born twenty-one months after me. She was an easy baby – perfect, even – although this would prove to be the antithesis of what she would become in her teenage years. She slept through the night the day she came home from the hospital and every night going forward. She didn't fuss, rarely cried. My mother would have to wake her every four hours to feed and change her and then she'd just fall back asleep. She wouldn't take a dummy, but enjoyed her thumb instead, maintaining the habit until she was eight years old (leaving a gap between her front teeth).

We were born different but raised the same. My mother did her best. She was determined to treat us as equals, giving us the same opportunities, the same amount of love and even sometimes the same clothes. She'd buy us matching outfits so we couldn't fight over who got what and she made sure that every Christmas gift under the tree was counted out, not one girl receiving more or less. We got haircuts at the same time and braces too, even though I didn't really need them: it was equal. Nina was long and lean and, even though she was nearly two years younger than me, we stood at the same height for most of our childhood. Put us together, with our matching blond bobs and our tandem outfits and people often mistook us for twins. But we were nothing alike. We weren't even friends. Our moments of peace and accord were anomalies, our differences so undeniable that they caused frequent clashes, bickering and the occasional hair-pulling. Together we were just a bad combination, like a peanut-butter-and-tuna-fish sandwich. When we were little girls, it was innocent sibling rivalry. But as we began to blossom into young women, our sour relationship and our stark differences became sharper, no matter how hard my mother tried to keep us equal. I was the introvert: serious, independent, secure, curious, worried, thoughtful and driven. Nina, the extrovert, the attention-seeking humourist: intelligent, insecure, emotional and passionate.

As a kid Nina loved to be the centre of attention. She would prance around the house, sometimes changing outfits as often as four or five times a day, singing songs from *The Sound of Music* or belting out Whitney Houston tunes at the top of her lungs. Her voice was good, really good. And for a while I even secretly thought, Maybe this girl will make it out of here with that voice – lucky. After everything that happened later in life, seeing how things fell apart, I realized I should have paid her that compliment and any others that had crossed my mind. It became clear with time that she was starving for my attention and I, as her older sister, had failed to recognize that duty.

The relationship that my sister had with my father differed from mine. From where I stood, it looked stronger, warmer, easier. Maybe it was because she was more like him; she had that same streak of 'born to be wild' blood in her. He seemed to expect less of her than he did of me, too. Dad wasn't shy about sharing his feelings about what he really thought about Nina and her prospects. He even found it amusing.

'Nina will probably end up a stripper,' he proclaimed on more than one occasion. She always took it in stride. She wasn't shy about her body, unlike prudish me. She certainly liked the idea of being onstage and the centre of attention. She seemed to love the shock-and-awe effect.

'But it better not be at one of those run-down Millinocket strip clubs. All I can say is that there better be stainless-steel urinals.' I wondered how he knew that classy strip joints had stainless-steel urinals, then quickly dismissed the visions running through my mind, accepting that there was probably a lot about this man that I didn't know – and probably didn't want to.

Nina never caught her big break to stardom with her big voice, but she broke away from Freedom long enough to catch a taste of what the rest of the world was like. Yet somehow she too found her way back to rural Maine, working a few bartending and waitressing gigs at a couple of local restaurants not too far from Freedom. Somehow neither of us could escape it. It was as if the day we both set foot in that diner as little girls, our future had been written for us both. The restaurant had gripped us and it was pulsing through our veins. Our DNA, much as we would deny it had anything in common beyond our blond hair, was intrinsically linked to our love for this place and for serving people. Before I had reopened the restaurant at the mill, we had been working apart, doing the same thing, but somehow couldn't quite figure out how to do it together. Until she came to work at the Lost Kitchen. It felt like a real chance for us to rekindle our broken relationship, right here in the very town that birthed us. I didn't know how long it would last, or even if it would, but the togetherness, the pride, the sisterhood we had right now gave me a good bit of hope that we had it in us to turn a new leaf.

The women in our village came with imperfections and a lack of major skills. But whatever it was that we lacked, we made up for with love. When we walked through the door each day, we brought with us our entire hearts. We weren't just co-workers; we weren't just neighbours: we were family now. We were stronger together, rooting one another on and lifting one another up. And we were falling into a smooth and effortless choreography around one another, serving out love, four nights a week.

31

THE AWAKENING OF A WOMAN

Among all the women, one came to life more than I could have imagined. I got to watch as she blossomed like a spring flower that had endured a long, cold Maine winter.

She had always been different from her six siblings. They were mostly towheaded and blonde, so she stood out with her auburn-tinged deep brunette hair. She always knew she was a little different, too. She had never been popular in school, never fitted into a clique. She had had one good true and honest friend once, Shelby. They shared a sweet and innocent connection until Shelby died of leukemia when she was just eleven years old. After that, she never really found her way into another group. She was liked well enough, though, because there was nothing you couldn't like about her. She was soft, kind and honest. That also made her an easy target to be trampled on by others who weren't as sweet, kind and honest as she. She took the occasional bullying quietly; she never stood up to anyone or called them out for their wrong-doings. She simply accepted every time someone would take advantage of her, swallowing it with the feeling that she somehow deserved it. Her father never hugged her or told her he loved her, but she just figured it would be selfish to expect it, as there were so many kids and not enough hours in the day to scatter love around like that.

But she found love in her own way. It was the summer of '78 when she met the man who would become her husband on a week-end trip to Maine. He was charming and flirtatious. It was attention that she wasn't used to and rather liked. He had long blond hair and a mustache that couldn't hide his big white smile. She had been to Maine before to visit friends at their rustic summer cottage on the coast in the sleepy summer village of Bayside. She had always been romanced by the ruggedness of this place and its bold, rocky shoreline; she craved it, even. It was a stark departure from the nondescript town she grew up in just south of Boston. That weekend she had come in search of cooler temperatures and found something burning inside of her instead. As she and this charismatic, easygoing man drank beer by the ocean he was wooing her, though nothing that made her feel uncomfortable.

Her trips north became more frequent. She liked his family and the way he flattered her. She didn't care that he was living in a hollowed-out, retired school bus on his parents' farm. And to him she was rare – the girl from away, so unlike the local women he had been with. He wanted to lock her down quick before anyone else could have the chance to snatch her up. She was a good catch.

They were married by the ocean in the summer of '79, just a year after they met. It was a warm and sunny August day, just like the one that brought them together. Deanna's dream had come true: she'd found love, but most of all, she'd never have to leave Maine. She could hardly wait to dig in and spread her roots, buy a little farmhouse, have a few kids, a garden, maybe even a few sheep. It was in an old farmhouse on a pothole-laden back road sixteen miles inland from the coast that they would start a family, two little girls with hair as blond as their father's. They planted vegetable and flower gardens that she would tend in the summertime while she wasn't teaching special ed at one of the nearby primary schools. Her husband found his own little piece of something to call his own, a diner just a few miles away. He always wanted to run his own business, but he never anticipated how much it would take out of him, how much it would shape him, grind him down.

Her husband became unkind. Maybe it was the sixteen-hour workdays, maybe it was childhood wounds coming back to haunt him. Whatever it was turned him miserable and mean. He couldn't compartmentalize his own pain or process it properly because he was raised like a true, stubborn Mainer to believe that therapy was for weak people. He did rely on alcohol, though. He started lapsing into fits of rage, his veins popping from his neck, his face beetroot-red. Once again she was trampled and once again she accepted it. Her husband would make demands of her, requesting that she wear certain clothes or style her hair a certain way. He would order her to make 'his' bed, refusing to take any part in it. He liked his sheets cleaned often and preferred them line-dried. He belittled her in front of friends, family and strangers – anyone and everyone – dumbing her down to keep her feeling weak. He didn't let her go out with friends and he questioned her whenever she left the house. She had always dreamed of owning sheep, but he forbade it. She never understood why, except that perhaps it was for the simple reason of holding that power over her. She felt like she couldn't complain – her husband worked hard and made more money than she did, even though he wouldn't share it. His money was his and hers was hers, although he expected her to hand hers over for half the bills each month. He bought her new cars whenever he felt like it, surprising her when she'd leave work to find a new car sitting in her regular parking spot – but not one that she would have ever picked out for herself. It was always something plain, something that wouldn't attract too much attention. She sometimes wondered how she ended up with a man who was so clearly different from her. But she felt selfish for even considering complaining, so she kept quiet.

Five years after the opening of the Lost Kitchen, my mother, Deanna, finalized her divorce from my father after more than thirty-five years of marriage. When she left my father she emerged from the shell that had kept her subdued for so many years. She was almost childlike, as if she had been living in a bunker somewhere that nobody knew about but was in plain sight. She was discovering who she was with her newfound freedom and I was getting to know her all over again. While I was reinventing myself, my mother was simultaneously experiencing her own transformation. There was something she saw in my own fight, in my own rise, in my ability to come through it all and be okay and she was inspired. She admitted that to me once and I found it strange to hear. I saw the tragedy in that, but I also saw the possibility. Together we were pooling our bits of strength and inspiration, becoming stronger women than we had ever been before. We had each other to lean on, we had the Lost Kitchen to push us and we had the women around us to support us. We had built our own village from scratch.

When I opened the Lost Kitchen, I couldn't have anticipated the fact that archaic and antiquated Prohibition laws still existed (the irony of this happening in Freedom was not lost on me). I suppose it made sense that they never had to change – there had never been a liquor store, bar or restaurant in town. As a result we wouldn't be allowed to offer wine, but if we were to form another 'small business' on the premises, we could sell it – and provide the glasses. We considered the problem from all angles and realized that we could put our unused basement space to use. It was a small, craggy, rustic cavern that had been naturally whittled from the granite foundation – just large enough to line the walls with handpicked bottles of wine and beer. The naturally cool climate was perfect for storing the spirits and the entrance was just around the corner from the restaurant's front door, so we could send guests over to purchase their selections, along with a corkscrew to borrow, before sitting down for their meal. We liked the idea of it feeling less fraught than worrying about whether your waiter was pressuring you into an unnecessarily expensive glass of wine or monitoring how much was left in your glass and more like arriving at a casual dinner party – walking through the door with a bottle tucked under your arm and filling up friends' glasses as you made your way through the meal. But while we had a space and a plan, I couldn't figure out exactly how it would work. We needed someone not only to curate the selection and run the business, but also to offer some guidance to anyone who needed help with their selections. There was but one person for this job: Mom.

She didn't know much about wine except that she liked it. She didn't know a Pinot noir grape from a Merlot grape, couldn't tell you about the appellations or terroir, or describe what a tannin was. She was terrified, in fact, of taking on a job that she felt so unqualified for. She was fearful of being a failure or a letdown. But she was patient and organized – two traits that had made her particularly well suited to being a teacher for the past thirty-five years. And her willingness to learn ran wild in her. When I was a kid, there was nothing she couldn't do, fix or figure out. She reglazed broken windows in our barn and built my bedroom door from pine boards she had picked up at the hardware store. She bought my father a table saw for Christmas because she wanted to use it to make things like tables from scraps of barn board. She taught herself how to shingle a roof and she mowed her sprawling lawn with a push mower, all the way around the flower gardens that she had built and tilled by hand. She built shelves and taught herself how to make slip-covers. And she learned some simple electrical skills so she could install her own light fixtures at home. She was more capable than she even realized and I was sure that taking on this challenge would show her just that. Now it was my turn to stand before her and tell her, 'You can do this'.

She began to devour wine books, teaching herself everything she could, studying and familiarizing herself with grape varietals she had never heard of, chuckling to think that, for so many years, she thought the only red wine that existed was either Merlot or Cabernet Sauvignon. She learned that Chablis wasn't a grape but an area and she had a small epiphany when she learned that if it was a red wine from Burgundy it was likely a Pinot noir and if it was a white wine from Burgundy it was probably a Chardonnay. From Mourvèdre to Falanghina, Nebbiolo to Pecorino, Gamay to Cinsault, she taught herself about wine from the ground up. She met with distributors and wine growers, sipping, tasting and testing her palate and nose. She learned how to swirl the wine round and round in the glass and then learned why. (She rarely, if ever, spat it out.) She wasn't a sommelier, she wasn't a wine snob, she wasn't a wine salesperson who intimidated you when you walked in the front door, flaunting how much more than you they know. She wasn't a sommelier, she was a mom and she knew how to pick out damn good wine. At first she was timid when she engaged with guests. It took time to believe in herself and her capabilities. For the better half of her life, she had spent her days interacting with schoolchildren and her own daughters. For the better half of her life, her husband had not allowed her to have much of a social life of her own. She wasn't sure she knew how to carry on a smart conversation and was anxious each time she found herself in that position. Eventually she learned how to trust her instincts and simply recommended things that she liked – Muscadet with oysters, Vermentino with halibut, or a nice Oregon Pinot noir if you really loved a red. For lamb it was nice northern Rhône, or maybe a Châteauneuf-du-Pape or a Gigondas; a Barolo couldn't go wrong either. And, of course, rosé, all day.

Discovering these wines led her to discover her voice, as well as a wider world. She still craved a simple life, but now she could just be herself, drive whatever car she wanted, wear whatever she felt like, wear her hair in an old-fashioned low roll, which her husband hated. She had lunch with friends and worked up the courage to take herself out to dinner. She travelled, finally visiting France, which she'd always dreamed of doing. She moved into a small cottage in the neighbouring town of Montville; she planted a small garden surrounded by a twig fence she made by hand. And she got a few sheep.

32

A HOUSE THE COLOUR OF STRAWBERRIES

It was a July morning and I was on my way to the pick-your-own strawberry farm on a back road in Freedom. I had a mission to fill the backseat of my car with flat upon flat of first-of-the-season berries for evening service. It was 6:30 A.M. and already damn hot, but I didn't mind – spending that time in the field would be a much-needed moment of quiet before my hectic day of prep followed by a full dinner service. I relished the brief pause as I mindlessly filled the green paper boxes with the warm fruit, daydreaming about how I'd serve them for dessert that night. Maybe a frozen custard with sliced berries and a dollop of cream, I thought. A cool respite from the midsummer heat. I snacked on the imperfect picks, realizing it might be the only thing I would eat all day and listened to the quiet chatter of the locals who were scattered around the neighbouring rows.

'Good pickin' this year, isn't it?'

'I'd say it's pretty fine, but they was sweeter last year.'

'Well, if the damn sun had a-come out more often this spring, I bet they woulda been a heck of a lot sweeter.'

I paid, placed the sweet red treats in the back of my car and made my way the few miles down the road to the restaurant. The traffic was heavy for the small country road – probably because of strawberry season. I hadn't been down this particular route since I was a teenager, teaching myself to drive the old Volkswagen Rabbit that I had nearly burned the clutch out of. I pulled up to the stop sign at the quiet intersection and remembered the very same sign from all those years ago. I laughed to myself, remembering rolling back at least twenty feet before I could figure out how to release the clutch, the nervousness flooding back but unmet by any real anxiety. And then it caught my eye – an old farmhouse perched on the hill at the foot of the quiet intersection.

It was greyed by weather and age, a few remaining chips of deep red paint the colour of strawberries clinging to the clapboards here and there. It looked dusty and vacant with its overgrown lawn and unkempt gardens. Some might have thought the effect was creepy, but I was drawn to it. I remembered the vision I'd described to my therapist earlier in the year, the dream I had of finding an old house that I could pour myself into and make my own. But in my dream it had been white.

From the outside it was tattered and worn down, maybe even abused over the years. But I could tell its insides were strong from its firm, proud stance on that hill. I could see inside the windows that its beams were thick and mighty. For almost two centuries it suffered through – and stood up to – countless nor'easters. So while it was crumbling in places, its doors had warped and its floors most likely creaked with effort, it deserved the chance to be fixed up and loved again.

A plastic bucket, tiny bike with training wheels and glittery streamers hanging from the handlebars and a collection of other children's toys were scattered across the yard: someone lived here. The realization surprised me with how sad it made me feel. From the moment I saw the house, the checklist of things I'd do to spruce it up and make it my own had sprung to life. In my mind I was already mowing the lawn, clearing out the garden, washing the windows and giving it a fresh coat of paint. I added a roof with cedar shingles, because – hey, it was my dream. It felt good to try it on for size.

A year later I was still living at my parents' farm. Strawberry season came back around again and this time there was a For Sale sign in the front garden of the house the colour of strawberries. It was almost as if once I had accepted Freedom in my heart, its love started to flow to me and things started to fall into place. I was timid at first about showing Jaim the house, fearful that he might think it was a run-down shack of a place. The house needed work and lots of it and the old barn that sat next to it even more so. But I brushed it aside as an afterthought, refusing to let the realistic amount of effort it would take to restore these buildings overwhelm me.

'I really like this place, Mom,' Jaim said as we stood at the top of the old stairwell, a genuine smile on his face. I felt relieved and comforted by his reaction. He had never been one to embrace big change and here I was showing him this ramshackle old place and introducing it as an idea for a home. I knew he meant it as he was peering into each bedroom, trying to decide which one to claim as his own. The thought of this house, one mile from the restaurant, becoming home felt like the final piece falling into place. We would make this house our own, our own patch of dirt that no one and nothing could take away. With all the work the place needed, we snagged it for a song. There were few people crazy enough to tackle the work it would take to make this place truly livable, but I wasn't scared, I was energized. And this time my name would be on the deed. I had learned my lesson.

We moved into the old farmhouse on a cold November day. A foot of snow had fallen just the day before, making it an even greater challenge to get to the front door. For the first time I almost felt lucky about the fact that I didn't have much furniture, just a few borrowed or broken pieces, which meant there was less to move through the banks of drifted snow. The house was cold and the oil tank had been condemned. I lit a fire in the big, old cast-iron stove that was in the centre of the living room with the armload of wood that remained in the shed. It seemed to take forever to warm the cold bones of the place, even though the stove had a good draw. For a brief moment I wondered, What the hell have I gotten us into? My mother, feeling my anxiety and seeing the tear I couldn't stop from trickling down my cheek, turned and said, 'Come on! Let's start vacuuming.' I watched her with such excitement as she used the vacuum wand to begin to suck up all the piles of mouse droppings that had accumulated on the dining room banquette. It was so ridiculous that I couldn't help laughing. I was on my way. Even if there was a little shit here and there.

As the seasons came and went, I poured myself into the old farmhouse, transforming it from a house to a home bit by bit. My mother would come by to help me strip away the layers upon layers of wallpaper, roll on a fresh coat of primer, or sand some floors. We painted all the walls a fresh coat of white because it symbolized a new beginning, a clean canvas. We sanded the floors back to their original sheen. It was exciting for her, I think, as if it took her back to thirty-five years ago, when she too walked into an old farmhouse in Freedom and turned it into a home for us girls. She had been lovingly doing the same for me and my soul, bringing me back from the brink.

With each coat of fresh white paint, I could feel my soul starting to settle in, settle down and find peace with my life. My divorce from Tom was finalized on a bitterly cold February afternoon, after a year-and-a-half-long battle, one that felt more like ten that might drag on for a lifetime. At our trial I sat on the stand for hours, publicly admitting to all my imperfections and fighting for the goodness that I knew was inside of me, to prove I was a deserving, good and genuine mother. The day in that courtroom was like a final lashing from Tom and I knew moving forward that after that day, he'd have no control over me ever again, so I took the beating willingly, knowing it would be the last. In the days and the months that followed, my blood slowly stopped boiling, my muscles and their great tension started to relax. I was no longer his possession. But my battle to regain my time with Jaim wasn't over. The courts ordered a one-week-on and one-week-off parenting schedule. I had come into my marriage with Jaim, a full-time kid and when it was over I was left with half, abiding by the fifty-fifty custody order. I'd have to learn to live with having Jaim under my roof only every other week. Through the tragedy of it, we found a gift: we would savour our moments together more than ever, realizing how precious they were now, never taking another day for granted again. I looked forward to the day when the ruling wouldn't matter anymore, when I wouldn't be forced to turn Jaim over every other Monday morning. Jaim's relationship with Tom had been forced. He had been a possession of Tom's, like I had been, for years, except Jaim couldn't divorce Tom. Even after the divorce was final, Tom continued to deny phone calls between us, while it was our week apart, banning us from being in any sort of communication.

As Jaim grew older, I knew it was only a matter of time before the day would come when his voice *would* matter. I knew it would come – with time, with age, his wishes would be undeniable. And it did come, with time, on a warm July day when a sixteen-year-old Jaim, who now stood taller than me, taller than Tom, said in a voice that no longer belonged to a child, 'Mom, I'd like to not go back there tomorrow.' I didn't stop him and Tom couldn't stop him either. Time was what it took to get here. And although I felt like we had finally reached the place I had hurt so hard to get to, realizing that all it took was simple time, I also knew that it was time lost with my child, who was no longer a child, that I could never recapture. And that I would forever regret.

The rebuild from the devastating war we had engaged in was slow and winding, taking years of our lives. Time was a major ingredient in the recipe of getting back and patience – much like a good soup. Day by day, bit by bit, board by board, we were coming home and sinking our roots deeper into this place that was giving us a second chance at a good life.

I also wanted to believe in a second chance at love. When I met him, I recognized the same pain in his eyes. He too had been battered and worn, the same as his eight-year-old son. He, too, felt the intoxicating pull of Maine, like a magnet, drawing him home. Its rugged coast, its sprawling farmland and its dense pine-and-maple-studded forests lured him from the city. There was something wild—frontier-like, even – that drew him as though back to a place he had once known.

He looked at me and saw past all my tattered bits. My skin was riddled with flecks of acne from the stress. My bangs were singed from a fire I got too close to once. My heart was bruised. My soul was battered. But my bones were good and he could see the beauty and strength in those imperfections. We moved tenderly around each other, well versed in the gentle care and consideration the other required.

For him the old farmhouse would become a beacon of pride and love and eventually home, where our boys became friends and then brothers. We saw ourselves and our past lives in the slumped, vacant-eyed barn sitting next to the house and together worked to bring it back to life, too. Board by board, shingle by shingle, we restored its strength. And on an August evening, surrounded by our own granite foundation of friends and family, it sheltered us as we said our vows. It was honest, it was simple, it was real. In our garden, with chickens beneath our feet, Penney and our boys by our sides and fried clam baskets filling us up, we celebrated, because we had found good, honest love.

33

THERE'S NO PLACE LIKE HOME

Four nights a week, I and the girls at the Lost Kitchen would open the restaurant that we had created together from scratch to a roomful of strangers, eager to taste what all the fuss was about. I was changing the menu every night, creating seasonal soups and salads, a handful of starters and four different mains for guests to pick and choose from à la carte. But on Saturday nights I'd serve a set menu with one seating, a menu that showcased everything that was in season that I wanted to eat. It was a nod to the old supper-club days. The success was instant and a bit baffling. I couldn't have imagined that every seat would book out every single night, the Saturday suppers booked weeks in advance, even. By year two all the suppers booked out months in advance. By year three I quit the à la carte menu and ran with the demand of prix-fixe suppers. We opened the phones for reservations for the new season on April 1. The phone calls started trickling in shortly after midnight. By the time I arrived at the office at 7:00 A.M., there were already twenty-six messages on the voice mail. Wow! I thought. The phone continued ringing all day long, until we'd booked the entire season in a single day. And when the following year rolled around, when the clock hit 12:00 A.M. on April 1, our three-line phone system was flooded with nearly ten thousand phone calls. We couldn't empty the voice mail fast enough as the requests came pouring through the lines, bogging them down to the point where our security system, unable to dial out for hours on end, set off alarms and alerted the fire department. Word spread around town about what was happening down at the Lost Kitchen and neighbours and loyal patrons dropped by with fresh-baked treats (a bottle of Champagne, even) to feed our staff as we manned the lines and dug out of the phone blizzard that was bearing down on us. There was a wild feeling of pride around the place that day, not from just the staff but also from all the supportive well-wishers who popped in to see how we were surviving. I broke into tears a few times that night. Tears because the influx of calls was mind-boggling and overwhelming, tears of pride that oh my God, this impossible little restaurant was a success beyond dreams. We were booked beyond capacity and with thousands still that we'd be unable to seat because we were just too small a place. I was awake for thirty-six hours straight, with an influx of help at my side, tending to the calls and enquiries. I crashed from exhaustion, knowing right then that we couldn't do it again like this next year. We couldn't put guests through that again either; hitting redial over and over again, only to get busy signals for hours on end and if lucky, eventually getting through to the voice mail, only to discover that it was full. Our simple reservation system of pencil to paper over the phone was no longer working. It had to change. We had to change.

Sure, we could have done like the rest of the world: resort to the Web. But the problems would persist, spots would fill in an instant and people would still be frustrated because there wouldn't be enough seats to serve the need. Was the answer to grow the place? I knew in my heart that to do that would mean risking the end of the magic that we had worked so hard to create. I knew in my heart that with this wild demand, my job might just be to protect it – to keep it small, simple and just the way it's meant to be. So I wouldn't double this restaurant in size and I wouldn't open a second restaurant.

The solution was born out of utter simplicity. It was as straight-forward as putting pen to paper, licking a stamp or postmarking a postcard on April 1 and sending it off to a town called Freedom in the middle of nowhere. We sent out the news of our new system and planned to toss the cards and letters into a bin and pull out winners, lottery-style, letting them know by phone if they had scored a seat for the season. No redial, no exhaustion, no rushing. It felt personal and honest, with the added benefit of reviving the sleepy Freedom post office, which had always been teetering on the verge of closing.

I didn't know what to expect when I showed up at the post office the first morning in April after our reservation process had begun. The chuckle that Joe the mailman let out when he saw me standing at the counter told me that something out of the ordinary was up. 'How big is your car?' He laughed again. There were stacks of full-size trays of mail that day, containing thousands of letters and cards. Hell, the combined towns of Freedom and Montville only see a half a box of mail each day for Joe's entire route. The most excitement he usually saw at work was the nip of whiskey my father would leave in a to-go cup in the mailbox for him every Friday when he was out for delivery. In the days that followed, the letters kept pouring in as though it were the North Pole. Twenty thousand postcards made their way to the little town in the middle of nowhere from every state in the country and from twenty-two countries around the world, all just for dinner.

Find your way to Freedom for dinner and my only hope is that I can give you a meal and a moment that will leave a memory to last for a very long time. Because like my mother told me, that's all life is made of: memories. From the pothole-laden parking lot, make your way over the gravel path embedded in the woods and follow the soft light guiding you to the footbridge that extends over

Freedom Falls. Emerge from the woods and the mill will come into view, nestled into its great granite bedrock perched above the rushing water. Wind your way around the side of the building, minding the path that leads you to the doorway of our wine cellar. Descend the stone steps and be engulfed by the tiny cavern carved into the foundation, lined floor to ceiling with wines from obscure and tiny vineyards with their own stories to tell, each handpicked by my mother. She'll greet you with a warm smile and conversation, hand you the evening's menu and help you find the perfect bottles to sip on through the night, before tucking them into handwoven baskets to be carried to the dining room above.

Upstairs Ashley will be waiting patiently for you. Like the rest of us, she'll be in her favourite black dress, the apron around her waist handstitched by my mother. She'll lead you through the barn board–lined dining room to the table that has been set just for you; handstitched linen napkins, vintage Blue Willow bread plates, mismatched estate-sale silverware, French water glasses, a milk jug filled with chilled water, a single candle and a bud vase filled with flowers that Ashley grew herself on her farm. Take your seats in the Windsor-like chairs that my mother and I painted a slate-like charcoal, uncork your wine as Alex graces the table with stemware to suit. Clink your glasses in celebration, sip, sit back and take in the sound of the falls rushing by the window beside you. For the table I want to share a marble board filled with local cheeses, a few whipped butters, grilled toasts, pickles and spicy radishes to nibble. This is what I would serve you if you came to my own home. I want you to feel like you *are* in my home – I want to serve you, converse with you and let you feel the warmth of an evening filled with food and candlelight, good company and laughter.

Let me bring you a platter of icy oysters served on a bed of frozen beach rocks I gathered from nearby Belfast, garnished with some freshly foraged moss. Sitting atop a vintage platter with a soft, brown floral pattern, the oysters that Carey plated with so much care and attention look as if they had just been found that way in the wild. Perfectly shucked and lightly dressed with a sweet and pickled shallot sauce and whatever fresh herb I could get my hands on that day. Once the shells have been sucked clean and every bit of briny and sweet liquor has been enjoyed, we'll deliver yet another treat I've been concocting in the small open kitchen. Atop a small milk-glass pedestal cake plate, tiny sandwiches so sweet in appearance they look like they should be dessert. An ode to my diner days: sliders made of local pork raised by my friends John and Emma, with homemade mayonnaise made from the eggs of my very own chickens, bread-and-butter pickles made this morning by Helen and a slice of good local cheese, all atop a fresh tiny bun dusted with poppy seeds. It's food you can recognize, food you can pronounce, food you can eat with your hands with your elbows on the tables (the tables I built with my own two hands). In between, a small dish of chilled towels soaked in rose water that Nancy tied with a bit of twine and a sprig of fresh lavender that Krista grew in her garden. Cool and refreshing, making the room smell like roses as the moist towels are unfurled and inhaled.

A tablespoon of homemade sorbet to follow, served in minia-ture glass hen bowls – like the kind my grandmother would put out around Easter and fill with pastel sweets that looked like eggs. One cool refreshing bite will leave you wanting more of the sweet tea–blueberry sorbet made from the berries that Maia harvested from her back field this morning. Yet to come: a soup of fresh celery with brown butter and crabmeat, garnished with tiny coriander greens and brightly coloured yellow brassica flowers; a salad – the baby butterhead lettuces that were still in the field next door at Polly and Prentice's this morning, tonight were on your plate – served whole with flecks of local blue cheese, fragrant fennel and bits of local bacon tucked between the leaves, drizzled with a bit of shal-lot vinaigrette and homemade buttermilk dressing, a scattering of violets over the top to finish; local hake, flaky and white, cooked skin-side down in a cast-iron pan until the skin was golden brown and crispy and finished in a bath of butter in the oven, served over a plop of creamy polenta and next to a potato salad of the tiniest fingerlings you have ever seen, some crunchy organic cabbage, a few salty olives and lots of fresh herbs. A squeeze of lemon and a spicy nasturtium blossom on top. Nasturtiums always reminded me of Gram and her smile.

We finish the night with a cold and creamy frozen custard, laced with a bit of homemade almond brittle, a dollop of whipped cream and a sprinkling of fresh blackberries. And at the end of the night, the only decision to be made: coffee or tea? A platter of fresh-from-the-oven stone ground-cornmeal-and-cherry cookies will adorn the antique dresser in the entrance hall – one last warm bite as you make your way back across the bridge, cloaked by the evening sky and the gurgling water below, bellies and hearts full.

The mystery of this place and its success still sometimes bewilders me. How could a restaurant in the middle of nowhere, run by all women (and one good man) with no formal training not only survive but thrive? Only one thing could explain it: love. We love our work because here, work feels joyful. We dance around the kitchen and dining room with a quiet grace – no yelling, no screaming, no put-downs. We are women, doing what we do best: caring for people. Caring for people with warmth and food. On the line I can sway back and forth between the stove and countertop, placing small cast-iron pans atop the blue flames. I move with the music wafting over the speakers as I grab big pinches of grainy salt, sprinkling each thick piece of fish with the perfect amount before placing them each in a pan, one by one, moving down the line with the rhythm, skin-side down in the hot pans, with a smoking coat of glistening olive oil. From pan to pan, turning each piece of tender fish gently but with conviction, revealing the crispy golden-brown skin before dousing each pan with a handful of butter pats. As they melt in a hot sizzle, I swirl the pan in a soft circular motion before sliding the pans into the hot oven waiting for them. I move as if I were dancing, keeping the beat, using it to time the fish in the oven. It's not a hustle or a grind because it's my joy, cooking here in this little kitchen surrounded by the laughter, the chatter, the flowers, the candlelight and the breeze coming through the open windows. I found purpose and light through my darkest days by doing something that I love so very much. I make mom food because I'm a mom and as a girl I learned from my father that good food could be a vessel, a way to say 'I love you' without words.

There are rare moments when I reflect on it all and think about what I have become and what I could have been. Times when I scrub my hands and arms in the basin of the big porcelain sink in the kitchen and I flash a thought about how things could have been so different.

Scrubbing my arms in that sink reminds me of my dreams, once, to be a doctor, to chase a different life. But by the time I've dried my hands with a kitchen towel, I've already glanced around the open dining room, realized who I am and the dream I *did* chase – the one I caught in my own backyard. Feelings of peace and contentment wash over me.

I'm not alone. We've all found some purpose together. In this place, this space, this little restaurant in the middle of nowhere, we grew stronger together. We formed our very own village and we had one another to lift up, root on and love. Together we survived divorces, makeups and breakups, affairs, deaths of people we loved so much and late-term miscarriages. Together we celebrated births, marriages, moments and yes, even new love – good honest, healthy, boundless, unconditional love. We found our place in this world, doing something together that we care so deeply about. Here you can taste our joy. The road to this place was winding, but it led me home. I found a good life, my own slice of heaven, right here in Freedom, where they told me nothing was possible.

On rare occasions my father would stop by the restaurant. Sometimes in the middle of the day during prep, showing a buddy or two around, breaking into the walk-in and stealing a few beers, cracking them open while he gave a grand tour while I somehow remained invisible to him. He still couldn't tell me with his words that he was proud, but I could see, through his half-smile and glazed eyes as he boasted to his buddy, that this might be the best he could do. And then there were his unannounced pop-ins during service: my dad, wearing his special-occasion sport coat, the one he wore to funerals or to gamble at the horse track, just like his father. With his buzz on, with that coat on, it may have been the closest to 'I'm proud of you' that he could manage. And I was okay. I had a village filling me up. I wasn't starving anymore. My belly was full with pride. And I was okay.

ACKNOWLEDGEMENTS

Writing this book was one of the most challenging things I have ever done. It meant going back to painful times and reliving them all over again and then recounting the details and moments that became these pages. It was always with the hope that some of my words might give others hope and strength in their own lives. There would be no pages without Deb Futter, my fearless editor, who took a chance on me and believed in my story. Deb, I am forever grateful to you and the entire team at Celadon for taking me on and shepherding me through this process. I can't wait to cook you a beautiful meal to express my deep gratitude.

To my agent, Janis Donnaud, the toughest gal in the biz. From the moment we met all those years ago, I knew that you would challenge me in all the right ways and that you would push me to reach higher and be stronger. You did it and I thank you from the bottom of my heart. Don't stop pushing me.

My love and thanks to Rachel Holzman, for holding my hand and supporting me infinitely throughout this process. You made me feel safe and confident even in moments when I doubted my work. You made me stronger. I'm so thankful for the work you put into this project and our friendship that carries on.

Deepest thanks to my family, for the love and support and understanding through the time it took me to put my story on paper.

Michael, my sweet husband, who was endlessly patient with me. I know my mood and emotions sometimes got wrapped up in the era of the pages I was writing about and you never stopped lifting me up with love and understanding. I love you with all of my heart and thank you for loving me back with such honesty and sincerity. Every day I am thankful we found each other. Every day I'm thankful for the beautiful life we are building together.

To my son, Jaim, being your mom has been the greatest gift of my life. You are finding your own path and I am so proud of the man you are becoming. I love you.

And to my own mom, you sat shotgun on this journey with me, recounting the memories and digging up the old photos. Thank you for raising me up right on that little dirt road in Freedom and for believing in all of my wild dreams.

To my dad. You may never read this, but without you I'm not sure who I would be. Thank you for introducing me to the kitchen. I found my life's passion standing at the stove and it's all because of you.